Venice West

VENICE WEST

The Beat Generation in Southern California

JOHN ARTHUR MAYNARD

RUTGERS UNIVERSITY PRESS

New Brunswick and London

Library of Congress Cataloging-in-Publication Data

Maynard, John Arthur, 1947–
    Venice west : the beat generation in Southern California / John Arthur Maynard.
        p. cm.
    Includes bibliographical references and index.
    ISBN 0-8135-1653-6
    1. Beat generation—California—Venice.   2. Venice (Calif.)—Intellectual life—20th
century.   3. American literature—California—Venice—History and criticism.
4. American literature—20th century—History and criticism.   5. Authors,
American—California—Venice—Biography.   6. Authors, American—20th century—
Biography.   7. Venice (Calif.)—Biography.   8. Lipton, Lawrence, 1898–1975.
9. Perkoff, Stuart Z.   I. Title.
PS228.B6M39   1991
810.9′979494—dc20   90-45114
                                                                                          CIP

British Cataloging-in-Publication information available

For Oliver A. Rink

CONTENTS

ACKNOWLEDGMENTS

Now that *Venice West* is finished, I would like to acknowledge a debt or two.

This book could not have been started, let alone completed, without the help of my family. I wish my father, Wallace John Maynard, had been able to see the end of what we had all considered a joint project, but I am grateful that he was able to read the first chapter. At one time or another I have called on my mother, Haro R. Maynard, and my sister, Marguerite-Louise Maynard, for every kind of support—moral, material, emotional, and, in my sister's case, bibliographic and electronic. They have always been there for me, and I hope I have not been too wrapped up in my academic fantasies to occasionally be there for them.

My doctoral committee members at the University of Southern California, Franklin D. Mitchell, Steven Ross, and Ronald Gottesman, showed extraordinary patience with an unorthodox project that often progressed in fits and starts. It is no exaggeration to say that Dr. Mitchell's belief in this work was the crucial factor in its completion.

Nettie Lipton, Lawrence Lipton's widow, gave me encouragement, vital information, and access to her husband's uncatalogued papers and tape recordings, which at that time were still being held, pending sale, in a basement at UCLA; if she had not decided to help me, I would not have known they existed until it was too late. I also owe a special debt to Bob Knutson, of Doheny Memorial Library, USC, for making it possible for me to meet Mrs. Lipton; to Professor Louis Stouman, who gave me formal permission to quote from Lawrence Lipton's books and papers; and to Anne Caiger and the staff of the Department of Special Collections, University Research Library, UCLA, who never seemed to tire of dragging the Lawrence Lipton Collection out of storage for me on ridiculously short notice.

Suzan and Rachel Perkoff, the poet's wife and daughter, lent me their confidence, their testimony, and the unrestricted use of Stuart Perkoff's journals, letters, and unpublished manuscripts. Neither they nor any of their friends who shared their experiences with me—Philomene Long, Tony Scibella, and John Thomas—have ever asked me what I planned to say about them. They simply told the truth, as they recalled it, and trusted me to do the same.

Marty Waldman, Sylvia Graham, and Steve Goldstein, of Brentwood Publishing Corporation, and Jerry and Sue Fisher, of *Tile & Decorative Surfaces Magazine*, gave me a different sort of trust. That is, they continued to employ me despite the fact that my mind was often far away. They knew I was writing "the book" at night in their offices, and had they not been supportive, this project might have been abandoned long go.

Joe Styles, the USC History Department's student advisor and procedural expert, ran bureaucratic interference for me at several crucial points in this project; I have no idea what I would have done without his help.

I would also like to thank Marlie Wasserman, Editor-in-Chief of Rutgers University Press, and Professor William O'Neill, who reviewed the initial version of *Venice West*; both offered encouragement, criticism, and suggestions that helped to turn a rather wild narrative into a publishable book. I also owe considerable thanks to Kenneth Arnold, Director of the Press, who edited the final version in about as painless a fashion as I can imagine.

Special thanks are due—a couple of decades late—to Professor James B. Inskeep, of the Bakersfield College Department of History, who made me want to learn to think like a historian, and to then-PFC Bob Hamm, of Company B, USAINTS, Fort Holabird, Maryland, who persuaded me to read *On the Road* and forget everything I'd ever heard about its author.

Finally, I would like to thank Oliver A. Rink, former chair of the History Department at California State University, Bakersfield, who recruited me for the historical profession and pointed me toward his own home institution, USC, and his mentor,

John A. Schutz. Dean Schutz, in turn, made it possible for me to embark on a full-time doctoral program at the advanced age of thirty-two, while Professor Richard C. Dales, in his role as pack leader, drill instructor, and spiritual advisor for the incoming graduate students of 1979, gave me the confidence to pursue my own peculiar historical visions.

This book is for Oliver, and I hope he enjoys it. He likes to joke about having "ruined my life," but it would be more accurate to say he gave it back to me.

J.A.M.
Simi Valley, California
October 22, 1990

Venice West

INTRODUCTION

Venice, California, has seldom been an entirely respectable place. Founded in 1905 as a genteel retreat for esthetically-minded Los Angeles businessmen, it quickly became the Coney Island of the West—and image-wise, at least, things have been all downhill from there. Although its property values are higher than they used to be, so is the price of everything else that fronts on the Pacific Ocean; recent crackdowns may have chased some of the drug dealers and squatters away from the beach, but there is still a fundamental raunchiness to the Venice Ocean Front that only the bulldozers will ever do away with completely.

The outward symbol of the boardwalk's economy is the mom-and-pop t-shirt stand; the outward signs of its culture include buskers, panhandlers, skaters, bodybuilders, esoteric healers, aspiring musicians, chainsaw jugglers, badly weathered murals, dirty-mouthed comedians and guitar-playing Sufi mystics on skates. There is something faintly threatening about it all, an energetic gutter craziness that no one really claims to have under control. Venice has always been a place where meanness and creativity run too close together for comfort. If there are no plaques dedicated to the poets and artists who made it famous as an enclave of the Beat Generation in the late fifties—no memorials to Stuart Perkoff, Charles Foster, Alexander Trocchi, "Mad Mike" Magdalani, or even the man who introduced "Venice West" to the world, Lawrence Lipton—it is because if they were still around in force, respectable people would undoubtedly be making plans to chase them away.

But there are signs that they and their culture were there. Not on the bookshelves, certainly; few of their works, with the exception of Trocchi's *Cain's Book*, were or ever will be published. At the height of their notoriety, when there seemed to be no end to the public's appetite for things "beat," the poets of Venice West congratulated themselves on sharing the "greatest drive for nonrecognition in the history of literature." (This book may be read as their collective recognition.) Even the Ocean Front's lone bookstore—the local counterpart to San Francisco's City Lights—lacks a section devoted to the Beat Generation, let alone to Venice West. No, most of the hints are subtle, and there is something conspiratorial about being able to recognize them. A hand-lettered sign in an apartment window reads "BIRD LIVES;" another quotes a line from the beat poet, Bob Kaufman: "Charlie Parker was an electrician. He went around wiring people." A small art gallery now occupies the storefront slot that once housed the Venice West Café, while a few blocks away, a single cast-iron column, towering above the Promenade like the mast of a sunken ship, marks the site of the Gas House, where the Beat Generation of Venice West briefly tried to take its case to the people. Across the lawn at the Pavilion, where the spray-painters come to write at night, it is sometimes possible to find the closest thing to a monument that the Venice beats are likely to get.

Graffiti may or may not have the high cultural significance that is sometimes claimed for it, but since it is a form of no-budget advertising, a few simple conclusions can sometimes be drawn from it. One of these is that it meant something to the writer; another is that the writer expected it to be understood more or less instantaneously by some imagined reader. That lends a shabby but defiant significance to the fact that every now and then, in place of the usual obscenities, passages from Revelation and threats to kill members of rival gangs, someone takes the time to draw a cartoon figure labeled "Maynard G. Krebs" on the wall of the Venice Pavilion. Almost thirty years ago, when "The Many Loves of Dobie Gillis" was one of the most popular comedies on television, almost any American would have recognized Dobie's beatnik sidekick, Maynard. Not one of Max Shulman's original characters, he is said to have been written into the show for the express purpose of capitalizing on an improbable national obsession with the exotic, "poetry-spouting" bohemian subculture of the late fifties and very early sixties. The show is back in syndication on some of the cable networks, but that hardly explains why, after more than thirty years, the old image, in the words of a Venice poet, still "makes a bridge to the eye."

But oddly enough, the cartoon figure seldom looks anything like the TV character. As played by Bob Denver, Maynard G. Krebs looked only marginally different from anyone else, except that he wore shirts with no collars and had the faintest hint of a goatee (but not a mustache, of course; that would have been too "masculine," and ineffectuality was the essence of his character). By contrast, the figure on the Pavilion wall is rather menacing, and brings to mind the unlikely fact that in his own time, the "beatnik," like any other "weirdo," tended to be laughed at in preference to being feared.

Like the cartoon character of the 1990s, the standard beatnik stereotype of the late 1950s was generally represented as a sly, knowing, physically unimpressive (read: weak and unathletic) young man, usually bearded, who dressed shabbily, wore his sunglasses indoors, went around in sandals all year long, and never seemed to do much of anything. A cigarette dangling from his mouth and a floppy beret on his uncombed head, he was almost never depicted without either a knowing grin or a hostile smirk pasted across his face. He was smug, inscrutable, rather silly, and utterly convinced of his own intellectual superiority; he spoke, whenever possible, in vague, smokey hip talk or rhyming couplets, and it was just as easy to see through his pretentions as it would have been to pull the "shades" away from his eyes. He seemed to embody two middle-class prejudices at once: the old one against intellectuals, and the even older one against "people who don't work." Since it was taken for granted that the beatnik "didn't wash," he was also an affront to the modern mania for going about with no more personal scent than a piece of china.

His female counterpart was the beat chick, who was equally silly but portrayed as considerably sexier. She tended to wear bulky sweaters, black stockings, and lots of eye makeup. Her hair could be long or short, but always out of fashion—no home perms or hairspray for the beat chick. Since she was principally a male fantasy, it was assumed that she was "available," although how she ever connected with a eunuch like the stereotypical male beatnik was a good question. What she probably needed, in the eyes of most observers, was a "real man." She was weird and spacey, sitting in coffeehouses all night with no expression on her face at all, so it was easy to imagine that she had never met one.

These may be laughable images, but they correspond to the ones presented in all seriousness by Reader's Digest in the illustration that accompanied Paul O'Neil's article, "Life Among the Beatniks," in the April 1960 issue. A line drawing, the picture was a collage of all the standard beat clichés—a pretty, tousle-haired, and obviously neurotic girl staring straight at the reader; an earnest-looking young man with a goatee reading poetry; a group of bearded, sweatshirted men playing chess late at night in a coffeehouse. Though certainly among the more innocuous scenes in the history of shock literature, they were meant to be disturbing, or at least lamentable, and Reader's Digest seldom miscalculated. Its readers knew the beats represented a kind of low-grade warfare being conducted against their way of life—a war all the more perplexing because it was pointless. It would have been bad enough if the beatniks were communists, out to abolish the good life for everyone; instead, they attacked the good life by refusing to acknowledge it as good. This was war on common sense. What was so bad about being normal? Or, as O'Neil himself asked, "What have we done to deserve this?"

Nor was this all. From these images there emerged a pair of sub-stereotypes, one "good," one "bad." The "good" beatnik was a harmless, funny fellow like Maynard G. Krebs—loyal, good-hearted and honest, but naive and given to panic at the thought of "work!" The "bad" beatnik, on the other hand, figured in crime story after crime story, especially after the San Francisco Police Department initiated a heavily publicized crackdown on the beat enclave in North Beach in the summer of 1958. The "bad" beatnik smoked marijuana and, by some accounts, took heroin, which automatically put him in the same category with another stock figure in fiction and crime reporting: the hopped-up, withdrawal-crazed dope addict. More often, however—since the broadcast media had strict guidelines about the representation of drugs, even in crime dramas, and the comics could not mention them at all—the "bad" beatnik was represented as a social misfit, perhaps a psychopath, but certainly a man who had rejected conventional society because he was incapable of succeeding in it.

In every one of its manifestations, the image of the beatnik posed the same question: why would anyone want to *be* like that? While for most Americans it was a question of how he could be so "wrong," it was inevitable that some should wonder whether or not he was "right," or at least right enough to teach them something about their own options in life. Even among those who rejected everything he stood for, there was just enough seductive power in the stock figure of the beatnik to make him an attractive nuisance. The best part about the temptation was that it could be indulged, if only in fantasy, on any number of levels. That was what Norman Podhoretz and other public-spirited intellectuals were afraid of, and they were right to fear it.

Behind the silly, opportunistic images, there were, of course, real people with real beliefs and a powerful and tenacious commitment to them. But perhaps because it is so hard to separate them from the trivialized images that linger from their own time, few historians have paid much attention to them. Allen J. Matusow presents a standard, and characteristically brief, description of them in *The Unraveling of America* (1984):

> By the late 1950s, a fully developed beat subculture had emerged not only in North Beach but also in Venice West (near Los Angeles), New York's Greenwich Village, and a few other hip resorts in between. The beats possessed deviant tastes in language, literature, music, drugs, and religion. Profoundly alienated from dominant American values, practicing voluntary poverty and spade cool, they rejected materialism, competition, the work ethic, hygiene, sexual repression, monogamy, and the Faustian quest to subdue nature. There were, to be sure, never more than a few thousand fulltime beats, but thanks to the scandalized media, images of beat penetrated and disconcerted the middle classes. Beats, like hula hoops, were a fad.

They were more than a fad, of course; they were a direct reproach to the consumer society around them, and since the people who laughed at them also understood this, it would be a mistake to dismiss their influence on the basis of the silly sensationalism that actually helped to spread it. But that is

largely what has happened. Thirty-three years after the publication of Jack Kerouac's *On the Road*, the beats are still a historical sideshow, studied in hagiographic detail by specialists
but ignored at little peril. Scholarship about them tends to take
the form of literary criticism, biography, or background material for studies of the events of the sixties. Thus there is a growing body of work on the poems and novels themselves, on the
lives of Jack Kerouac, Allen Ginsberg, William Burroughs, and
their friends, and on the beats' contributions to the better-
publicized and more attractively photographed movements that
came after them. Even the historians who do take them seriously tend to show them the same sort of appreciation usually
given to a good opening act at a rock concert: not bad at all,
guys, and thanks for warming up the crowd.

As already noted, Allen Matusow is one historian who does
take the beats seriously, although his admiration for the counterculture in general is fairly restrained. He identifies the beats as
the vanguard of a revolution in the relationship of mind to body,
or, more precisely, of the libido to the rational mind. Applying
Norman O. Brown's mid-sixties concept of the Dionysian ego
("a new ego, a body ego . . . overflowing with love, knowing no
limits, affirming life") to the bohemians who had helped to
make Brown's ideas acceptable, Matusow sees them as the
founders of a latter-day paganism whose exaltation of the non-
rational has pushed its way into everyday life. "The creation of
the Dionysian ego, the ego in service of liberated Eros," he
writes, ". . . was a project millions of mothers would soon understand implicitly and fear with good reason." Lawrence Lipton,
the self-appointed "Shaman" of Venice West, would have been
happy to endorse his conclusion that by the end of the following
decade, "Dionysus had been absorbed into the dominant culture and domesticated, and in the process routed the Protestant
ethic." Since his primary concern in *The Unraveling of America*
is with liberalism and public policy, Matusow does not explain
this transformation in detail, but he comes close to seeing the
Venice beats, at least, in the way they saw themselves.

The cultural historian William O'Neill seems more concerned
with the momentum and direction of the counterculture than
with its origins. He does give the beats credit for contributing
to the movement its uniform and its marching order:

Even in the 1950's and very early sixties, when people still worried about conformity and the silent generation, there were different drummers to whose beat millions would one day march. The bohemians of that era (called "beatniks" or "beats") were only a handful, but they practiced free love, took drugs, repudiated the straight world, and generally showed which way the wind was blowing.

O'Neill concludes this observation with an astonishing throwaway line: "When the bohemian impulse quickened, dropouts knew what was expected of them." Why should nonconformists need to know what is expected of them? For that matter, why should millions of young people in the late sixties have expressed their individuality by making themselves look almost exactly like one other? O'Neill acknowledges conformity as a conservative force but neglects its role as a force for raising hell. Despite his tendency to equate popularity with validity, he overlooks one of the most interesting differences between the beats and the hippies: the beats instinctively distrusted publicity, while the hippies, raised in the age of television and saturation advertising, seemed to think it proved they were right.

In *The Fifties: The Way We Really Were*, Douglas T. Miller and Marion Nowak contribute more substantially to an understanding of the beats in their own time, and especially in relation to their critics. Although their book is weakened by an all-too-obvious loathing for the tastes and aspirations of ordinary people—as well as an over-eagerness to define middle-class culture only by its excesses—Miller and Nowak do a convincing job of explaining why the mainstream intellectuals of the late fifties felt justified in using strong-arm, or, as the authors put it, "McCarthyist" tactics against the beats. That was the way of intellectual power struggles in an era of consensus. The intellectuals' exaggerated hostility made it "all right" for others to attack the beats, just as their acquiescence had made it easier for conservatives to put the Old Left out of business. Miller and Nowak also believe the media chose to focus on the beats because other, more significant manifestations of dissent might have been harder to ridicule; by calling them "the only rebellion around," Paul O'Neil implied in *Life* that rebellion itself was childish and inconsequential.

On the other hand, I think Miller and Nowak have failed to recognize the extent to which the media acted against the presumed interests of mainstream society—or succeeded in having it both ways. For example, where they see "bland journalese" in a *Life* article contrasting bohemian life in Venice West with middle-class life in Hutchinson, Kansas, *I* see carefully crafted language that made it possible to promote the one while pretending to uphold the other. The fact is that despite its celebration of middle-class values, the essential message of the commercial media, then as now, was not "you never had it so good," but "you're *missing* something." Why would anyone spend good advertising money on a medium calculated to make people satisfied with what they have? Can such a massive engine of dissatisfaction always be assumed to be fully under control?

As for the beats themselves, Miller and Nowak consider them an important step, but also a dead end. They see in the beat fad a sign of mass dissatisfaction which called for political action, not artistic withdrawal. Their epitaphs for the fifties are drawn from C. Wright Mills, H. Stuart Hughes, and Paul Goodman. The new day they see dawning in the closing pages of their book is one of a "radicalized," decidedly elitist political consciousness. This interpretation "works," by the airtight logic of the New Left, but it denies any independent power to the beats' own persuasive brand of illogic. I suggest that not to explore that illogic is to ignore a great deal.

In *The Making of a Counterculture* (1969), Theodore Roszak tends to treat the intuitive and antipolitical aspects of the sixties counterculture in exactly the same way. But much of the counterculture was not about political consciousness at all; it was about the possibility of a completely transcendant state of mind. To dismiss the beats, as Roszak does, for "failing" to do their political duty is not only to write history in terms of a desired ending, but to ignore most of what they themselves said they were trying to do. It also ignores the possibility that there *are* more forms of power than are yet accounted for in political theory.

There is certainly no denying that the beats arrived on the scene at a time when middle-class culture seemed triumphant— and when most Americans, regardless of what kind of work they did, are generally agreed to have thought of themselves as middle class. While a good many middle-class Americans felt insulted by the diet of ideas they were served—by high-pressure commercials, low comedy, and questionable moral standards—few would deny that most of the books, phonograph records, films, magazines, newspapers, radio programming, and television shows of the fifties were intended for mass consumption and professed, at least, to celebrate middle-class values. As Miller and Nowak demonstrate, popular culture made a point of telling the majority of Americans that they were good, honest people who worked hard and deserved everything they got as a result. In return, middle-class Americans were expected to spend more of their earnings than they had dared to part with in the past. That was not all. Mass culture also served the more arcane purpose of helping the nation's intellectuals define what they were *not* and simultaneously reaffirm their claim to the moral and esthetic leadership of the big, boorish, clumsy, tasteless country from which they felt so isolated.

The leadership issue helps to explain why professional thinkers like Norman Podhoretz, Diana Trilling, and even one early ally and sponsor, Kenneth Rexroth, reacted so violently to the literature of the Beat Generation. It was one thing to condemn materialism and crassness in American life; it was another to do so without the slightest sign of respect for those who normally worked that side of the street.

As Miller and Nowak point out, most American intellectuals had reconciled themselves to approving of their country in at least a ritual way—so long as it conceded them their status as a cultural elite, and not a very friendly one at that. "Until the day dawns when a democratic elite will be welcomed and listened to in this country," Bernard Iddings Bell wrote in 1952, "the American who would escape from slavery to crowd culture must expect to have a difficult time of it." The beats hated crowd culture and consumer values as much as Bell did, but in claiming to find the alternative in the untaught human mind, belly, heart, and crotch, they also threatened to put their cultural betters out of business. Who needed a cultural elite when the purest poetry and fiction sprang out of the typewriter with the spontaneity of thought itself?

Jack Kerouac, it must be said, was extremely proud of having gotten an "A" in English from Mark Van Doren at Columbia, and Allen Ginsberg was just as pleased when his friend William Carlos Williams (who never found his medical practice an impediment to writing poetry) contributed the foreword for *Howl and Other Poems*. Few of the beats really rejected literary tradition as ferociously as the keepers of that tradition rejected the beats. The real source of the quarrel was that both parties, the beats and the mainstream intellectuals, believed strongly enough in literature to fight over it. The intellectuals thought of the beats as charlatans and barbarians; the beats thought of *them* as members of a worn-out cultural gentry who had held power for so long that they had forgotten what to do with it. After John Ciardi, James Dickey and John Hollander wrote devastating attacks on *Howl and Other Poems* (1956), for example, Allen Ginsberg responded with the same cordiality: "Poetry has been attacked by an ignorant and frightened bunch of bores who don't understand how it's made, and the trouble with these creeps is they wouldn't know poetry if it came up and buggered them in broad daylight."

To its credit, the Southern California literary establishment was initially friendlier. It was mainly the Venice beats' association with the writer Lawrence Lipton that turned them into pariahs—as the Malibu poet Curtis Zahn called them, "the Great Ungifted." The principal local reviews, *California Quarterly* and *Coastlines*, usually made a point of endorsing all serious literary efforts in the area. Lipton himself had once spent a great deal of energy getting himself accepted into this harried little inner circle of writers, which included Lawrence Spingarn, Thomas McGrath, and James Boyer May—after a lifetime of writing potboilers for large sums of money. Once accepted into the literary fraternity, Lipton seemed determined to get himself thrown out—and when he finally succeeded, he took his Venice protégés with him, effectively cutting them off from any hope of acceptance. Time and Lipton's death have healed some of the damage, but Venice West still represents something of an outlaw strain in Southern California letters. The poet Stuart Perkoff's editor, Paul Vangelisti, draws a hard line between the writer he admired and the tradition he considered pure moonshine.

Where the general public was concerned, it was certainly nothing that the Venice beats wrote or painted that made them the objects of ridicule and even fear. Nor was bohemianism really the issue; if the beats had merely been eccentric, they might have slid along. The Southern California "nut," with a bottle of goat's milk and sign predicting the end of the world, was already a well-established stock figure, and the Los Angeles basin had a long tradition of congeniality to the odd and unconventional. Vedanta, Theosophy, Rosicrucianism, spiritualism, New Thought, and the Self-Realization Fellowship had all found homes there, right along with Krishnamurti, Paramahansa Yogananda, Ernest Holmes, and Aimee Semple MacPherson. Nudism, spiritualism, bodybuilding, ethical vegetarianism, Theocracy, and homeopathy all coexisted more or less amiably with circus-tent revivalism, militant atheism, the Nation of Islam, and the Church of Wicca. The city's older, pre-Forest Lawn-era cemeteries were studded with crypts bearing the sun disk, wings, and cobras of ancient Egypt, while the vast industrial complex collectively known as "Hollywood" housed three of the most powerful crypto-religions of modern times, the American motion picture, television, and record industries.

For more than fifty years, Hollywood had been the world's great channeler and shaper of mass fantasy, with its own inscrutable doctrines of beauty, perfection, reward, punishment and deification. Though not particularly systematic about it, the industry tended to emphasize the marks of virtue that showed in pictures—material goods were easy to photograph, inner peace somewhat trickier—and because of its presence, the fabrication of dreams and beliefs was as calmly accepted in Los Angeles as the harvesting of cotton in Fresno County.

Paradoxically, none of this made Los Angeles a really tolerant city. It was not an easy place to defy convention; it simply tolerated a great many odd conventions. As late as 1959, local authorities were still trying to root communist teachers out of the public schools, and the police department had acquired a national reputation for persecuting homosexuals. But personal eccentricity, if not political or sexual unorthodoxy, was a long-standing tradition, and much that was culturally foreign, cranky, and strange routinely slipped into the realm of tolerated behavior before the gates, as gates will, slammed shut.

The gates slammed hard on the Venice beats. It was one thing to harbor strange ideas; it was another, in the language of the theater, to "kid the show." In Southern California, the show was economic growth—and the unquestioning belief in its goodness. From 1953 to 1963, the Los Angeles metropolitan area added 300,000 new residents a year, or not quite one thousand per day—and there was a reason why people were coming.

Between 1950 and 1957, at least 15,000 new single-family houses were built each year in the city alone; in the same time frame, manufacturing jobs in what had been an overwhelmingly service economy more than doubled, growing twice as fast as the population itself. In adjacent counties, housing-tract construction made possible by state and Federal veterans' benefits from two wars swallowed up prime agricultural land. Communities with names like Dairyland, Dairy City, and Dairy Valley incorporated valiantly to save themselves, only to vanish. By 1960, the "Southland" held seven and a half million people, and there was no reason for most people to think it would ever end. Growth was nature's way, and the best thing about it was that there seemed to be something in it for everybody.

That makes it particularly ironic that the Venice beats, preaching the virtues of having nothing in a place where everyone expected to have more tomorrow, should be left out of most accounts of the Beat Generation. They were the movement's point men where the attitudes it challenged were strongest, and yet the inference seems to be that they were not "real" beats—just amateurs from the no-class end of California who never did anything but attract publicity. They certainly attracted plenty of that, but, then, so did that born-again marketing researcher, Allen Ginsberg.

The fact is that the Beat Generation as a whole enjoyed a curious relationship with its own hype. It was always the cultural equivalent of that old science-fiction standby, the cyborg—part human, part manufactured, and no one, least of all the creature itself, quite able to say where the organism left off and the contraption began. It also included more than one biological generation. Kerouac, Ginsberg, and Burroughs were old enough to have served in World War II, and Charlie Foster was a combat veteran. Most of the original Venice beats were Korean War-era enlisted men (except for Stuart Perkoff, who resisted the draft in 1948). The beatniks who flocked to North Beach, Greenwich Village, and Venice West in 1959 and 1960, however, tended to be very young people who had read about the revolution and wanted to join it. Kerouac's biographers usually treat the publicity, the hangers-on, and the rebellion's worshipful younger recruits either as aberrational (Jack never meant *this*!) or as a skewed confirmation of his power to inspire. While that was certainly true from Kerouac's point of view, it avoids the issue of who and what the Beat Generation really was—let alone explain its pull on the public's imagination.

As the "third" beat community—third, that is, after North Beach and Greenwich Village, which continue to draw most of the scholarly attention because of the "star system" that necessarily characterizes literary history—Venice West may supply some fresh answers. In its own time, it actually provided the detail-hungry public with most of what it thought it knew about the beat way of living. Even if nobody knew the names of its artists and poets, everyone seemed to be aware of what they wore, how they talked to each other, and what strategies they used to support life without holding jobs. That was Lawrence Lipton's doing—and the mass media, with their preference for eye-catching symbols and explanations of twenty-five words or less, decided to run his version of the story. Lipton's book, *The Holy Barbarians* (1959), became the outsider's handy one-volume guide to the beat scene, complete with photographs, capsule biographies, transcribed conversations, a ready-made historical context, and even a glossary of beat jargon in the back. It was a distorted picture but a vivid one, and it has stuck.

That is one reason for studying the Venice beats. Whatever else it may have been, the phenomenon of which they became a part was an example of something real merging with something fabricated to produce something totally unforeseeable: a new branch of popular culture dedicated to the *rejection* of popular culture. Its life cycle was interrupted and transformed by public awareness, and the effects of that awareness are more easily seen in the story of Venice West than in any accounts of the two better-known beat enclaves. Long before the beats, San Francisco and Greenwich Village had well-established traditions of cultural revolt and experimentation; Venice had only a local reputation for cheap thrills and oddness. Yet its tiny community of dropouts was living the "beat" life long before Lawrence Lipton pulled that label out of the headlines and forced his neighbors to wear it for the rest of their lives. Though his book was an honest attempt to describe a simpler and perhaps truer way of living, his street barker's instincts prevailed. No one actually did more to sell the Beat Generation to the American people—and when something is sold, it becomes a commodity.

The fact that Lipton was telling an essentially true story is another reason to look closely at Venice West. Before "the book," Larry's neighbors were genuinely dedicated to a code of ethics, ideals, and behavior they had largely invented for themselves. If they were trying to measure up to anyone, it was Charlie Parker, not Kerouac's hero, Dean Moriarty. They lived on subsistence incomes in the shabbiest part of Southern California's tackiest beach town, held jobs no longer than they had to, and considered the sacrifice worth it if it freed them from the false values and phony satisfactions of conventional life. They used illegal drugs to draw themselves even farther away from respectable society, and even closer to each other. Instead of amassing possessions and staring into the television set, they wrote poetry, painted pictures, made collages, and tried to burrow into each other's minds through endless hours of self-revelatory talk.

Their contempt for middle-class people and their values was the equal of any New York intellectual's, and they cheerfully paid a higher price for it—complete and voluntary obscurity. By their own transmuted version of the Puritan ethic, a fully realized human being was one who lived for art, friendship, love, and candor, and whose devotion was expressed through undistracted, unrelenting, unrewarded work. They even agonized about the temptations of fame within their own closed circle. All of this was hard enough to bring off in isolation, when the outside world neither knew nor cared, but when the eye of the public turned their way, in 1959 and 1960, the results were both cruel and bizarre, if occasionally heroic. Their history is one of struggle—to survive and create in a materialistic society; to imagine, construct, and sustain a competing version of reality; and to keep faith with each other despite the worst that publicity, notoriety, the herd instinct and their own self-destructive tendencies could do to them.

This study devotes most of its attention to the beats themselves, and inevitably invites comparison to a pair of well-known books on pre–World War I Greenwich Village, Arthur Wertheim's *The New York Little Renaissance* (1976) and Robert E. Humphrey's *Children of Fantasy* (1978), focusing, as they do, on the lives of key individuals. It is not, strictly speaking, a community study, since Venice West was not a community. It was, like Humphrey's prewar Villagers, an "island of art and freedom surrounded by a hostile world of crass materialism and hypocritical respectability"—or at least a collection of like-minded rebels who tried to make it so.

There were, of course, crucial differences between the Little Renaissance and Venice West. In the first years of the century, Greenwich Village lay within easy striking distance of the literal center of American culture, popular as well as elite. Small but determined intellectual guerrillas could choose their targets, strike, and fall back to the relative safety of an established, tolerated bohemian community. The Venice beats, by contrast, lived near but tried to ignore Hollywood, and in the end, it was Hollywood that pounced on them. Nor did Venice, that embarrassing stepchild of Los Angeles, offer them any support; after 1959, its solid citizens were always trying to drive them away. If the Village of Max Lerner and Floyd Dell was the perfect staging area for guerrilla raids on the dominant culture, Stuart Perkoff's Venice was an untenable place to retreat from it. Besides, the Village rebels really expected to transform American civilization; the Venice beats did not. They dreamed about changing people's consciousness through art, but they knew the people better than that. What they really wanted to do was to write their poems, paint their paintings, take their drugs, love their friends, and keep from getting busted by the police.

The prewar Villagers were also extremely well-connected. They were, in fact, elitists who never doubted their own superiority. They had studied at first-rate universities and often remained close to their professors. Unless they were "excessively eccentric or uncouth," they were as much at home in Mabel Dodge's strategically located salon as in their own romantically shabby rooms and cheap bars. They had that much in common, moreover, with the better-known members of the Beat Generation—Kerouac and Ginsberg had studied at Columbia; Burroughs was a Harvard man and a member of the business-machine family; Gary Snyder had been steeped in a new kind of elitism at Reed College; and even Gregory Corso eventually got himself "adopted" at Yale. Kenneth Rexroth, who initially shared his literary connections with Ginsberg and his friends, was connected to practically everybody in the literary world, especially the influential East Coast journals through which he later denounced his protégés. By comparison, the Venice beats were complete outsiders. Tony Scibella was a housepainter's son who chose poetry in preference to "the lunch box forever;" John Thomas was a computer programmer who hated computers; Stuart Perkoff was a dedicated misfit who seldom got anything right except his poetry. Lawrence Lipton, who willed the myth of Venice West into existence, was a hack writer, an obscure novelist and poet, and an immigrant from Tsarist Poland. Of all the Venice beats, only Charlie Foster started out with any substantial advantages in life, and he spent his whole life making sure they would do him no good.

The Village rebels also tended to go on to bigger and better things—Walter Lippman to the deanship of American journalism, Eugene O'Neill to near-godhood in the American theater, John Reed to a grave at the foot of the Kremlin Wall. They could plausibly claim to have "helped change the entire course of twentieth-century American painting and literature"—not only by producing art and literature, but by decisively influencing those who bought, exhibited, and published it. The Venice beats, for the most part, remain unpublished and unhung. The best of them were very good indeed, but that is almost beside the point. What they really contributed to the culture of the fifties was their example of lives based on art, poverty, and a separate arrangement with reality, at a time when that amounted to an assault on common sense.

But millions of Americans did find them irresistible, if only as an alluring source of consternation. This was not entirely Lawrence Lipton's doing. From 1948 through at least 1962, Henry Luce, that staunch upholder of Protestant values in Asia, was in the habit of receiving a fortnightly briefing paper on the activities of the avant-garde throughout America, prepared for him and his senior editors by a shrewd and very canny researcher named Rosalind Constable. Ms. Constable, who apparently had no other responsibility (and was also said to be the only person at Time-Life with an office, Room 2221, but no title), regularly scanned some 160 obscure publications, including *Contact, Evergreen Review*, several English and French journals, and the *Village Voice* (whose columnist John Wilcock obtained a copy of one briefing in 1962). The purpose of her report, as she herself wrote, was to "draw attention to the more off-beat events, sometimes the very ones that are causing such consternation among the critics. . . . And the weirder the better, if there is reason to believe that the author knows what he is doing. It is just possible (as history has sometimes proved) that he is inventing a new language which takes most people, including most critics, time to learn." It is therefore not surprising that the relationship between the Luce Publications and the Beat

Generation should have been as close and often perverse as that of, say, Robert Capa and the wars of the twentieth century—although what *Time, Life,* and their close competitors chose to make of the beats is a more complex issue.

It is also interesting to note that while everyone seemed to have an opinion about the beats' mental stability, no one seemed to take much notice of the only formal psychological study ever devoted to the issue: Francis J. Rigney and L. Douglas Smith's unpretentious little book, *The Real Bohemia.*

Dr. Rigney, a San Francisco psychotherapist, had spent every night from October 1958 through January 1959 in the Grant Street section of North Beach, getting to know the people and persuading them to take a battery of standard psychological tests. Fifty-one bohemians cooperated fully, out of a total beat population he estimated at between 180 and 200 persons. While his standards of sickness and health were understandably skewed in favor of conventional society—one was, or was not, able to "function" within it, and was therefore healthy or not healthy—Dr. Rigney found much to intrigue him and to admire among the Grant Street bohemians.

Yes, he said, many of them were "sick":

> Sickness stalks the Beach. The largest number in our group were found to be lonely, depressed, anxious, only ocasionally *able* to work despite, in the cases of some, real gifts. . . . But unlike many communities, they do not *conceal* these problems. . . . These Bohemians have created a combined artistic and therapeutic community whose inhabitants are trying to help themselves, but only in their own way.

While the beats scored high on the parts of the tests which indicated "psychic and physical distress," they also showed a strong capacity for "self-acceptance." While Dr. Rigney certainly felt it was better to be cured than to stay sick, he also came close to saying that the beats' psychic troubles and their honesty about them tended to balance each other out, especially in comparison with members of ordinary society.

He did note a certain hostility to women, who were viewed by the men as an "encumbrance" and a "source of problems for man." Few of the men expected anything but sex out of a relationship with a woman, and most had trouble imagining one that was "warm and enduringly human." As for drug addiction, or what we would now call substance abuse, he found that while there was more of it among the beats than in the general population, it was still a "minority phenomenon," and the chief difference was that the beats still treated the addicts among them as human beings. Besides, the real destroyer among them was, of all things, alcohol.

What did "real" beats look like? What did they wear? Despite the general impression that there was a beatnik "uniform"—beards, grubby clothes, and sandals for the men, leotards, bulky sweaters and basic black for the women—Dr. Rigney found no evidence of it among his subjects. Of the thirty-three men he studied, nineteen were consistently clean-shaven, four had mustaches, and ten had beards; twelve went about in sandals much of the time, but fourteen, or nearly half, wore ordinary business suits practically every day. Twelve of the eighteen women were seen to wear black stockings "more than once," and seven wore black dresses on a fairly regular basis; but only six wore leotards. Three were "very chic"; the rest "varied," with eight described as "very neat" and only five as "shabby to sloppy." This, of course, was in the winter of 1958–59; it would have been interesting to see what the costume mix was like one year later, after the real media blitz and the publication of the *The Holy Barbarians*, but Rigney was interested in committed bohemians, not worshipful seekers who had practiced in front of mirrors in San Leandro, Daly City, or Bakersfield.

But where had the beatnik come from? While the stereotype contained no hint of his social and economic background, it was never suggested of him, as it would be of the stereotypical hippie, that he felt free to defy convention because he had been born with privileges that he could not imagine losing. Perhaps because the beatnik was, by definition, a failure, it hardly occurred to anyone to ask how far he had fallen. On the other hand, since he was also, by definition (*Partisan Review*'s as well as *Time*'s), unlettered, some of his hostility toward the prevailing culture had to be presumed to have sprung from envy. *Of course* he rejected high art and middle-class morality—what did he know of either one? Yet 16 percent of Dr. Rigney's subjects were the sons and daughters of "professionals and big entrepreneurs," compared to a national average of 2.7 percent; 20 percent came from "educated semiprofessional" backgrounds, compared to 9.8% percent of the general population; 30 percent described their parents as "white collar," as opposed to the standard 18.9 percent; 28 percent were of "blue collar" origin, despite the fact that fully 48 percent of the people answered to that description. While the government still counted a fifth of the nation as "unskilled" or unemployed, only 4 percent of Rigney's beatniks came from such a background.

What did Rigney's findings mean? At the very least, they meant that the stereotypical beatnik was a repository of fantasy. On the one hand, he represented the absurdity of arguing with "real life"; on the other, he offered a way out, if only in the imagination. That was probably why the popular media, which were perfectly capable of getting their facts straight about Amazonian Indians, trapdoor spiders, and the Battle of El Alamein, preferred exploiting the comic-strip beatnik to finding out about the real one.

"Why this interest?" Dr. Rigney wrote. "Why this simultaneous fascination and repugnance?" He thought the answer lay with the onlooker. His subjects' behavior represented only an "exaggerated and prolonged" version of the "dynamics common to everyone." But if everyone went through the same "search for identity and contact," especially in adolescence, why all the fuss? "It is the intensity—real or fancied," he wrote, "which disturbs the onlooking outsider. The open sexual or angry material that threatens the stabilized attitude systems and defenses of those ordinarily *hiding their own own such impulses*."

He hastened to add: "But the ability to hide problems is not synonymous with health."

The beats of Venice West, as already noted, tended to come from a little further down the social ladder and to look a little more like the stereotype. But, then, Larry Lipton had essentially fashioned the stereotype around them. The fact is that the public liked and, as Dr. Rigney suggests, probably needed the fantasy image. By the time *The Real Bohemia* appeared, of course, the fad phase of America's relationship with the Beat Generation was largely over; the beatnik had become a part of the national folklore, if not its demonology. The interesting thing is that even at its high-water mark, only one social scientist seems to have cared enough about the truth behind a popular obsession to find out how much of it was based on fact.

The immediate result of Larry Lipton's book, on the other hand, was an influx of tourists, reporters, photographers, criminals, law enforcement officials, and would-be beatniks that overwhelmed Venice, anticipating San Francisco's Summer of Love by nearly a decade. Among the long-term results of the beat mania, in turn, were the installation of the far-out artist as a durable and extremely influential fixture in twentieth-century popular culture—and of the dropout life as an ever-present option for the younger members of the middle class. The beats, of course, can hardly claim all the credit for making alienation the presumed attitude of the young—or the preferred means of packaging things to sell to them. Part of the significance of the Beat Generation was that it proved rebellion sells, and Venice West, even without its cooperation, helped provide one of the earliest examples of how the culture of perpetual dissatisfaction could be profitably turned back on itself.

On the other hand, the Venice beats were real rebels whose message of personal revolt survived its exploitation by friend and enemy alike. Most of them remain unknown because they refused to cash in on themselves; even Larry Lipton, a man seemingly born with commercial genes, never allowed the fad he helped create make him rich—notorious, yes, but not rich. And while *Time, Life, Look, Newsweek, Reader's Digest,* the sagging movie industry, and the hungry television networks all borrowed his ready-made clichés to exploit the beats as clowns, they also succeeded in spreading the beat message of art, community, simplicity, spiritual independence, and freedom from possessions to a vast and surprisingly receptive audience. It was an assault on the American way of life promoted by the same people who manufactured its images. The irony was that it could only have been done in the course of selling soap, since, as the early fifties had clearly demonstrated, there were laws against trying to subvert the Republic on purpose.

"Where there's smoke," John F. Kennedy is reported to have said, "there is usually a smoke-making machine." This book can be read, in part, as a case study in the relationship of the smoke to the machine, and as a suggestion that the two often work together in ways more complicated, perverse, and ungovernable than most of us prefer to imagine. On the other hand, there was far more to Venice West than sensationalism and manufactured images. It really *was* a collective attempt to live outside the way of life other Americans considered normal, if not divinely inspired. To a surprising extent, it succeeded. Many of its founders died young, and nearly all of them allowed themselves to be driven away from Venice, but few of them lost their faith in what they had tried to do. Most of the ones who survive, in fact, are still trying to do it.

Accordingly, *Venice West* takes the form of a collective biography, with the narrative intentionally written, for the most part, as if nothing similar had ever happened before. In the fullest sense, nothing like it had. The significance of Venice West lies less in its artistic achievements—although there were quite a few—than in the audacity of its people in trying to live for art *and nothing else* in a city that adored, and still adores, its status as the world's biggest, gaudiest, and wildest symbol of material success. In its high-floating, quirky visions and stubborn, offhanded poverty, Venice was a brave and deliberate affront to an American Dream that worked.

In a sense, the beats served as a kind of spiritual Rorschach test for their fellow Americans. Intellectuals and middle-class working people alike tended to see their worst fears for society confirmed in them. Both sets of fears were based on the still greater fear that the beats and their approach to life might prevail. To mainstream intellectuals, they were childish, irresponsible, barbaric, self-indulgent and unworthy of moral leadership. To the coalescing New Left, they were childish, irresponsible, barbaric, self-indulgent, and incapable of revolutionary action. To millions of people who harbored traditional values, they were deviants who "don't work." Not only did they not work, they got away with not working because they had no desire for the things other people worked to get. In each case, what the beats did with their own lives was probably less important than the doubt their example cast on the validity of life as lived by others. In each case, the underlying fear was the same: "If the beats are right, we and all we strive for are nothing at all."

To which the beats themselves might have answered: "No, perhaps not. Why not start over?"

CHAPTER ONE

The reporter from *Time* was clearly annoyed. Sent out to California to interview mystery writer Craig Rice for a feature article on detective fiction, he found himself listening, instead, to her husband, Lawrence Lipton, a mildly successful novelist with pronounced opinions about practically everything. Lipton talked and talked; Rice herself, though usually memorable in conversation, scarcely opened her mouth. This was not what the reporter had come for, and he took his revenge in print. His article, which ran as the cover story for the issue dated 28 January 1946, celebrated Craig Rice as a gifted "professional" who had worked her way to the top of a tough, competitive business—and her husband as the kind of self-important "serious" writer who deserved all the obscurity he could get.

The article, "Mulled Murder, with Spice," described Rice as a wacky but disciplined craftswoman, hammering out best-seller after best-seller for a specialized readership that knew exactly what it wanted. It portrayed her husband, on the other hand, as an egghead, and a noisy one at that. *He* did his writing in a downtown office; *she* was content to work at home. While Rice seemed likely to become the first woman to win a "Gertrude" award for having sold a million copies of a single title in paperback, neither of Lipton's novels had won a Pulitzer, "much less a Gertrude." While she was pictured surrounded by her adoring teenaged children on the front lawn of their Santa Monica home, he was shown gesturing at his captive audience with a cigar, a pencil stuck behind his ear and a manuscript open in his lap. "A man of letters, he," the caption teased.

What the reporter failed to wring out of either of them was that Larry Lipton *was* Craig Rice—or at any rate, he was 50 percent of her. The Craig Rice books were a collaborative venture, and for the last two years, with Rice drinking again after six years of sobriety, Lipton had written practically everything. It was actually flattering of *Time* to call him an egghead who longed for readers, since he was, in fact, an unusually talented commercial writer who longed to be known as a thinker.

A forty-eight-year-old bohemian in a suit and tie, a veteran of radical literary and political movements in New York, Detroit, and Chicago, and the co-author, with Kenneth Rexroth, of an extraordinary document called the "Escalator Manifesto," Lipton was also a past editor of the Detroit *Jewish Chronicle*, a former director of national publicity for the Fox Theatre chain, and the well-paid author of stories, screenplays, and potboiler novels that almost never appeared under his own name. In his youth he had even worked briefly for Frank Harris, who had taught him a thing or two about resourcefulness. Upon learning what the Chicago Public Library had paid for an original manuscript of one of Oscar Wilde's books, Harris had ordered everyone in his office to start copying his own books back into manuscript form.

In his heart, Lipton despised hustling for money, but he was simply too good at it to leave it alone. He believed an artist could only succeed by being the world's idea of a failure, but that kind of failure, as he would later complain to Rexroth, came more easily to some people than to others. "I always *looked* like everything I was not," he complained to a friend, "and worse: I was capable of doing the very thing I had the most contempt for—and doing it well!"

He and Rice had worked well together. He wrote the rough copy, then she added the jokes, the little twists and turns, and the final polish. Their partnership had transformed Rice from a bright, hard-drinking, thirty-year-old failure into a confident, hard-working novelist who succeeded brilliantly in a field dominated by men. Since 1938 they had shared a life of sobriety, affection, good humor, and enormous literary output. The offbeat, engaging little novels had taken right off from the start.

The standard Craig Rice novel was a hard-boiled farce of the Dashiell Hammett variety—realistic on the outside, skewed on the inside, and with even less respect than Hammett's for the laws of probability. They were also full of drinking, which served as both a trademark and a standard plot device. Powered by alcohol, Rice's typically unheroic characters managed to muddle through some of the most hopeless situations in commercial fiction.

Each title normally sold between fifteen and twenty thousand copies in hardcover, which put Rice and Lipton in the same league with Raymond Chandler, Erle Stanley Gardner, Rex Stout, and Ellery Queen. At the rate of 10 to 15 percent of a standard cover price of two dollars, plus one to one-and-a-half cents for every paperback copy sold, the books earned enough to provide a better-than-comfortable living—so long as they continued to appear on schedule.

This was obviously the kind of success that earned a writer the respect of Time-Life, Inc. There was a double irony in the image of Lawrence Lipton, the "man of letters" whose ideas sold no better than his books. While he had every intention of becoming a full-time professional intellectual, he also meant to be read by large numbers of people. What good was it to have important ideas if nobody knew what they were? Some cerebral types might consider mass acceptance a sign of failure in itself, but not Larry Lipton. As much as he hated commercialism, nothing could shake his faith in the assumption that underlay it. If a book were good enough, people would buy it. If an idea were really right for its time, millions of people would change their ways of thinking to accommodate it—of that he was as sure as a man might ever be.

His performance for the *Time* interviewer was probably staged for the purpose of keeping the man away from Rice, whose alcoholism made it into the story by innuendo anyway. It was also a kind of out-of-town tryout for the persona of the new, undivided Larry Lipton, the one who signed his name to his books and wrote only the things he really meant to say. The mystery novels had finally made him secure enough to write "real" novels. The private man would now become the public man, while the truly secret man—the one who hated his own talent for making money—would be transformed by stages into the man who never was.

Almost six years before, Lipton had taken the first step by writing his "first" novel, *Brother, the Laugh Is Bitter*. Produced in seven weeks in the summer of 1940, it was a grittily realistic portrayal of two worlds he knew well, the Jewish slums and the glittering department store empires of Chicago. The book's hero, Max Levinsky, was an ex-bootlegger who had turned legitimate only to find himself excluded, conspired against and driven to murder by "respectable" anti-Semitism. The plot was rather contrived and the ending particularly hard to swallow, but that was Lipton's style. Though not a "cheap" writer, he was not a particularly deep one, either. Novels only interested him as vehicles, and where "serious" fiction was concerned, intellectual argument came first, social backdrop second, and plot and characterization dead last. He felt *Brother* deeply and believed in it ferociously. The anger it contained was real—real enough to overwhelm its artificiality, and real enough to give the book an enormous capacity for outraging others.

To handle such an important book, only a first-class New York publisher would do. It was not the prestige he wanted so much as the promotional resources of a major house. He liked to compare the situation of a first novel with that of a "B" picture in Hollywood, and he wanted to be assured of at least as much support as the average "B" movie got from the studios. When the book was still only half-written, he sent the manuscript to his friend at Vanguard Press, James T. Farrell, along with a "treatment" of the second half that proved to be equal parts synopsis, exegesis, and hard sell. He was still using the working title *With Fire and Flame*, but he thought he might change it to *He Killed Hitler*, because, as he confided to Farrell, "that's what Max really does when he kills Tod." But Farrell declined to read it, pleading near-blindness, and his colleague, James Henle, flatly rejected it. Lipton's next step was to answer a newspaper ad placed by Doubleday, Doran and Company, which had sent an editor, Ken McCormack, to recruit first novelists in Chicago. Lipton appeared at the Palmer House, manuscript in hand, and pressed his attack so fiercely that McCormack only escaped by promising to take the novel back with him to New York. Safe at last in Manhattan, however, McCormack, too, rejected it.

The next target was Simon and Schuster, which had just brought out Rice's latest title, *The Wrong Murder*, as an Inner Sanctum Mystery. At first he seemed to have a chance. Rice's editor, Lee Wright—who had no idea he was Lipton's editor too—reported that his fellow editors were already calling him "Jerusalem's Richard Wright." But when Joe Schuster himself returned from vacation, he personally spiked *With Fire and Flame*, and that, no matter what the boys in the back room thought, was that.

After major revisions and a change of title, Lipton finally sold the novel to Harper's—only to see its publication unaccountably delayed until 1942. On the other hand, Harper's paid him the extraordinary compliment of assigning *Brother* to Edward C. Aswell, who had been Thomas Wolfe's editor. Aswell, a patient man, had fashioned *The Web and the Rock* and *You Can't Go Home Again* from the tangle of manuscripts Wolfe had left behind at his death. But he was totally unprepared for Larry Lipton, who impressed him with the passion of his work but dismayed him with his apparent crassness. Aswell had never heard, for example, of hiring two literary agents for the same book—one to handle the publishing end of things and the other to sell the rights to the movies. But he expected brisk sales for *Brother, the Laugh Is Bitter*, especially among Jewish readers.

Just as the promotional campaign for *Brother* was getting under way, the publisher's Chicago salesman panicked. Anyone familiar with Chicago, he said, would immediately recognize "Bisset's" department store as a cryptogram for Marshall Field's, "Silverstein's" for Goldblatt's, and so on. Any or all of the city's real-life "class store" owners could be counted on to sue, especially when they read the part about a polite conspiracy to drive a Jewish competitor out of business. Virtually every page of *Brother, the Laugh Is Bitter* carried references to real people, real places, and real establishments—along with Lipton's opinion of their quality. Had anyone back in the New York office actually *read* this book? Did any of them know what "libel" meant?

Lipton refused to be alarmed. "Bisset's," he tried to explain, was not Marshall Field's. It was only a department store *like* Marshall Field's—which, now that the lawyers mentioned it, *did* happen to be known for its anti-Semitic business practices. It was also true that when most people from the Midwest imagined a department store, Marshall Field's tended to spring to mind. But *libel*?

Harper's attorneys were not amused; what people *tended* to think was precisely the point. It was no defense, either, to point out that none of the events in the book had actually happened; from the legal point of view, the less factually true a libelous book was, the greater the libel. The only way out was to purge the novel of all objectionable material. Since the first edition had already been printed, although not yet bound, it would have to be scrapped. If Lipton really wanted to be published that badly, and if he were willing to bear the expense himself, he could still produce a second edition, using a procedure that amounted to a parody of the creative process. Aswell explained:

> You will have to figure, with the greatest possible care, the exact number of characters, including spaces and punctuation marks, in the lines that are removed, and in drafting new copy, you will have to substitute words that will fill the exact space of the matter that is taken out. Then this new matter will need to be set, and plates of the new lines cast, and these lines then plugged in to the page plates. It will not be possible simply to cut anything, nor will it be possible to have over-runs or under-runs.

In short, Lipton would have to reconstruct his novel with one eye on the courts and the other almost literally on his fingers. Nor was that all. By now the lawyers, as lawyers will, had begun to worry about unseen dangers. Take, for example, the matter of "Little Meyer Silverstein": the reader who identified "Silverstein's" with Goldblatt's was also likely to mistake the fictional Mr. Silverstein for the real-life Mr. Goldblatt. "If Goldblatt is a little man," Aswell warned Lipton, "Then for God's sake don't call Silverstein little. Make him anything else but little. And that's the principle to follow throughout . . . change the descriptions purposely so they won't fit the real characters. Then you'll be safe."

What the lawyers really wanted was for Lipton to *imagine* possible objections and cave in to them in advance—if he wanted to see the book published, that is. Lipton objected, but he obeyed, and in less than two weeks he returned a bowdlerized version. "Is it okay?" he asked hopefully.

"All I can say is that you astound me," Aswell replied. "Of course it is not okay. It is libel in its simplest, purest and most pristine form." Since Lipton was clearly not up to the task of castrating his own novel, Harper's engaged an attorney—a *Chicago* attorney—to finish it. The results were truly extraordinary. It was decided, for example, that the entire city of Chicago had to come out. The story must be set, instead, in a mythical place that was essentially nowhere at all, like Superman's Metropolis.

lace would simply be called "The City," and if Lipton
it to be a Midwestern city, it would have to be rendered
tree of all identifying features. There could certainly be no mention of a Gentile conspiracy against Max Levinsky. Far better,
from a legal standpoint, that only one "bad" store owner should
be an anti-Semite; that way, "bad" people everywhere could be
condemned without implying that prejudice was ever more than
a matter of wicked individuals.

When the lawyers were through, it was still Lipton who had
to make the changes, space by space. He hated the whole exercise, but not enough to withdraw the book from publication.
He still thought it retained most of its original message, and that
like all good books, it deserved to sell. He had even decided that
John Garfield should play the lead in the Hollywood version.
He saw no particular irony in trying to sell to the movies what
had barely been rescued from the courts, or in expecting a novel
about bigotry in respectable society to do well with the respectable buyers of hardcover books.

Though good at first, sales of *Brother* soon shrank to practically nothing. Lipton cried foul, blaming halfhearted promotion, but Aswell had another explanation. Had it ever occurred
to Lipton that his fellow Jews might not like the book? "If you
have seen any favorable comments from that quarter," Aswell
wrote, "I'd like to know what they are, because I have none. No
Jewish person to whom I sent it has been willing to comment
on it."

In fact, many Jews hated it. Sydney B. Lavine, writing in
behalf of the Chicago branch of the Anti-Defamation League,
scolded Harper's:

> The filth and sex that drips from these pages are abominable,
> particularly as they concern the Jewish people. The book is not
> only insulting to the Christian, but also to the Jew. . . . Please
> understand that there is no desire upon our part to censor the
> publishers nor tell them what to publish. It is only because we
> are anxious that your company retain the good-will relationship
> without Christian and Jewish contacts that we bring this matter
> to your attention.

The League also considered 1942 a bad time to charge American society at large with anti-Semitism; there was a war on,

after all, and the sides were very plainly drawn. Lipton hastened to assure Aswell that "opposition by Anti-Defamation League is sure proof of approval by vast majority of Jews," meaning that the League was made up of stodgy, unimaginative old worriers who spoke for practically nobody. He also sent a reply to Sidney Lavine, whose attack had hurt him deeply. But he knew he needed substance, not arguments, to save his book— numbers to counter the League's numbers, prestige to counter its prestige.

He also recognized that timing *was* part of the problem with *Brother*, though not in quite the way its critics charged. Much that was "wrong" with his book was also wrong with his friend Richard Wright's *Native Son*. Both novels defied the oppressor by rejecting his moral standards, and both, in so doing, had made themselves unacceptable to millions of potential friends. To black and Jewish organizations that had worked for decades to promote an image of conventional respectability, it seemed only reasonable to expect black and Jewish writers to remember whose side they were on. Instead, Lipton and Wright had created heroes who were at least as morally repulsive to many thoughtful readers as prejudice itself. It was a predictable response, and the only really surprising thing about it was that it certainly surprised Larry Lipton.

On the other hand, some prominent Jews agreed with him. Nathan Rothman came to his aid with a friendly review for the *Saturday Review of Literature*, observing bitterly that whenever Jews wrote about Jews, caricatures seemed to result—some derogatory, but most so lofty as to be past belief. Why, he asked, was it only the Jews who had to be "good, talented, worthy, in order to earn existence?" Another admirer of *Brother*, Lewis D. Browne, wrote to volunteer his support, his good offices, and unrestricted access to his own formidable network of literary contacts, which included Thomas Mann, Lion Feuchtwanger, Emil Ludwig, Upton Sinclair, Norman Cousins, Ben Hecht, Max Lerner, Sinclair Lewis, and Rabbi Bernard Brickner, of Cleveland's Euclid Avenue Temple. Browne also advised Lipton to look to the masthead of a Zionist publication, *The Fighting Jew*, for the names of potential allies.

Together, he and Lipton launched a frenzied campaign to gather endorsements which they hoped would make the Anti-Defamation League's objections seem parochial and even childish. Browne wrote the first letters, asking his friends to read *Brother* and comment on it for attribution. Aswell then sent each of them a free copy, and Lipton followed up with an uncharacteristically deferential letter describing himself, his work, and his embattled situation.

The results were mixed, but, on the whole, gratifying. Lipton, the lifelong hack writer, soon found himself respected as a novelist by some of the great living men of letters. Emil Ludwig, the biographer of Goethe, admired his nerve, and Ludwig and the co-author of *Having Wonderful Crime* spent a friendly and collegial afternoon together in Santa Monica. Thomas Mann, another Santa Monica neighbor, spoke highly of *Brother*'s "strong and verisimilar narrative." Lion Feuchtwanger, whose home in Pacific Palisades had been the capital-in-exile of German letters since the thirties, became a strong friend as well as a powerful supporter. But Lipton's most gratifying endorsement was also the one that hurt the most.

"You have the true eye and ear, and they are not common," wrote Sinclair Lewis, who was the one American novelist Lipton had expected to understand his position completely. He was also Lipton's kind of artist: fearless, uncompromising, honored in his lifetime, and a popular success only *after* he had made up his mind to write nothing but the truth as he saw it. Lipton had actually sent him copies of his choicest replies to his critics, which Lewis, to his complete surprise, considered a very bad idea. "People get so easily bored by other people's defense of themselves," he wrote. "You could not be more attacked than I was for 'Elmer Gantry'—and even 'Main Street' and 'Babbitt' were pounded pretty well. I made a rule of never answering anything, and where I have broken this rule, I have, if I remember, always been sorry."

He meant it in genuine friendship, but the rebuke stung. The truth was that Lewis was dedicated to the novel in a way Lipton was not. Lipton wrote to provoke controversy, which was not *exactly* the same thing as pursuing the truth for its own sake. He seemed to live for a good fight. When Rabbi Bernard Brickner expressed the opinion that Max Levinsky was an unfit representative of the Jewish people, Lipton replied that it was just this kind of narrow-mindedness that made people turn to novelists for their education about life, "and not to the sermons of rabbis and preachers." In his rapture at being handed such a straight line, he managed to forget that it was he who had approached Brickner for support.

Oddly enough, while Lipton and his fellow Jews continued to fight over *Brother*, no anti-Semites bothered to attack the book. None of Lipton's critics, Jew or Gentile, tried to deny the strength of anti-Semitism in America; no one even claimed that Lipton had told a lie, only that he had expressed an ugly truth in ugly terms. For Lipton, the struggle transcended the issue itself. He was a man born to fight recklessly for ideas, and the more those ideas offended the comfortable and the well-adjusted, the better. He loved being the center of controversy *almost* as much as he hated being attacked, and he fought for his way of telling the truth as if the telling were the truth itself.

The novel itself had become strangely unimportant to Lipton by the time Harper's decided to cut its losses. His blood was up, and the momentum carried him along into a brief but passionate involvement in Jewish-American politics. Unfortunately, he never quite came to grips with the positions of all the competing factions; after writing an article about the future of the Jews in Palestine, for example, he was reminded politely but firmly that such expressions as "the new Hebrew people" should not be tossed about without regard for their rather precise political meanings. Inevitably, his interest faded. Even Zionist politics were too conventional to hold him for long—and besides, the ground rules had been written by others. The only kind of controversy that could really hold his attention was one he had helped to start himself, and that he had grafted so firmly onto his own personality that no one could say for sure where he left off and the cause began.

His devotion to the novel was beginning to fade, too. He wanted to use his next one, *In Secret Battle*, to strike a blow at isolationism, but by 1944, when he got around to finishing it, any private citizen who wanted to denounce the isolationists had to wait in line behind all the heartland politicians. He had been scooped by events, just as his mildly radical hero, the "common man," had been scooped by the war propaganda effort. He had also rushed the book into print, and it showed. After missing all his deadlines, he had waived the right to see the galleys, so he never even knew where the publisher had inserted the chapter breaks until the first edition was in his hands. As usual, the promotional campaign was not energetic enough to suit him, but the whole exercise reflected nothing so much as his loss of patience with the "serious" novel itself. After *In Secret Battle*, he would always be starting new ones, but he would only finish the potboilers he needed to earn his living.

On the other hand, he was beginning to think his real vocation lay in poetry. Even that would have to wait for a while. He could only afford to write "real" books because the Craig Rice titles were selling. In fact, they were selling too well. Even at the rate of a quarter of a million words per year, he and Rice could not keep up with the demand. The unreasonable pace was at least part of the reason Rice had begun to drink again in 1944. As the pressure mounted, their marriage, anchored in work, turned destructive.

They separated early in 1946, shortly after giving the interview to *Time*. Their divorce was unpleasant, but hardly more wrenching than their final two years together. While Lipton took a beating from the lawyers, and Rice began to throw herself into one hopeless emotional venture after another, the wacky little whodunits continued to appear. In February 1948, the two of them signed an agreement to share the income from all Craig Rice properties, past, present and future, on a fifty-fifty basis. In practice, Lipton did most of the work and Rice collected somewhat more of the money, since publishers' checks were usually issued in her name. But it was her name, after all, that had the selling power; she needed him because her cycles of work, drink, and helplessness were growing steadily shorter.

Lipton had health problems of his own, but neither they nor the reduction in his income seemed to discourage him. He moved from a beachfront hotel in Santa Monica to a cottage near the boardwalk in Venice—a distinct, and, in its own way, satisfying step downward. It was the right sort of venue for a poet-philosopher who despised commercialism, even if he did need to hustle commercial jobs to pay his bills.

Lipton liked to say that Venice, unlike other slums, had been *built* as a slum. But it had no more been built as a slum than he himself had set out to be a mystery writer. Abbott Kinney, the developer, had built it as a genteel fantasy, with seawater canals, graceful, arching bridges, and gondolas imported from the "real" Venice, gondoliers and all. Stockbrokers and sales managers from Los Angeles could keep summer homes there, or even commute all year round—and that was the whole idea.

Kinney wanted solid, acquisitive citizens to be able to live slower, more cultured lives in the Los Angeles basin. He had chosen the Venice motif because, like millions of other Americans who read magazines and peered through stereoscopes, he knew exactly what it looked like and found it almost unbearably romantic. It would have been hard to find a better symbol of business and esthetic values triumphing together—except, perhaps for Florence, and lots on the Del Rey salt marshes were cheaper than land that looked like Florence.

The trouble with Kinney's scheme was that after he had sold the land, he could only impose his vision on the community by dominating its politics. After his death, Venice property owners behaved much like other property owners in Southern California. When it became expensive to maintain their own city services, they voted for annexation by Los Angeles, and promptly saw half their canals filled in. When oil was discovered, a forest of derricks sprang up overnight. Instead of a retreat for those who had already arrived, Venice became one of the places newcomers to Los Angeles stayed first. Kinney's Venetian facades, built of standard California building materials—plaster, pipe, two-by-fours, and stucco—weathered quickly. The surprising thing was not that they crumbled so soon, but that so many of them lasted so long.

The same could be said for his dream; a rougher, hardier version of it did endure. Venice did not become an ordinary suburb of Los Angeles—or even an ordinary beach town. The people who preserved Kinney's fantasy were not necessarily of the sort he had in mind, but they clung to it like any other object of civic pride. Grocers, realtors, roustabouts, airframe welders, ice cream makers, and petty criminals conspired to make at least *some* of the laws of ordinary reality unenforceable. Gambling was illegal in Los Angeles, but it had *almost* been legal in the Venice bingo parlors for decades. The automobile tyrannized the rest of Southern California, but in Venice, people parked their cars and walked. The old hotels with their arches and tilework made Windward Avenue look like a movie set. The people often seemed to have wandered in from a number of different productions, but they shared what other California communities only issued proclamations about, a sense of tradition. It was an oddball tradition, more in the spirit of the Emperor Norton than of Father Serra or Pio Pico, but it was real, it could still be felt, and no one had to pay a public relations agency to keep it going. Although Venice would never be the esthetic preserve Kinney had hoped for, it had reached its own rough understanding with the arts. It never subsidized them, but with its respect for the eccentric and its crude, ripe, Elizabethan mixture of people, it made them possible in other ways.

By the time Lipton moved to Venice its central lagoon had been a traffic circle for thirty years, but Windward Avenue, Kinney's grand double *galleria* copied from St. Mark's Square, still ran unbroken from the circle to the Ocean Front. At the promenade its archways opened outward, and the fantasy remained more or less intact for another fifty yards to the south and a hundred and fifty to the north, toward Santa Monica. Alternating male and female faces grinned from the bolted facings of the cast-iron columns, which Kinney, looking ahead, had sunk into the concrete when the lots were laid out. He had planned the convergence of Windward and the Ocean Front as a formal gateway to the sea. Instead, its arches and ornate facings had lent a crackpot dignity to the wildest amusement pier and toughest midway on the West Coast. With the pier dismantled now, the broad open space remained, a gateway to the sand, if not, in any practical sense, to the sea.

To the south the Ocean Front narrowed to an ordinary sidewalk, as commercial property gave way to weatherbeaten beach front houses. It ran north all the way through Ocean Park, still known in some circles as "O'Sheeny Park," with its battered but still profitable amusement pier, its solid brick apartment houses, and its community of refugees from East Coast winters, the Germans, and the Tsar. During the tourist season, the half-mile from Venice Boulevard to the Santa Monica line was a natural place for families to lose sight of the city, for suckers to lose their money, for drug users to score in relative safety. Now that the bingo parlors had finally been shut down, the beachfront arcades featured skee-ball, pinball, miniature bowling, pop-up baseball, electric-eye shooting galleries, dart throws, ring tosses, mechanical contraptions for winning worthless prizes, and, carefully guarded from minors, "art shows"—viewing boxes with still or moving pictures of naked women, posed with a timid lasciviousness that approached real innocence. Above all, the Ocean Front offered outsiders a mildly titillating seediness, a sense of risk without much risk, in the same way that bingo had offered the opportunity to gamble—not for the money, really, but for the feeling of getting away with something.

Lipton felt renewed, and his literary output showed it. By November 1948, he was far enough ahead to marry his former secretary, Nettie Brooks, and to start thinking seriously about publishing a book of poetry, to be called *Rainbow at Midnight*.

He still drew the same line as ever between his life's work and his livelihood—and as before, his two creative halves hardly seemed to take notice of each other. He wanted to phase out the literary whoring as quickly as possible, but it was expensive to be sick—and he and his wife were sick much of the time. At the end of 1950, when it again seemed possible for Lipton to devote most of his time to serious writing, Craig Rice began to write, wire, and call as often as once a week for money—ten dollars here, fifty dollars there, usually to help her out of one impossible situation and into another.

Rice's life had become a nightmare of bounced checks and unpaid rent. Her publishers were still willing to buy whatever she had to offer, but Lipton had all the old stories in his files. Rice could rarely concentrate long enough to produce new ones. The money she did make from reprint royalties and movie work tended to vanish within days—gone for back taxes, back rent, and petty day-to-day living expenses.

Lipton sent her money every third or fourth time she asked him for it. It added up quickly. He kept a tally of what she owed him, but he seldom pressed her for it. He was doing reasonably well writing radio and movie scripts, including all the episodes of "Grand Motel," a thirteen-week, five-nights-a-week series for network radio. The only way he could keep going was by not stopping, and he could afford neither the extra drain on his income nor the extra work it took to make up for it. Besides, it soon became clear that each time he bailed Rice out on a piecemeal basis, her life took another lurch toward its next crisis.

"You know I'll never let you run short of money as long as royalties are coming in, no matter *what* our contractual arrangements are," he wrote. "So stop tormenting yourself about it." But milking old properties had its limits. There were only so many stories to be dusted off and so many magazines available to run them. Only a source of income that did not rely on new material would enable Rice to pull her life together—or to live with some dignity if it came completely apart. While Rice sounded out stage and comic strip syndication prospects in New York, Lipton turned to the television industry, whose long-term possibilities might prove to be unlimited.

Within six weeks he had all but closed a deal with Meredith Productions, which was offering a six-month option on thirteen stories in exchange for an advance of $250, $200 in cash each time a story was made into a television episode, and the understanding that each option exercised constituted an option purchased on yet another story. If the price Meredith Productions got for each episode went up, so did its payment for the story on which it was based. Lipton and Rice would also receive a "producer's profit"—7 percent of everything the series earned above its production costs and sales charges—*in perpetuity*. As he reminded Rice, "These things go on for years in television."

In New York, Rice's personal life careened on as usual. She even had to pawn her own typewriter and rent another—and four days after that, she pawned the rented typewriter. Lipton sent her some money along with the good news that an even better deal was in the works—same terms, more money, and 10 percent "producer's profit." He had to shanghai a mutual friend, Jack Lewis, into making sure Rice signed the contract in front of a notary. While the deal threatened to go soft more than once between the signing of the contract and the airing of the show, it held firm. That and Simon and Schuster's publication of the definitive Craig Rice anthology, *Forty-nine Murderers*, seemed to make them both secure.

In fact, Lipton had learned enough to be more than secure. He had always known how to wring money out of popular culture, and the last few months of hustling had taught him exactly what it would take to earn a great deal more, especially from television, a young industry ravenous for good material. But he could not bring himself to do it. Write scripts for money, yes; cut deals for a living, no. The entertainment industry would just have to keep its money—or *most* of it, at any rate.

In the year of frenzied work he had written two motion picture screenplays, ghostwritten a popular science book called *The Air We Live In*, produced no fewer than sixty-five radio scripts for the "Grand Motel" series, sold two packaged deals to television, and given Craig Rice security, if she could keep it. By the end of 1952, the project he cared most about was the one that promised to pay nothing at all—*Rainbow at Midnight*, his book of poetry. He had committed himself to closing his own divisions; the side of himself that he respected would emerge as the entire man. He would always write for his living, but he would never write again for more than just enough.

CHAPTER TWO

Lawrence Lipton had no intention of being an obscure poet. He meant to be known and read. For that to happen quickly, as he hoped it would, *Rainbow at Midnight* would have to be published well. The fifty-four-year old poet also knew what an extraordinary sales effort that might require on his part. He took it for granted that "poetry, an amateur game in which it is against the rules to get paid," was "as full of petty politics as amateur tennis," and that he was going to have to learn those politics from scratch. He assumed that quality counted for something, but when it came to his future in American letters, he was not a gambling man.

From a marketing point of view, *Rainbow*, like any book of poems, enjoyed one major advantage over a first novel: parts of it could be sold without hurting the sales potential of the book. In fact, that was one of the best ways of getting a book publisher to take a chance on it. There were scores of tiny markets for poetry in the early fifties. Though none of these "little" magazines paid anything, it was possible to build a reputation through them—always remembering, as Lipton did, that a small publisher had to be worked just as hard as a large one.

He submitted copies of the whole book to James Laughlin, the owner of the publishing company, New Directions, and to *California Quarterly*, the Los Angeles-based literary review that he planned to cultivate in person. He also started sending individual poems to such avant-garde reviews as *Goad, Flame, Embryo, Olivant, Inferno*, and, in Paris, Alexander Trocchi's expatriate journal *Merlin*. To cushion himself against failure, he assured his friends that these truly tiny magazines were only interested in poetry by "crackpots," but within a year, his work had appeared in all of them.

He knew, of course, that there was more to being published than being printed, so in November 1952 he approached a New York literary agent, Lucy Kroll, about handling *Rainbow*. She seldom represented poets—10 percent of nothing was still nothing—but Lipton sweetened the deal by throwing in his still-unfinished novel about a Venice gambler, *Gimpie*. Kroll had been impressed with *Brother*, and her skepticism vanished when she actually read his poems. "*Rainbow* magnificent," she wrote. "Advise your preference publishers."

Lipton was not particular; any of the big houses would do. But Kroll agreed with his friend and former Brentwood neighbor, Christopher Isherwood, that a book by an unknown poet needed a preface by a known one. The trouble was, he hardly knew any. His literary friends were all novelists and screenwriters, and he knew almost nothing about very recent poetry. Isherwood, on the other hand, knew practically everyone. His immediate circle included W. H. Auden and Gerald Heard. Dylan Thomas had been his house guest in the spring of 1950, and it was Isherwood who had done the driving when Dylan, like any other tourist, had wanted to meet Charlie Chaplin. Lipton, on the other hand, had managed to miss the Welshman's cockeyed but powerful reading at UCLA, even though he lived only a few minutes away.

Isherwood thought enough of *Rainbow* to suggest that Lipton approach one of his own friends, Selden Rodman, about writing the preface. Rodman also wrote long narrative poems, and he owed nothing to any of the tight little circles whose tastes and personal connections seemed to dominate the art.

To his regret, Lipton sent Rodman a copy of the book and asked for a "critical appraisal." Everyone else, he said, had been "too full of praise to do me any good at all." Rodman had a cure for that. "Neither the style nor the point of view," he wrote, "are sufficiently matured for a poem of this scope." It was probably the first time in Lipton's adult life that anyone had called him an amateur, and he answered Rodman, as he once had Sinclair Lewis, with a point-by-point defense of his work. Less stinging, but more discouraging, was the comment Lucy Kroll relayed to him from Louis Simpson, the poetry editor at

Bobbs-Merrill. Simpson found *Rainbow* at once derivative and out of date; poetry had taken some rather dramatic new turns in the last few years, and Lipton seemed to have missed them all. "I do not think," he concluded, "that Mr. Lipton is really an original poet."

How could a man be unoriginal if his ideas were his own? The poetry was admittedly topical, external, cerebral; there was almost nothing in it of the inner life—or of what the inner life was currently supposed to be. Yet Lipton's most coldly intellectual thoughts *were* his inner life. Part politics, part anthropology, part old-fashioned mystery play, *Rainbow* effectively summed up a lifetime of self-education and, more importantly, self-construction.

It was not so much a book of poems as a long essay written in verse *about* poetry. Its central theme was the ancient and admittedly savage role of the poet as society's shaman, communal speaker, and mystical explainer. Lipton thought poetry could renew the modern world by restoring the moral and spiritual authority of the bard; he wanted poetry to "be what it once was," a cultic exercise which *did* things as well as *said* things. "In short," he wrote, "it should be an *experience*."

It should also be an experience involving two parties, the reciter and the listener. Although poetry was essentially outside time, the ceremony through which it was invoked and made to work should be very much of the present, like all the other experiences people took seriously. Lipton himself had started reading his poems aloud to small groups; Lion Feuchtwanger was trying to arrange a dramatic reading of *Rainbow* "in the manner of 'Don Juan in Hell.'" Lipton was particularly interested in performing for the very young, whom he considered more receptive to the "sound" rather than the mechanics of poetry. He wanted to give them an older, deeper, psychologically truer experience than they could find in their books—one that had nothing to do with the publishing industry, and only a little to do with the printed page.

In the future, he said, "the Word" would re-authenticate human experience, while the poet would again become "the world's remembrancer." True poetry was a performance art; the words on the page were only the score for a communal and essentially nonliterate ritual of speaking and hearing. The goal of all *real* poetry was to leap across the barriers of civilization to the "savage source" from which everything spiritually and psychologically authentic in the human experience proceeded. Accordingly, the hero of *Rainbow at Midnight* was the "New Barbarian," a full-blooded pagan who came to the city as a destroyer, yet entered it humbly as "The Postulant."

"Good omen," said the poem's old, effete, helpless priests, "We have watched for such a one to come." The New Barbarian's methods might be crude and bloody, but they were pure, final, and, most important, irresistible. What society could resist the power of the unrestrained id?

Lipton was calling for nothing less than a great spiritual leap backward—for a restoration of the ritual life and of the many gods that had once presided over it. It might seem irrational and even pitiless, but it was the only truly *human* way in a world rapidly civilizing itself to death. "Rededicate our lives," he charged the New Barbarian:

> restore
> The sense of wonder; men made brothers
> Not in name alone, but deeper,
> In the ritual ring. Fresh sacraments,
> New meanings valid for our time,
> A world reborn, a new hierogamy.

Lipton's view of the art as a shamanistic exercise was not, to say the least, the one shared by most of those engaged in criticizing, subsidizing, and publishing poetry. Yet at precisely the time he was expounding it, thousands of Americans, many of whom had no patience with ordinary poetry, were packing themselves into university auditoriums to partake of something very like the experience he had in mind. At the center of this extraordinary development, though hardly in control, was the Welshman with the archetypal voice, Dylan Thomas, whose readings of his own and others' poetry proved that there was an appetite for the spoken word that no one, least of all himself, had ever imagined.

Although he had frankly come to America for the money, Thomas became an instant symbol of the ancient world reinvigorating the new. Not considered Welsh enough by the Welsh-speaking purists in his own country, he was more than Celtic enough for the Americans. His densely written poems had a

rich, bardic semi-comprehensibility that gave them an almost
sensual power to move the listener, even if he or she had little
rational sense of what they were about. He rose all too readily
to the role of the virile, careening, "pure" artist, and to the un-
funny, self-destructive behavior that went with it. In that sense
he was a peculiarly American poet, a seemingly undisciplined
nose-tweaker who worried academics, threatened the genteel
order of things, and still managed to earn Dame Edith Sitwell's
seal of approval.

Thomas's premature death in New York City turned him into
an American tragic hero. There was something primeval and
even arcane in the American response to the man, and it went beyond the usual fascination with offbeat celebrities. Dylan Thomas
really did have the power to make words come to life for others
and to make his own surprisingly small voice speak with an
authority long since conceded to the artificial media—and the
artificial idea.

Lipton kept a picture of Dylan Thomas on the wall of his
study, but he knew the symbol better than he did the poet. He
had only begun to read him recently, in the course of trying to
cure his relative ignorance of contemporary poetry. It was an
unabashed cramming session, and one of his texts, an anthology
called *The New British Poets*, proved to have been a lucky
choice indeed. Its editor was Larry's old friend from his bohemian days in Chicago, Kenneth Rexroth, and somewhere between reading the man's comments on his fellow poets and
listening to Isherwood complain about them, Lipton decided
that "Rex" was the ally he needed.

The author of *The Dragon and the Unicorn* and *The Art of
Worldly Wisdom*, Rexroth was also a skilled translator and a
critic with a fearsome reputation on both coasts. More important to Lipton, however, was the fact that Rexroth had kept on
writing to please himself long after *he* had gone commercial.
Lipton knew a lot of prominent writers, but hardly any "pure"
ones, and he took it for granted that Rexroth would be just as
happy as he to revive their friendship. In December 1952, he
assembled a clean copy of *Rainbow at Midnight*, prefaced it
with a long letter of re-introduction, and sent it off to Rexroth
in San Francisco, urging him to "hack away to your heart's
content."

There was no other poet in America with whom he had so much in common, or whose criticism he would accept so readily. Their original friendship ran back to cold flats, hard streets, and dangerous politics in the Chicago of the middle and late twenties. Rexroth had been an organizer for the IWW, Lipton a working journalist with ties to the Wobblies, the Communist Party, and the inner circles of Technocracy. In those days Lipton had given refuge to Big Bill Haywood on the first leg of his flight to Moscow. He and Rexroth had founded Escalator, one of the last manifestations of a movement that had begun with Carl Sandburg and Vachel Lindsay. ("Escalator is the backfire of the hindbrain against the conflagration of reason," their "Escalator Manifesto" had read).

"We're both bastards of the same dam," Lipton reminded Rexroth, "and her name was Escalator." Now that his friend was perhaps the best-established poet in San Francisco, and something of a literary arbiter there as well, he was the logical person to help him get through the final stages of own evolution. Besides, Lipton's affection for him was genuine, and as usual, it showed. He had actually mailed four long, intellectualizing letters to Rexroth before his old comrade found time to answer the first. "Do you write so many letters to everyone?" Rexroth protested gently. "Mercy, when do you sleep?"

"I write letters to nobody," Lipton replied solemnly, meaning that for now, at least, he wrote them to nobody *else*.

Lipton's side of the correspondence represented an onslaught of friendship, literary theory, and intellectual politics. Rexroth, on the other hand, preferred the friendship without the freight. "I do this stuff 'for a living,' " he protested, "even if it doesn't pay very well." He preferred to share "jokes, gossip & family news" with his friends, and as for the burning intellectual issues of the day, "my interests," he warned, "lie almost completely outside of the universe of discourse into which you wish to lead me." He only read contemporary poetry, he said, "out of sense of duty," since most of it was no good at all. In much the same way, he despised capitalism, fascism, the Communist Party, and the *Kenyon Review* with equal violence. Even back in Chicago, his best friends had been anarchists who would stand up and speak for the Wobblies, but would never sully themselves by carrying membership cards. He had as much contempt for

Auden, Isherwood, and the other "Hollywood swamis" as for
the "swimming pool Soviets" he himself had helped found during the Depression. He hated the Stalinists as much for driving
poets to suicide as for betraying the Spanish revolution. He disliked Ezra Pound, "sane or mad," although he had visited him
in St. Elizabeth's Hospital because, as a former war resister,
he knew what it meant to be to be locked up. Most of all,
he hated "official" anarchism, especially after "comrades from
New York" had deliberately sabotaged the West Coast pacifist
organization he had kept going throughout the war.

On the other hand, Rexroth was prepared to like any sort of
good poetry, and while he still supported the idea of revolution,
poetry had in effect become his life. He was deeply involved in
the San Francisco Poetry Center, based at San Francisco State
and headed by Ruth Witt-Diamant, and he felt as strongly as
Lipton did that poetry was most effective "when it communi-
cates orally." He earned most of his living, such as it was, by
reading aloud to college audiences, and spent most of his time
on such nonpaying projects as the translation of one hundred
poems each from the Chinese, the Japanese, the ancient Greek,
and the French.

While Rexroth wanted to encourage Lipton, he was forced to
admit that times were hard for poets. While his own work
usually found a publisher—and his East Coast connections
were better than he sometimes cared to admit—poetry in general was "almost impossible" to publish, and it never hurt to
have an angle. He thought Lipton was right to approach all the
little magazines, "just like a pulp writer," but wrong to seek an
endorsement from another poet. Instead, he offered a list of all
the little reviews in San Francisco, the "capital of the new Bohemia," and urged him to tell the publisher of his next novel,
"poetry too or I won't play."

His assessment of *Rainbow* was brief: "The idiom is not
mine." He found it too bookish and sentimental, and he agreed
with Selden Rodman about Lipton's rather heavy-handed use of
very long words. "Harden it up," Rexroth wrote. "Every place
you can substitute something concrete & specific for the general
or abstract, do so—and keep doing it." He also thought Lipton's eschatology depended too much on the wrong sorts of
people. "Where you say 'We,'" he wrote, "I should say 'They,'"

by which he meant the craven and treacherous power-seekers of all political persuasions.

The renewed Lipton-Rexroth friendship never did become the kind of long-distance symposium that Lipton, with his long letters about art and higher meanings, had hoped to make it. On the other hand, Rexroth tended to write people off rather easily, and it was probably a measure of his affection that Lipton stayed off what Dennis McNally has described as his "passionate and constantly shifting 'shit list.'"

For his part, Lipton fairly idolized Rexroth, who had never even been tempted to sell out. He fed a growing family on $3,500 a year, owned a radio and no other consumer goods, "not even a toaster," and rebuilt his own twenty-year-old car once a year. Before long Lipton managed to convince himself that far from turning down good jobs in order to write, Rexroth had never even *looked* for a job.

Rexroth tried to restrain this disturbing new development in Lipton. It was true that he considered poverty a "positive virtue," but by "poverty" he had never meant "indigence, pauperism or squalor"—only "being aware of and uninvolved in the Social Lie—hip." Lipton seemed to think Rexroth was still starving for his art. In fact, he was living quietly in a house with his wife and simply spending as little as possible. He had lived at the same address for the past fifteen years and held most of his paying jobs for five to ten years at a stretch. "I don't think I have ever owed a landlord rent," he wrote. "It would give me nervous prostration. I have a horror of debt. I have never owed anybody any money for more than a few hours and I am probably the only American who has never bought anything on time." In short, he was an ideal citizen of a very old-fashioned kind. He thought Lipton underestimated "the degree to which quite ordinary people can cut themselves off from the evils of a commercial society." To him, living in "respectable" poverty simply meant maintaining life without accepting a price for it.

Lipton lived that way too, but it was not enough for the preacher in him. When he said poverty, he meant poverty. The difference was that while Rexroth had the better literary connections, Lipton had the better commercial ones; a moment's weakness in the face of temptation, and it might have been back to the tax accountants again. Rexroth was probably making all the money there was to make from poetry readings and translations, while Lipton flirted with the devil every time he accepted an assignment from the studios. Many of his troubles could have been solved by only a *little* more money. His wife Nettie Brooks, now forty-six, had suffered a recurrence of tuberculosis, which had once cost her two years in an Eastern sanitarium. The cure was slow and expensive—$250 a month for the first few months and $150 a month thereafter, not counting drugs. So he stepped up his production of adventure stories for the pulp magazines, but refused to consider a regular job in Hollywood. Instead of cranking out another Inner Sanctum mystery, he wrote whodunits "with a working class background" for a union-owned book club that paid him $1,000 per title—roughly a fifth of what he had been used to getting as an advance.

Yet he and his wife were entirely happy. They were together all day, and Lipton was able to work without disturbing the absolute quiet her cure required. Gentle and deferential, with a faintly Southern accent and manners acquired through her upbringing in Washington, D.C., Nettie believed completely in her husband and his poetry. "If she had her way," he told Rexroth, "I'd write nothing else."

Now thoroughly established in Venice, they lived an essentially middle-class life on Park Avenue, a kind of elongated court lined with homes of a type still found all over Southern California—deep, high-roofed, generous with wood and space. Their house was slightly larger than most, with a shallow, overgrown yard and two tiny sitting porches, one upstairs and one below. It stood fifty yards up from the Speedway, a broad alley running parallel to the beach which served as a semi-official boundary between the sunbeaten, vomit- and urine-stained Promenade and a quieter world of sandy lawns, wooden baffles, bouganvillas, railroad ties, climbing plants, porch railings fashioned from steel pipe, and everywhere, as might be expected, cats. Most of the streets that ran to the beach permitted nothing but foot traffic; reality, stoplights, and three-digit house numbers began on the *other* side of Pacific Avenue. It was a good place to get over something, and it was not at all a bad place to write.

It was also a fascinating place for anyone who believed, as

Lipton did, that slums were uncommonly honest places. The year-round Venice economy, with its tiny corner markets, warehouses, liquor stores, fleabag hotels, strange little factories, and old-fashioned Jewish bakeries, was essentially a skid row proposition. The rents had always been low, and between the smell of the Hyperion sewer outlet and the promise of deafening air traffic at the new international airport, they seemed unlikely to go any higher. It was still possible, in 1953, to rent a storefront apartment for forty dollars a month—and to go for months without even paying that. Venice was not the only slum in Los Angeles, but it was probably the only one that was not a good investment.

It was also a slum with remarkable amenities. With its benches, chess tables, archways, empty buildings, and broad expanses of lawn and sand, it was a playground for the idle poor. A man who slept in a doorway could literally awaken to his own private beach; as the day wore on, he might find himself sharing it with Charles Eames, the architect, Stan Laurel, the actor, Mickey Cohen, the gangster, and a strolling party of great-grandmothers from Lublin.

While Lipton's term, "voluntary poverty," might have been an overblown way to describe it, Venice was also home to a distinctive style of doing without. Its practitioners, most of them young, a fair number of them artists, had ended up there because they simply could not be bothered to make money, and because in Venice, as in few other places in America, it was *almost* possible to live on imagination alone. They lived in cottages, sheds, garages, warehouses, and empty stores, observing a cheerful and offhanded ethic of noncompetition, nonacquisition, and disrespect for established values, however or by whomever established. They wore shorts, sweatshirts, and sandals because they lived near the beach, and because there was no one in particular they wanted to impress. Some of them grew beards to make themselves completely unemployable. Many were "students" on the GI Bill, and some were veterans of Korea or even World War II. Almost none of them were poor for lack of opportunity, and many had walked away from what most Americans would have called good jobs. A loose group numbering around twenty or thirty, they shared an elaborate set of principles, rituals, and suppositions about outsiders—"squares."

"Squares," a term borrowed from the lore of the jazz musician and the big-city hipster, referred to everyday citizens who worked, owned property, raised children, and presumably never questioned the values they had received from parents, religion, government, and others in authority. For "success," the young Venice bohemians substituted "art," and there was some irony in the stern work ethic and absolute reverence with which they pursued it. Like success, art served as both an authenticating ideal and a reward for righteous activity. Like the Law and the Prophets, it was assumed to infuse every aspect of the believer's daily life. The boardwalk area of Venice was not, in any traditional sense, an artists' colony. A few people, like Wally Berman, were already working artists before they settled in Venice, but most took up painting or drawing or writing poetry because it was what their friends were doing, and because they believed in the creative act as an end in itself.

Anyone could be an artist, they told each other; it was a matter of belief, not talent or preparation. When Saul White, for example, discovered Jackson Pollock, he immediately went into his backyard, set up a stepladder, and began to pour paint onto canvas. *Anyone* could do it. White, in turn, introduced Tony Scibella to Abstract Expressionism; Scibella encouraged Stuart Perkoff to draw, paint, and make collages; and Perkoff taught Scibella to write down the words he heard in his head. The idea was go ahead and do it—to "just blow."

They meant "blow" in the sense of a jazz musician's blowing, without artificial preparation. Jazz served as the ultimate point of reference, even though, or perhaps even because, few among them played it. From it they adopted the mythos of the brooding, tortured, solitary artist, performing with others but always alone. They talked the hip talk of jazz, built communal rituals around using the jazzman's drugs, and worshiped the dead jazz musician most fervently. The musician whose music was fatal represented pure spontaneity. When Charlie Parker killed himself through several kinds of excess, including heroin, it became as obligatory to produce a poem about it as it would soon be, in other circles, to eulogize Dylan Thomas. "What about that horror, man?" Stuart Perkoff wrote. "What about that pain?" But it was an *admiring* "what about that pain," and it concluded with the benediction,

but he'd been there, man
& he blew
& he flew, man
like
high

The cult of art included a side-cult of death, which was also borrowed more or less whole from the jazzman's world. Death, alienation, and addiction were all part of the mystique, and a proper reverence for them was essential to being "cool." They represented the dark side of creative compulsion, with the same fascination death always holds for the romantic. For most of the Venice bohemians, however, shooting junk was still a mighty leap of faith away; it was still enough to celebrate the sacrament of the spike in endless rounds of reverent, frenzied talk.

The scene shifted from garage apartments to sedate little cottages to old shacks and storefronts on the Promenade. The bohemians played new jazz LPs and old blues 78s, drank wine, beat drums, blew kazoos, smoked marijuana, and took benzedrine to help them stay up and shout their revelations through the night. It was all dark and cerebral, but it was also young, vital, and intoxicatingly new, with a saving good humor and a freedom in obscurity that the media-ridden hip scenes of the future would never know.

One by one, Lawrence Lipton got to know the bohemians. Their faith in art was almost identical to his, and their example confirmed his belief that the eyes of the young could see through the falsity of the acquisitive society around them. As soon as his wife was healthy again, Lipton began to have the neighborhood's "young people" over for long evenings of poetry and free-swinging, wide-ranging talk. Since few of his guests had had much formal education, he undertook to fill them in on the history and traditions of what it seemed perfectly obvious to *him* that they were trying to do. They sometimes joked about him afterwards, but they were genuinely in awe of his knowledge. He had a theory about everything, and he had seen more than one bohemia come and go. It was hard not to be flattered by the attention he gave them, and harder still to stand up to him in an argument—even, or perhaps especially, when he was wrong.

The young poets, artists, and "poet-painters"—Lipton's term

for a writer who also produced paintings and collages, although not necessarily on a level with his verse—became a kind of private resource for him, a confirmation that he was still on the right side of history. That knowledge, in turn, made it easier to deal with timid publishers, egomaniacal editors, and narcissistic literary circles. If they accepted him, fine; if not, it would ultimately be their loss, not his.

After more than a year of hard lobbying, he had actually won a tentative acceptance from Southern California's highbrow literary establishment. The spring, 1953 issue of *California Quarterly* contained a twenty-six-page excerpt from *Rainbow at Midnight*, and in June of that year, largely through the good offices of Lion Feuchtwanger, the entire poem was given a full-scale dramatic reading on a Beverly Hills stage. Lipton had also struck up a friendship with James Boyer May, the poet who published a fairly influential little journal, *Trace*, in London.

A naturally modest and helpful man, May tried to introduce Lipton to some of the younger Los Angeles poets, one of whom, Curtis Zahn, shocked him with his aggressive informality. "I don't know what to think of him," Lipton remarked afterward. "You know, he listened while lying on the floor, and he wears sandals and a beard." He could accept those things from his brash young neighbors, but he still thought of public literary gatherings as suit-and-tie affairs. It was also May who connected him with the Paris-based *Merlin* and its editor, Alexander Trocchi, and got him the assignment to write an article on "the state of the arts on the West Coast" for Louis Brigante's *Intro: A Magazine of the Arts*.

Lipton turned the hastily written piece, "Secession: 1953," into a polemic against commercialism and in favor of what he now called "dedicated poverty." Most of the essay dealt with the movie industry and the writers it betrayed, corrupted, or broke. Despite its seductive reputation, Lipton wrote, California's dream assembly line offered nothing to creative people but the opportunity to estrange themselves from their own creative processes. The system was actually at its most cruel when it kept its promises. Political witch-hunting might claim its victims from time to time, but for real ruin there was nothing like success. For anyone with integrity, the only solution was to refuse to benefit from any of it:

For the writer that means back to the typewriter, the slum or near-slum studio, library books instead of limited special editions, and checks that are small enough to cash at the corner grocer's. For the actor it means back to the stage, the dramatic school classroom, the little theatre—or nothing.

As far as Lipton was concerned, there was no "safe" level of participation. Staying pure meant rejecting the whole thing—by which he meant the *whole* thing—institutions, conventional values, foundation grants, and all. "One has to get out of *himself*," he wrote. "The rottenness of a society is *in* us, in the very air we breathe, from birth. . . . Yes, in order to see our world as it really is, not as we have been indoctrinated, we must *come out* of ourselves."

The essay impressed Rexroth so much that he asked the author to write something similar for an upcoming issue of James Laughlin's magazine, *Perspectives*. He had been asked to edit the entire issue and wanted Lipton to address himself to the topic of "alienation," stressing the idea that "the young have rejected the official culture of the professors & the literary magazines *in toto*." He also told Lipton that "Secession" had been "too good for a little magazine," and urged him to aim higher—perhaps at *Discovery* and *New World Writing*, for which he himself often wrote. It was the first gesture of artistic equality he had ever made toward Lipton. He did hope a better word could be found than "alienation"; it was *Partisan Review*'s favorite word, and "by it," he reminded Lipton, "they do *not* mean utter rejection of the Social Lie."

Lipton settled on "disaffiliation"—as in John L. Lewis's declaration upon leaving the American Federation of Labor, "I disaffiliate." He re-defined it as the "repudiation of sonship," the severing of ties that had never been consensual to begin with. By combining art and disaffiliation into a single moral issue, he also upped the ante on his friend. Rexroth opposed the Social Lie, but Lipton wanted to go further. He had begun to view art less as something to be kept pure than as a *means* of promoting purity in a vastly larger sense. The one thing the Social Lie demanded was assent; the one weapon that worked against it was refusal. If disaffiliation really made the artist free, it could also turn him into the prototype of a new kind of free human being.

Thus, instead of disaffiliation being good because it purified art, the real value of art might be that it promoted disaffiliation.

This was not at all what Rexroth had in mind. He certainly wanted people to reject the Social Lie, but not by trading it for the illusion that anyone could be an artist. Lipton continued to expand his argument in essay after essay. When he believed in anything that strongly, he believed in it for everyone.

Rexroth tried to persuade him that it was a mistake to let the issues of poverty and integrity "overlap unduly." For one thing, most of the writers Lipton cited as examples of "dedicated poverty"—such as J.D. Salinger and Ralph Ellison—were actually doing rather well for themselves. For another, Rexroth was still his primary source of information about up-and-coming literary developments. Rexroth knew how selectively Lipton absorbed what he told him. It was he who had made Lipton aware of Salinger ("*Catcher in the Rye* . . . a paperback . . . I think a Mentor—all the cats are reading it"), and it was he who had been passing him information for months about an entirely new generation of poets, most of them from the Bay Area. For now, Lipton knew only the names of Kenneth Patchen, Denise Levertov, Philip Lamantia, Robert Duncan, and William Everson, but it was anyone's guess as to how he would incorporate them into his argument.

When Dylan Thomas died of drink on 9 November 1953, Lipton, like so many American poets, wrote an elegy which invested the doomed poet with all of his own ideas about the mission of poetry. Perhaps because he *was* so out of touch with intellectual fashion, some of Thomas's real friends thought he had come unusually close to the man himself. It was Rexroth who wrote the Dylan Thomas elegy for the time—a self-righteous blast of anger and class hatred that had nothing to do with the real Thomas and everything to do with poetry as an outlaw province of American life.

Who killed Dylan Thomas? Someone had to be responsible. A tragedy of such magnitude required a perpetrator as well as a victim, and only a very large culprit would do. Back in Laugharne, the dead poet's friends blamed his death on free whiskies and excess adulation, neither of which he got at home. Rexroth, however, blamed American philistinism. He wrote his elegy, *Thou Shalt Not Kill*, within a few hours of hearing the news from New York; almost immediately, mimeographed copies marked "not for publication" were being distributed throughout the city and the world, soon to be augmented by versions in French, Greek, and Japanese. The effect was immediate and overwhelming, as if an injection of radioactive iodine had revealed the presence of miles and miles of unsuspected veins in a patient's body. Most of the pirated editions were hack-and-slash abridgements that left out vast chunks of context and went straight to the point: *who killed Dylan Thomas?*

> "You killed him! You killed him.
> In your God damned Brooks Brothers suit,
> You son of a bitch."

It was an ugly and even a silly poem, but it became an instant classic. For a short while, at least, it seemed an inseparable part of the tragedy itself. It impressed Lipton so much that he wrote Rexroth six letters about it in ten days. He considered the poem an antidote to the "sentimental drivel that is sure to be written on the subject." Rexroth had not desentimentalized the poet; he had *re*sentimentalized him as the Joe Hill of a class fable based on sensibility rather than politics. Coming, as it did, from a life-long believer in the pacifiability of man, it was a remarkable assertion of the right to hate. The whole affair showed that it was possible for a noncommercial writer to create an immense and *popular* sensation in America in the early 1950s. It was almost as though political dissent had gone into hiding under the skirts of the Muse. What could make so many Americans get their blood up about a poet? What might the right sort of poet do with such authority?

Rexroth himself seemed reluctant to find out. He was always far more comfortable writing for an enlightened few. Poetry might be *his* way of life, but it was not for mass consumption—or participation. He wanted revolution, but not at the cost of allying himself with bad art, which was what most would-be artists, world without end, tended to produce.

Larry Lipton, on the other hand, chose to defer the question of ability. What counted was moral authority, and he no longer felt quite so inclined to defer to Rexroth's. While he still had a long way to go to match his friend's literary output, he was not doing badly for a late-bloomer. *Rainbow at Midnight* had found a British publisher, and was even being translated into

Greek. Rexroth reported seeing his poems "all around. Fame at last, huh?" Now that Dylan Thomas had created a market for spoken poetry, some of Lipton's poems had been included on a long-playing record that was selling rather well, while his articles on disaffiliation had launched what amounted to a third career (or a fourth, depending on how one was counting): social critic. All of his essays said roughly the same thing, but the effect on his reputation was apparently cumulative, while the cosmic stakes rose with each retelling.

In 1955, moreover, he found an American publisher for *Rainbow at Midnight*. The Golden Quill Press was not a Scribner's or a Random House, but its printers were master bookmakers, and its distribution network surprisingly good. Most of the initial thousand-copy press run went to the members of the Book Club for Poetry, and Lipton worked hard to help move the rest. His success at getting local booksellers to display the little octavo volume amazed Rexroth, who reviewed the book for KPFA radio and even began to play tapes of Larry reading from it over the air. After three years of struggling with a completely new career, Lipton could think of himself as a professional again.

With the appearance of the definitive version of "Disaffiliation and the Art of Poverty" in *Chicago Review*, Lipton considered himself Rexroth's full equal. He even wondered why Rexroth insisted on living in the past ("Why do you keep harping on that old Chicago crowd?"). Rexroth, at work on an essay of his own about "disengagement" for *New World Writing*, conceded that Lipton was "better at that sort of thing" than he was, adding that between them, "I think we may have launched a 'movement.'"

As Lipton discovered upon reading "Disengagement: The Art of the Beat Generation," Rexroth had been holding back on him. For over a year, he had been acting as sponsor and father figure for a group of earnest and devilishly talented New York writers which included the poet Allen Ginsberg and the vagabond novelist Jack Kerouac. They were disaffiliated in thought, deed, and especially in body; Rexroth had even granted them air time on his weekly KPFA radio program. He had also introduced them to the right people in the Bay Area, including such like-minded poets as Gary Snyder, the young "beat hipster monk" who lived in Berkeley. Rexroth had put his own reputation on the line for these men—yet somehow he had never gotten around to mentioning them to his corevolutionist in Venice. He had never even told Lipton about the reading at which, by his own reckoning, the young barbarians had launched a revolution in American poetry—and perhaps in American thought.

In the spring of 1955, thoroughly divided as to his future, a clean-shaven, unremarkable-looking market analyst, Allen Ginsberg, had decided, like so many thoughtful Americans, to take his psychiatrist's advice. After months of hearing the young man agonize about his sexuality, his poetry, and his fraying attachment to conventional society, the doctor had asked him simply, "Why don't you do what you *want?*" And so he had. After deliberately engineering his own replacement by a computer, he had moved in with his lover, Peter Orlovsky, and spent the summer in Berkeley learning to write his poems, as Kerouac had always urged him to do, straight from the mind to the page.

Kerouac himself was a practitioner of "spontaneous prose." After publishing one traditional novel, *The Town and the City* (1948), he had forsworn all conscious premeditation and revision and begun to write his novels nonstop on long rolls of telegraph paper, filling them with real events, real people, and all the raw contents of his memory. One such book, *On the Road*, was now under consideration by the Viking Press; the rest were in his rucksack in Mexico City, where he had spent the summer of 1955 drinking himself sick, taking benzedrine to stay awake, and writing an astonishing work of American visionary poetry, *Mexico City Blues*. When Ginsberg sent him the long poem he had written over the summer, with the assurance that it was pure and untouched, Jack packed his gear and started hitching north. "Let's shout our poems in San Francisco Streets," he wrote Ginsberg. "Predict earthquakes."

That October Ginsberg and Snyder had organized a reading at San Francisco's Six Gallery, near the Embarcadero, with Rexroth happily volunteering to serve as their "established poet." Three of his Bay Area protégés, Michael McClure, Philip Whalen, and Philip Lamantia, had made it "six poets at Six Gallery." Ginsberg had publicized the reading with mimeographed postcards promising "wine, music, dancing girls, serious poetry, free satori. . . . Charming event."

It was also a predominantly male event, despite the presence of Ruth Witt-Diamant. The seventh celebrant was Kerouac, who was too shy to stand up and read. Instead he acted the chorus and the holy fool, roaming the gallery floor with a gallon jug and turning the "rather stiff" listeners into shouting communicants with raw California burgundy. The poets, who had started drinking hours earlier, roared their visions while Kerouac clapped, chattered, beat out time on the jug, and stirred up the crowd into chants of "Go! Go! Go!" By the time Ginsberg rushed up at eleven-thirty to read his long poem, "Howl," the night was outrageously transcendant.

"Howl" was a jeremiad, a litany of defiance, an act of war. It poured out its images like plagues: drugs, buggery, devastated minds, slum alleys, "angelheaded hipsters," exultant madness, sexual anarchy, and a terrifying landscape of joy. Where Dylan Thomas had made ordinary words powerful and mysterious, Ginsberg turned them into clubs and axes. His enemy was materialism, and he identified it with the insatiable god of the Canaanites: "Moloch! Moloch! Filth! Ugliness! Ashcans and unobtainable dollars!"

But Ginsberg's Moloch, like Elijah's, was a false god, a bogeyman who brutalized the imagination so as to keep himself from being seen clearly. The violence implied in "Howl" was no more than what was necessary to negate a false concept of reality. It had to be total, because Moloch claimed total dominion, and pitiless in its sense of truth, because there was no other way to fight the house-to-house combat of the mind. But the mind that could bear such a war could win it.

"It was a mad night," Kerouac later wrote. Rexroth, wiping away tears, told Ginsberg he had started a revolution in American poetry "from bridge to bridge." Ruth Witt-Diamant was upset about all the dirty words, but what was good for poetry was good for the San Francisco Poetry Center—and the Six Gallery reading proved to be very good for poetry indeed. Word began to spread eastward that something new, and, with any luck, dangerous had been launched by the "San Francisco poets"— although Rexroth, for whom being a San Franciscan was a serious matter, preferred to call Ginsberg and his friends by the name Jack Kerouac had invented for them: the Beat Generation.

They were certainly not everyone's idea of a revolutionary vanguard. They took their lunacy seriously and often indulged it a bit too self-consciously to suit Rexroth. Their chattering, constantly shifting "scene" was like a Marx Brothers movie, and they kept it up no matter who was trying to work—or who had been soldiering for a new consciousness before they were born. Rexroth soon conceived a violent dislike for Kerouac, who tended to drink himself soppy, and while he stayed on better terms with Ginsberg, it irritated him to hear the younger man belittle his Dylan Thomas elegy. Ginsberg told him, "Rexroth, I'm a better poet than you, and I'm only twenty-[nine] years old."

Seeing it all in print, Lipton was beside himself. "Is Big Sur the southern frontier beyond which lie the lands of the Barbarians?" he wrote angrily to Rexroth in a letter which he somehow persuaded himself not to send. "Evidently I can't belong by mail order. But I'm willing to negotiate before I set myself up as the anti-pope in these parts." Two months later, in June 1956, he was calm enough to try again: "Your poets are a little too concentrated around the Bay Area, don't you think? Are there no hopefuls south of Big Sur? Me, for instance."

He left that letter unsent as well; better not to betray his resentment—or his determination to found his own counter-empire. From the summer of 1956 on, he and Rexroth were rivals. He, too, would assemble a critical mass of youth, rebellion, and creativity around him; he, too, would create a "movement" based on his own unerring visions. Rexroth, of course, had only "discovered" the Beat Generation, not created it, but Lipton was happy to allow him full credit for an achievement he meant to surpass.

Later that summer, Allen Ginsberg set out to visit Kerouac in Mexico City, but he decided to stop in Los Angeles first. He had relatives in Riverside, and he and his traveling company— Peter Orlovsky, Peter's brother Lafcadio, and Gregory Corso— wanted to "dig Hollywood." He also knew that Anaïs Nin, the not-so-secret heroine of Henry Miller's Paris novels, lived there, so he wrote to introduce himself. Did she think she could persuade Marlon Brando, Christopher Isherwood, James Dean and Aldous Huxley to hear him read his poetry? If not, "strange beat citizens" would be sufficient. Whatever else the evening might turn out to be, it would not be "just a big nowhere bore . . . we promise to be the only poesy in Hollywood or anywhere else for that matter, in eras, or seasons."

The reading, with Larry Lipton officiating, was staged in the Hollywood boarding house that served as the headquarters of the journal *Coastlines*. Anaïs Nin brought her own friends, not

Brando, who was a stranger, or James Dean, who was dead. Lipton arrived with a small contingent from Venice, including the young poet Stuart Perkoff. Representing the host publication were Gene Frumkin, Mel Weisburd and the two editors who actually lived in the house. None of the *Coastlines* people had read Ginsberg's *Howl and Other Poems*, which was still unavailable in Los Angeles, but Lipton had persuaded them that Ginsberg was the real thing. After their introduction, Ginsberg and Corso sat down at a table, opened a gallon jug of wine and began to read.

The evening reminded Nin of "Artaud's mad conference at the Sorbonne." "Howl" impressed her as a "great, long, desperate wail, a struggle to make poetry out of all the objects, surroundings and people he had known." Not everyone in the hall saw even a mad purpose in it. Before the poet had finished reading, a friend of one of the *Coastlines* editors—not, as Lipton would later insist, a drunk from the street—stood up to challenge him.

Why, he wanted to know, must Ginsberg write about filth and ugliness? Why must he write about the slums? "Isn't it enough that we have them?" The two men proceeded to argue about nakedness—naked confessions, naked beauty, and "naked values"—until Ginsberg, furious, decided to define his terms. He started by removing his coat, which the heckler took as an invitation to step outside. Off came his jacket as well, but Ginsberg kept right on stripping. *That* was what he meant by naked. Tossing his clothes to the audience—a friend of Nin's caught his jockey shorts—Ginsberg demanded that the heckler come up and do the same. "Come and stand here, stand naked before the world," he shouted. "I dare you! The poet always stands naked before the world!"

To Nin, it was a profound gesture; to Gene Frumkin, it was shameless exhibitionism. Lipton, still ostensibly in charge of the proceedings, rushed to the front. Instead of demanding order, he quietly pointed out that there were "women and children upstairs." Most of the audience laughed; it broke the spell. The heckler, booed and hissed by some of the crowd, stormed out, and Frumkin gathered up Ginsberg's clothing, "stitch by golden stitch." The poet showed no inclination to put them on again. Instead he sat back grandly on the couch, slugged down some more of the wine, and went on reading.

It was nothing new for Gregory Corso, who knew that all

questions of poesy aside, Ginsberg always enjoyed taking off his clothes. It was strong stuff for the Southern California literati. For Larry Lipton, who had struggled so long for their acceptance, it was a turning point. "L.A. will never be the same again," he wrote triumphantly to Rexroth. Nor would he. He had seen the future, and it worked. Tonight it was back to Venice with his protégés, but tomorrow, the world.

For the next few days Stuart Perkoff, poet, painter and boxcar loader, struggled to sum up the evening for all of them in a poem dedicated to Ginsberg:

> blind as roses
> we sit in the evenings in rooms of our own choosing
> rooms filled with intricacies of many delicately structured
>   parts
> which dazzle & fascinate, & alter appearances & statements
>
> everything with its clear limits
> everything marked & classified
> all aspects known
> all new structures viewed with distaste
> everything of the utmost seriousness
>
> what are we to say, then, of a man
> who takes off his clothes in someone else's living room?
> are we to applaud?
> what is his nakedness to us?
> what do we care about his poems?
> do you realize that he is in the lite? how can i
> be expected to read?
>
> he makes too much noise!
> he says dirty words!
> he needs a bath!
> he is certainly
>   drunk!
>
> i hope he soon realizes that this is, after all, now
> & we have many wonderful things to amuse us
> when we want to see clowns
> we go to the circus
>
> *is he gone yet? can i come out now?*

CHAPTER THREE

Stuart Perkoff was what Lawrence Lipton wanted more than anything to be, an original poet and a leader of poets. A visionary who helped others develop their own power to see, Perkoff often saw himself, with characteristic humility, in the role of Moses. He did have a few traits in common with the prophet whom God "knew face to face." Like Moses, he could be tortured by doubt; like Moses, he was only interested in knowing God—"the numinous"—directly. He wanted to give the people rituals without becoming distracted by them himself; that was the difference between a prophet and a priest—or rabbi. Most disturbingly like Moses, Stuart sensed that he had no choice at all about his vocation. He had been "called," not invited. He could always choose to resist, and to accept suffering as a consequence, but every other alternative was an illusion.

Raised in a relatively liberal Jewish household in St. Louis, his favorite childhood story was about Moses, and about choice. Sitting on the Pharaoh's knee in the palace, so the tradition went, the young Moses reached up playfully for the great king's crown. To the chief priests and diviners, this, like everything else, was a sign. "The child is ambitious," they said. "Kill him or he will grow up to overthrow you." But the king loved Moses, so he decided to subject him to a test. He ordered his servants to set two trays before Moses, one holding a golden crown and the other a glowing coal, to see if it he were attracted to the gold or merely the glow. Moses tried to reach for the crown, but an angel pushed his hand toward the coal instead; he grasped the coal, burned his fingers, and thrust them into his mouth. And that, said a hundred generations of rabbis, was why Moses lived to lead his people out of Egypt—and why he stammered for the rest of his life.

Perkoff was not a stammerer, but he spent his life torn between natural rebellion and hard obedience. He wanted to create "visions for the tribe," poems that would call men and women back to a primitive sense of themselves. In "Feasts of Love, Feasts of Death," written in his middle twenties, he turned the memory of a summer camp in Michigan into an image of the physically, spiritually, and communally whole life:

> sitting on the benches, bodies warm & throats filled with
> joy & love
>
> we offered worship
> sitting warm, eyes & skin touching, love flowing
> we offered worship
>
>   we sang
> & spoke languages & poems
> offered worship & love
> mixing the birds of passion & the swords of God
> in our beautiful young eyes

In the poem, the sudden knowledge of death changes everything—yet invalidates nothing. The rituals of God and adolescence remains true, but for a fifteen-year-old who demands to know how everything works together, the news of the Holocaust has put them permanently out of reach. Nothing can be so simple, natural, and clean again. Now it is necessary to know how death works, and why. So Perkoff (the poet in the poem) takes the matter to a distinguished rabbi. Why did the six million die? Was it part of God's plan?

"*God's plan?*" asks the rabbi—who then tells him of his own days and nights of fasting and prayer, trying to find an answer to the same question. What did he find? "Only hope that came from the realization of the cleansing & purification of pain."

In his poems, at least, Stuart was less inclined to shake his fist at God than to question his own ability to bear the pain of knowing as much as he intended to know.

As a young man growing up in St. Louis in the thirties and forties, Perkoff was rebellious in school and argumentative at home, although his parents were willing to accept that as the price of his being bright. His father, who had brought the family through the Depression in relative security, believed in working hard and playing later; his mother believed in putting art before work *or* play and encouraged her son to do the same. One of his brothers became a doctor, the other a jazz musician. Perkoff resolved the conflict the way he resolved all of the important ones, by swallowing it whole.

He started writing poetry in high school, at about the same time he decided to join the Communist Party. He also began to roam the city on his own, trying to find the proper venue for his one-man rebellion. In a disintegrating neighborhood near the riverfront, "pressed in by warehouses & bitter men," he discovered poverty, desperation, and an artistic tradition that seemed to be bonded to them. It was slumming, but it was earnest slumming. He and his friends spent their evenings in a bar called Little Bohemia, whose jukebox selection included Beethoven and old organizing songs. There they baited old Stalinists, drank themselves drunk, made their first real-life sexual connections, and learned to express their own chaotic hopes in the language of revolution.

The owner of the bar was a young painter with a Slavic name and a beautiful wife, and, as Perkoff later recalled, "the fact that she wore no brassiere & that they were not really married was very important to us." For a while Perkoff worked hard for the party, but his poetry—which, by his own admission, "aped [Kenneth] Patchen badly"—was too stubbornly personal to suit the comrades. When the Party ordered him to stop writing about love, he resigned instead. Just as abruptly, he decided to leave St. Louis for New York City. He had vague notions of becoming an actor; he was still not quite eighteen.

Alone and hungry for strangeness in the city of Wolfe and Melville, Perkoff worked in a drill press shop, wrote poetry, started an ambitious novel, and spent long hours arming himself in the library for interminable late-night arguments in bars, coffeehouses, and cold Bohemian flats. He was brash, intense, and short with people; "you could easily hate the dude," one friend would later admit. He had a zealot's temperament without an ideologue's gift for consistency, arguing strongly but rather haphazardly for whatever position seemed right according to his own furiously evolving standards. He read history, anthropology, sociology, and back issues of *Partisan Review* to build a command of facts and principles that even the old coffee-house revolutionaries usually found overwhelming.

He loved the city for what it offered him: hunger, the comradeship of other artists, and the press of other creative minds. He learned to be a poet among poets in Kerouac's and Dylan Thomas's bars and on Ginsberg's stained, electric streets. He was surprisingly slow to learn about two of the things the city taught best—modern jazz and illegal drugs—but he had already settled into a life of more or less serious hipness when the political "realities" of the Cold War intervened.

Perkoff would later claim to have been the first draft resister of the postwar era, and he was almost certainly the first to turn himself in. When the peacetime draft law went into effect in 1948, he calmly waited for the grace period to expire, then walked into the nearest federal building and announced that he wanted to report someone for failing to register—"me." They arrested him, of course, but no one knew what the drill called for next; the law was simply too new. They put him in jail and telephoned his father, who was in the midst of starting a new family business out in California. Eventually Nat Perkoff flew back to New York, convinced his son that if he did register the army would not want him anyway, and dragged him back to Santa Barbara to flip hamburgers and consider his next move.

Perkoff was still working at the Twin Burger stand—and writing poems with a heavy though acknowledged debt to T. S. Eliot—when he met Suzan Blanchard, a student at the old Santa Barbara campus of the University of California. Six feet tall, with a long, handsome face and short brown hair, she towered over him by nine inches and could more than hold her own with him in an argument. Although she had spent the last two years in a TB sanitarium instead of at Berkeley, and a bout of childhood polio had left her with a limp, Perkoff always saw her as a personification of strength, independence, and grace. An old boyfriend of hers had introduced them because he knew she liked bohemian types and because no one else seemed to be capable of making Perkoff close his mouth. Suzan Blanchard was quick and crafty and had a disarming laugh that she used as a standard part of speech—a wild laugh full of chaos and power that was enough to put most brash young men out of business. The two of them fascinated each other from the start, and in the same year, 1949, they were married.

Perkoff's family had no objection to his marrying a Protestant girl from Inglewood; they liked her and were happy enough to see him married at all. Only six months after they had set up housekeeping in Santa Barbara, however, Perkoff succeeded in talking his new wife into moving back to New York City, where they sublet a one-room apartment on 87th Street. There she became pregnant with their first son, Sasha, and her husband began a life of trying to support a family on the kinds of jobs that would allow him to concentrate on writing poetry.

For a while he worked in a Manhattan bookstore that hired only poets—and paid them poets' wages. He made more money as a short-order cook, but they were still so broke that when his parents paid her way back to California so that they could see the baby, Perkoff considered coming back too, for good.

"Forget it," his wife told him. "We have to stay in New York—you'll go *crazy* out here." They compromised by moving to San Francisco, which was supposed to be a poet's city, but it was not city enough to suit Perkoff. After two months, he decided he was in love with a woman he had known back in New York. That was the only honorable pretext he could think of for leaving his family, who spent the next year living with Suzan Perkoff's mother in Inglewood. When Perkoff finally returned to his wife and child, San Francisco was no longer an option. They had barely enough money for Santa Monica, and the next couple of years passed in a slow-motion economic slide down to Venice. His wife refused to think of living anywhere but near the beach, and for a poet who really wanted to be nothing else, Venice did have its compensations.

One of these, of course, was the company of other creative people—or, more to the point, other *hip* creative people. It might not be the Village, but the bohemian community of Venice was both self-contained and isolated enough to make a poet with no understanding of "real life" feel at home. There were even enough bottom-of-the-barrel jobs available that when he really felt the need to work, he could usually find employment right away.

There was also pot, which the Perkoffs somehow never had gotten around to smoking. They made, in fact, only one serious attempt to try it in New York, but what they puffed on all night was not marijuana. In Venice, however, the stuff was all around them, buried in coffee cans under doorsteps, and produced, as if from thin air, for any serious social gathering. It was more than just a way of getting wasted; it was a communal ritual. Marijuana was the amateur outlaw's social drug—strong, mysterious, good for several years in prison, yet essentially benign. You could go to jail for using it, but you could never kill yourself with an overdose. While it was not considered a heroic drug, like heroin, it had its own cerebral mystique. The user was enabled to feel brilliant all night; it was hard to say whether its chemical or its social effects were stronger.

It was also as illegal as a substance could be. Anyone who bought it, sold it, planted it, watered it, smoked it, buried it in a coffee can in the backyard, or was even present in a place where it was being smoked could expect to do serious time if he or she were caught. Gene Krupa and Robert Mitchum had gone to prison for possessing it; in the black neighborhoods, experienced users made a habit of tucking in the ends of their joints so that not a single speck of weed could be found in the lining of their pockets. Among white, middle-class users, the sort who "should have known better," marijuana reinforced friendship with conspiracy, and the very harshness of the laws against it tended to transform intellectual reservations about the system into heartfelt contempt.

In the early fifties, marijuana was cheap but sometimes hard to find in Los Angeles. While Venice had not yet been singled out for any special attention by the police, there was no sure way of recognizing a nark until it was too late. That made the question of who was cool a very serious one and created new rituals of its own. Everyone agreed not to bring outsiders to pot parties, but someone always did, and no hip gathering seemed to be complete without an argument over the coolness of some stranger.

With the approval of the group, Julia Newman took Perkoff aside at a party and turned him on; his wife had to wait another week or two. Predictably, once initiated, he became both a true believer and an overnight expert, with a supposedly infallible instinct for knowing who was cool and who was not. Except for benzedrine, which hardly counted because even the squares used it, pot was as far as he planned to go. He liked the high and the feeling of living dangerously, but he still had an absolute taboo against the needle.

On the other hand, he quickly came to the conclusion that marijuana had its limitations. It lacked the power, after all, to move him to a "different level of perception." It certainly worked some changes, if only in his manner, because his mother, who had always tolerated his moods in deference to his art, soon told him, "I *hate* what you've become since you started smoking pot!" Even if it got him no farther than "the outer court of the temple," better there, he wrote, "than in the yard with the broken tombstones!"

By day, he was still trying to be a "mensch," to fulfil his "responsibilities, responsibilities that spring from love & are accepted out of love." He now had a second son, Ben, and Perkoff was determined to do a better job of providing for his family, even if it meant not writing poetry anymore. Two developments conspired to prevent his giving up poetry. Early in 1956, his New York connections finally paid off. Jonathan Williams, the publisher most respected by the hip poets of the Village, accepted his first book of poems, *The Suicide Room*, for publication. At roughly the same time, he began to develop a real friendship with Larry Lipton, who used all of his powers of persuasion to keep Perkoff from forsaking his art.

Lipton was now a well-known and very visible figure in Venice, striding confidently to the post office every day in his old sport jacket, string tie, and old-fashioned, snap-down visor golf cap. Now that he had hired a collaborator to help with the screenplays and mystery stories, he had plenty of time for poetry—and for making radio appearances as a literary expert and social commentator. He had been completely serious about becoming the literary "antipope" of Southern California, and he liked the fact that *his* protégés tended to be younger and angrier than Kenneth Rexroth's. While less accomplished from a technical standpoint, they were truer to Lipton's own savage ideal. They were real barbarians, not just literary ones, and he sensed that in time, with the proper guidance, they and others like them could sweep away the world's outdated ways of living, right along with its outmoded ways of thought.

The gatherings in the Liptons' living room now assumed a certain formality. Though sometimes attended by friends from Hollywood and the recognized literary world—so that it was hard to say who was on display for whom—these events usually consisted of long, rambling discussions featuring the local talent. Lipton tended to dominate the proceedings, but the younger poets did learn from them, especially when they heard themselves on tape.

Stuart Perkoff, impressed with the range of Lipton's knowledge, came regularly. Lipton, in turn, began to see in Perkoff the potential for the kind of spiritual leadership he had been preaching. There was never any humility lost between them, but Lipton's encouragement was important, perhaps crucial, to the younger poet, who thought of him as an older, wiser writer who knew so much that he deserved to be heard out—no matter how long it took. Often Perkoff would labor for days over one of Lipton's ideas, until he finally managed to work the answer into his poetry. In the end, Lipton succeeded in convincing him that he was a poet above all—not a man who sometimes wrote poems, but a man with a calling, a man with the power to "send thoughts thru germinations, carrying the signs & meanings of the Rituals of the Fathers hidden in their sounds."

As a sacred speaker, Perkoff wanted "to recreate a civilization in simple things on stretched skin & chewed out hollowed wood." He insisted on an unbroken link with the past, one that took account of all spiritually useful knowledge. He studied the Hebrew and Greek alphabets for hidden meanings and connections, drew charts plotting the progression of reality outward from the soul, and stubbornly insisted:

> Now I see that the art & craft of poetry takes much more knowledge, discipline, time to become proficient at than I wd ever have suspected.
>
> Perhaps I never saw this before because I was incapable up till now of conceiving of myself, except in a kind of horror, as a way of torturing myself, as unformed. Now it is an excitement to me, the things I have to learn, looking at them. & every day now I learn more (& more consciously) about my craft.

He considered playing the role of the poet an essential part of being one. He read solemnly and often harshly in a low, powerful growl that pulled at his vocal cords and gave his speaking voice an undercurrent of overwork and pain. His friend, Charlie Foster, compared his poetry to a dwarf star—"a matchbox full of the stuff weighs a ton." He wrote his poems not to be spoken, but *as if* spoken, with the physical act of speaking incorporated into their timing, spacing and progression down the page.

Open house became an unfailing Sunday event at 20 Park Avenue. Lipton thought of them as terribly serious events; Suzan Perkoff thought of *him* as Doctor Dolittle, talking animals and all. Poetry was to be read, food served, ideas spun out, tapes made, and big sketch pads left out for those who drew whenever they felt like it on whatever came to hand. For inspiration, Lipton had accumulated a respectable jazz collection, and he hoped to get the poets accustomed to reading with a live musical backup, as he knew Lawrence Ferlinghetti, Kenneth Rexroth, and Kenneth Patchen were doing up north. The one thing he did not allow was getting stoned, but no one would have done that anyway; as cool as he was, Lipton was not considered that cool. He liked to shock the squares with his talk about drugs and creativity, but no one ever saw him smoke or drink anything. He got high enough, he liked to say, on poetry, sex and the right kind of conversation.

To young men as serious about poetry as Perkoff, Bruce Boyd, Saul White, Maurice Lacy, and Charlie Newman, Lipton's open houses offered more than food and endless talk. They offered a sense of history. Lipton tried to make them imagine themselves in a long tradition of revolt and regeneration. He tended to lecture rather than converse, and he could be abusive to anyone who contradicted him. But when he managed to give his ego a rest, a thoughtful, unselfish man rather shyly emerged. Nor did it bother him that some people came as much for the food as for the intellectual stimulation. It cost him more than he could afford, but he knew that on any given Sunday, his wife's sandwiches would be all that many of them would have to eat.

What did the shaman himself get out of it? Surrounded by youth, ideas, respect, and a feeling that the times, with the benefit of his guidance, were changing, Larry Lipton was exactly where he had wanted to be all his life.

No one seemed to know who invented the term "Venice West," but Lipton was quick to make it his own. In his ever-more-frequent radio and platform appearances, he began to refer portentiously to "what we are doing in Venice West"— implying that something radically new was under way and that those not willing to embrace it had better be prepared to step aside. He took pride in bringing outsiders down to Venice for a look, but not everyone who came felt the magic. "The first time I went to his cottage in Venice," Anaïs Nin wrote, "and saw a little man whose glasses magnify his eyes and give him a fixed stare, whose teeth are blackened by cigar smoking, I was faced once more with what I call the antithesis of creation. The definition of creation for me was turning dross into gold. The definition of Lawrence Lipton and his friends is to give voice to the ugliness." It was also true that for any bohemian who remembered Henry Miller's Paris, Lawrence Lipton's Venice was strictly down-on-the-farm stuff. Nin even complained that when she was there, he "played records of poetry readings instead of letting the poets who were there read."

The recordings were essential to Lipton's plan to go public with Venice West. He wanted to stage large-scale performances of jazz and poetry—like those that had become a tourist attraction in San Francisco, only bigger and slicker—but he doubted that many of his poets were up to it just yet. There was no problem with the jazz musicians, who were used to improvising in front of people, but to be safe, Lipton thought it might be best to throw in a few actors or disk jockeys for the first event. Stuart Perkoff and Saul White were effective performers, but Perkoff distrusted the entire concept. As he saw it, either the poet or the musician would be forced to compromise. It would be some time before he came around to the view that jazz and poetry could be fused into a powerful new art form. In the meantime, he had more pressing things to worry about.

On the surface of things, Perkoff, with his contempt for material possessions, was a textbook example of "dedicated poverty." He bounced from low-paying job to low-paying job, usually working only as long as it took to qualify for unemployment; every time he quit or got fired, he insisted it was part of his *system*. In fact, he tried as hard as he could to earn a living for his family; he was simply not very good at it. When he worked, he worked hard—unloading boxcars, driving trucks, cooking short orders, and painting houses. He even borrowed a double-breasted suit, slicked back his hair, trimmed his mustache, and tried to sell used cars. Only once did he stay at a job long enough to earn a paid vacation; in due time, that job evaporated too.

Work was not the problem; it was *employment* he could

never quite get the hang of. Taking a conventional job meant spending the whole day with people who entertained hysterical notions about his way of life. By living outside the rules most Americans took for granted, he lacked the most ordinary mental survival skills for getting through a working day. Other men and women managed to leave their working selves at work, but not Perkoff. Either he took his real attitudes to work with him, which was a good way of getting fired, or he came home and inflicted on his wife the ones he had conned himself into accepting during the day.

Besides, if it was all just a matter of making money, the only difference between working and drawing unemployment was that unemployment paid less. Or so he liked to say—but he knew better. Intellectually, he told himself he was staying "pure" for his art; as a man, he knew he was neglecting his family. Suzan Perkoff, who believed in his art as much as he did, saw no reason a poet's children should not have enough to eat. Occasionally, but only occasionally, she managed to get the idea through to him. He quoted her on the subject in his anniversary poem for 1956:

> "I'm tired of poverty! I'm tired
> of not having enough to eat
> & nothing to wear
> for me or the kids
> & always dirt & hunger
> I'm tired"

He preferred to think of their marriage in terms of "madness & love," but fear was woven all the way through it. Perkoff had sought to build a "refuge of bone, & flesh, & carriers of the blood, attempting to swallow myself, & hide." That was not substantially different from any man's reason for starting a family. His wife's feelings about home, children, and basic personal dignity were even less exceptional. The daughter of a successful career woman, Suzan Perkoff was determined to be a mother who was present, *at home*, with her children. It was fine and courageous to renounce material ambition, especially for two people who had never really had any, but it was something else to have less than enough to live on. Sophistry would only go so far toward making that bearable; after that, fantasy had to take over.

Like everyone in Venice West, the Perkoffs knew there was a difference between imagination and delusion, but it was getting harder and harder to remember what it was. It had been so easy to liberate themselves from what *should* be that they now regarded what *might* be as a firm point of reference. "Lifestyle" was not the issue, although Larry Lipton, with his fixation upon the trivial, seemed to think it was. The truth was that Stuart and Suzan Perkoff, Tony Scibella, Bob and Anita Alexander, Milton and Bunny Bratton, Charlie and Julia Newman, Saul White, Bruce Boyd, and the others had knowingly committed themselves to a collective suspension of reality, a redefinition of what really is. They could still be good-humored about it, but the work of dissolution and re-creation, reinforced by love, self-denial, and an alternative mythology, went on all the time. The tricky thing was that *their* version of reality could be just as unforgiving as the other one—and far less predictable.

Everyone seemed to be "flipping out" in the summer of 1956. They joked about it, but it kept happening. Perkoff could use his poetry to turn the strangeness back on itself, but his wife had only her sense of adventure—and competition. They were like characters in a Warner Brothers cartoon, chasing each other off a cliff onto empty air, but safe until they looked down. In the end, it was Suzan Perkoff, ranging far ahead of her husband in her own quest for "the numinous," who looked down.

They were sitting around stoned with their friends one evening in June, and Perkoff was describing a particularly convoluted and enlightening dream he had had only a couple of nights before. Suzan Perkoff was resigned to hearing about it all over again, but as he began to talk, the thought came to her that if she let him get all the way through it, he would go crazy. So she cut him off and launched into an excited monologue of her own, a kind of filibuster against madness. When it showed no signs of stopping, he sat back and listened. It was an astonishing stream of talk even for a stoned person, and it mesmerized the speaker herself. Whatever she said seemed to become real; when she talked about birth, she could feel herself being born. "Shit," she cried, "I have to be born as a girl, 'cause my mother wants grandchildren!" She could feel what seemed to be an iron ring coming down and tightening around her head, and she screamed to Bruce Boyd, whom she somehow identified as the doctor, to pull it off. Boyd, however, had a vision of boils popping out all over Suzan Perkoff's body and ran away instead. So with the pressure building in her head, her hallucinations fusing together, and her husband watching in fascination, she shrewdly detached a part of herself to watch and remember, as the rest of her mind gave way to whatever was tightening the ring.

She managed to sleep that night, but when she woke up in the morning she was still crazy. It was partly self-dramatization, but the core of it was real. She and her madness came to a quick understanding. As long as there was no danger of her frightening or hurting anyone, especially her children, she agreed to stop resisting. Word had already gotten around that she had flipped, and friends were starting to drop by to pay their respects and to listen to her talk. She spent the next week as an oracle, a witch, a "walking poem."

Stuart Perkoff was transfixed. He and Lipton had theorized endlessly about getting back to the "savage source," the font of truth from the "time before the time." Now Suzan Perkoff sat speaking that murky truth in his living room, and whatever she saw he wanted to see too. He was afraid for his wife, but he adored the seeress, even if she did make him feel like something of an amateur.

At the peak of her madness, Suzan Perkoff announced that Sasha, their firstborn, would have to be born a second time. It was only fair. Ben's birth had been easy, but even though she had studied all the books on natural childbirth, her second son's had gone wrong in almost every way. So she led her husband and their friends down to the beach, commanded them to dig a hole deep enough to bury a five-year-old, and put Sasha into it. Then she covered him with just enough sand to make the rite a serious one and let the summer sea roll in and wash it off him. It was all so innocent and pagan, but thirteen years later, when Sasha himself went mad, he would tell the doctors in all seriousness that he had been born on Venice beach.

That evening the Perkoffs went to the Dome Theater, on the old Ocean Park pier, to see a cheap Hollywood "youth" comedy. Suzan Perkoff was able to predict every tired twist of the plot, which she proceeded to analyze in the same deep, oracular terms that had kept her husband transfixed for days. Everything was starting to have the same cosmic weight for her; it was all a joke *and* a mystery—which meant that neither joke nor mystery had any of its usual power to protect her. All of her fears and ambiguities now came to her wearing ritual masks, which made them easier to name but harder to resist. The nearer she drew to a state of pure acceptance, the more they threatened to overwhelm her.

She began leaving the house at any hour, day or night, and surfacing in other people's beds. It was a variant on a theme in their marriage; he "went out," she "went out," each ostensibly in response to what the other did. In the past, they had always been calculating or offhand about it. Everybody they knew did it at one time or another, and some did it constantly. It was not so much a matter of betrayal as of people acting out roles with and through their friends; sooner or later, most of the men and women of Venice West got around to each other. This was different; Suzan Perkoff was obsessed. As her husband, the "onlooker of love," wrote,

> inflated with the Divine Mother
> reliving traumas of her births
>   searching the wild beds & hatreds of the world
> for her twin
>   her strength
> her unhad power

>   david, david
> the tears that flowed!
> that there cd be such tears!

One of the people Suzan Perkoff ran to was a lesbian friend who had always told her she had a reckoning to keep with her own sexuality. The advice now was the same as ever: she "had to have an orgasm." It was solid post-Kinseyan reasoning, but Suzan, hearing it from the other side of the mirror, accepted it as a higher command so final and terrifying that nothing could reassure her—not people, ideas, conventions, or her own structure of love.

> there were too many things for her to see
>   she cd not sort them out

> into herself, & me, the world & time
>   into space & history
>   she sent her eyes & vision

> the warps & stones & enveloping structures
>   she saw thru
>   or around

until she came to that point in her mind
     where they were of enormous size
          & shapes completely without reference

& she sd: "hit me, feed me, rape me, touch me
     do something real to me, that i may know, touch, have
     something real to hold to. i
     must have something to
     hold to."

One morning Suzan Perkoff found herself on the porch at 20 Park Avenue, taking off her jewelry and hiding it under the Liptons' welcome mat. After the rings and earrings came off, it seemed logical that her clothes should follow, but she managed to tell herself, "No, that's crazy. I can't do that." Just then Larry Lipton, shopping bag in hand, cap on head, came shambling down the walkway from Pacific Avenue. She began to laugh. She put her rings back on and told him what had been going on. He seemed to know some of it already. "Larry's not gonna solve me nothing," she concluded almost gratefully, and accepted his invitation to come inside for coffee.

According to the account Lipton would publish in *The Holy Barbarians*, he left her alone for a while, then returned to find her on the couch with her knees drawn up under her chin and most of her clothes strewn fetchingly about his living room. With a "little-girl-lost" look on her face, she pleaded in a "tremulous," "desperate" voice: "You can help me, Larry. I *know* you can help me. Like you've been helping [Stuart]. We've been making a swinging scene every night. *Far out!* But I can't seem to come *back*. Like I do things . . . I don't know why I do them. And I just can't *stop*! You've got to help me come down . . . come *out* of it."

The way Lipton had heard it from Stuart Perkoff, the Perkoffs had been staying up all night, every night, carrying "pot, sex, Benzedrine and mystical self-searchings" past physical limits. They were brave, he concluded, but reckless. He took it for granted that it was the wife who had been trying to keep up with the husband, not the other way around; he felt for Stuart, who was probably "running around all over Venice looking for her." As he listened, Suzan's story "poured out of her breathlessly."

She began to philosophize about sex, in its pure, undifferentiated form, as the creative principle of the universe, invoking Bacchus, Priapus, Dionysus, and even the Shekina, the feminine emanation of Jehovah who hovered over the marriage bed. The gods themselves were originally conceived of as androgynous, hermaphroditic; how was a mortal supposed to experience "the numinous enlightenment ... nirvana ... satori ... except by going far out? How could you know in these other ways of knowing unless you explored your unconscious ... disassociated ... broke up, and through, and beyond ... beyond ... far out ... through pain ... through sex ... through pot ... Benzedrine ... *anything* ... *everything*?*"

As reconstructed by Lipton, it was the sort of monologue that made perfect sense at three o'clock in the morning, assuming the listener shared some of the speaker's points of reference. It was also the kind of talk that terrified people who had never chanced to think about such things, and it tended to make them pull their intellectual wagons into a circle. The trouble was—and Lipton, the old advertising man, knew this—that for such people, the far-out held a titillating fascination that could be freely enjoyed so long as it was condemned at the same time. When he came to write of Suzan's madness, Lipton's prescription would be shock therapy for the reader and condescension for the patient. He would turn her into an archetype of rebellion whose life just happened to revolve around America's favorite dirty secret—and he would also take most of the credit for her insights.

As Lipton saw it, Suzan Perkoff's problem was not so much that she had taken on more visions than a human being could handle, but that she had not been paying close enough attention to his lectures on the subject. That could be corrected. He gave her a book that he thought would keep her busy, then dashed out the back door and up Park Avenue looking for Stuart Perkoff. He found him, but by the time the two husbands rushed back, Suzan had gathered up her clothes and left.

"Did I *really* do that?" she would later demand of Lipton. Oh, yes, he would assure her, she had. But memory lapses were not, in fact, a part of her ordeal until *after* she had signed herself into "The Place." That happened a few nights later, when, after taking her younger son into her bed to stop his crying, she began to feel violent stirrings in her hands and arms. That was

enough; convinced that she would hurt her children, she shook
her husband awake and bullied him into driving her to the
county hospital. It was thirty miles one way through the bright,
alien city, but he, too, sensed the need to sue for peace.

Not that she seriously expected the doctors to help. No one
could convince her they ever helped anyone. She had run out of
weapons. She wanted to be in a place where they would keep
her from hurting anyone, where they would feed her, put her to
bed, and take every other responsibility away from her—a place
where there would be other damaged people to talk to. Los Angeles General Hospital had a clean and peaceful psychiatric
ward in which the doctors, all things considered, could be endured. She had always heard that the best thing to do was to get
one of them to like her, and eventually she settled on the department head, who seemed to be worth the effort it took to be
charming. By that time she had alienated everyone else, and
since the head was not allowed to serve as her therapist, she
ended up getting packed off to the state hospital at Camarillo
anyway.

There her memory lapses began. After she fell asleep, a second
Suzan Perkoff seemed to come on duty, doing things the original
would have to be told about in the morning. "Jesus Christ," she
thought to herself, "I let you do all these things, the least you
can do is let me *watch*!"

She knew she was still far from well when her husband
checked her out on a weekend pass two months later, pronounced her cured, and refused to take her back. After that, on
top of being crazy, she had to *pretend* to be sane. Since she was
firmly convinced that having an orgasm would make her "dis-
solve into pure air," she also "pretended" to have sex. She tried
explaining that to her mother, but to her that was simply what
a woman did. "God," Suzan thought, "don't I *ever* get to be
myself again?" Worst of all, the fear of orgasm only became
unbearable when she was moments away from having one. The
solution was to make herself "very dull." Stuart Perkoff responded by throwing himself into a hammer-and-tongs affair
with Susan Weire, a stunning young divorcee who worked with
him at the machine shop. He told himself he was "drug" with
Suzan's "not caring attitude," but he was also terrified at the
thought of her going back to Camarillo.

Susan Weire was "spooky." When one of her lovers would tell his wife about the things she had done or said, the wife usually recognized them as the things *she* would have done or said. Weire had an uncanny ability to become what a man wanted her to be, whether or not he knew what he was asking for. She became his "ideal girl," and if he still idealized his wife, she would even adopt his wife's mannerisms, whether or not she had ever met her. Ironically, she was probably the reason Stuart Perkoff stayed at the machine shop long enough to earn a paid vacation.

As always, he made no particular effort to hide his distraction, and it brought Suzan Perkoff at least part of the way back to herself. She decided to start an affair of her own with Danny Farber, their pot connection, and began to keep a journal that Stuart was not allowed to read. In practice, the two of them read each other's journals all the time, and they had long, screaming fights. They were trying to be very modern about the whole thing, but the simple absence of hypocrisy was apparently not enough.

One night, after Stuart had gone out, Suzan dumped the entire contents of his desk onto the floor—ink, glue, paint, papers, pencils, and the old-fashioned composition books he wrote in—*everything*. She had had enough, and on top of it all, she "just couldn't stand not being able to be real." She could still sense "voices and things" tugging at her, but she had had all she wanted of those, too. She sat down in her living room and shouted, "Fuck it! I can't stand this, you know! I'm going to stop holding on. And all I have to say is, if you have any messages to give me, *give* them to me. No more symbols. Just tell me what you want to tell me!"

Apparently it had all been said; the pressure in her skull began to lift. It occurred to her that this was taking a chance, too, but not much of a chance, after all. Whatever she did from now on, they would be things that *were done*; never again would she try to do what *no one* had ever done before. She clung to that thought, and it worked. She spent the rest of the night wandering through her home, or just sitting—peering approvingly into rooms, watching her boys sleep, looking at her husband's things scattered over the floor, feeling clean and high and seeing beauty.

The Perkoffs spent their vacation in San Francisco, where they met Kenneth and Marthe Rexroth and Stuart read with Bruce Boyd at the San Francisco Poetry Center. ("Seems a nice guy," Rexroth reported to Lipton, "full of ideas and good will. I'm anxious to hear his poems.") Poetry was certainly alive and well in the city, but Perkoff felt a little uneasy. It was pleasant to feel a part of something big, but the scene's code words, little orthodoxies, and elitist mentality made it obvious that even poetry could be made to work against thought.

Larry Lipton, ever the territorialist, had no such misgivings; he could hardly wait to get something like it started in Los Angeles. LA had its coffeehouses and poetry dens too, and better yet, it had Venice West. To set the record straight, Lipton actually challenged Rexroth to a debate. Which city was the *real* center of the West Coast Renaissance?

In a two-way hookup arranged by CBS Radio, Rexroth walked right into the ambush. He spoke calmly of San Francisco's Mediterranean cultural origins, of its tolerance for the eccentric, and of the practical advantages of being far from New York. It was "a very free and easy city," he concluded, "and very hospitable to the artist. Always has been."

Lipton, as usual, came out swinging. North Beach, he insisted, was nothing more than a "warmed-over, left-over Greenwich Village." If San Francisco was so "hospitable" to the arts, why was Lawrence Ferlinghetti fighting an obscenity charge for publishing Allen Ginsberg's *Howl and Other Poems*? Real artistic movements, he said, only prospered where artists saw through the illusion of popular acceptance and relied on each other. "Only artists are hospitable to new art, and to one another. In Venice, in Los Angeles—'Venice West,' *we* call it— such a community of poets and artists is working. . . . Venice West is to Los Angeles what the Left Bank once was to Paris."

Rexroth came away with no hard feelings; he hardly seemed to know he had been set up. Lipton, moreover, still valued his friendship and longed for his approval. He wanted Rexroth to see the LA scene for himself, and Rexroth, who despised Southern California on principle, but resented the fact that Ruth Witt-Diamant never got him any bookings there, was agreeable. When some friends in Hollywood proposed to arrange a reading for him there, he let Lipton know he would be available for other bookings. Lipton, with his customary energy, threw himself into preparations for a jazz-and-poetry extravaganza such as no one had ever seen.

Rexroth made his way south in December 1957, but not without a great deal of fussing. He balked at Lipton's choice of musicians; he hated "Pacific (i.e., LA) jazz in general," and Shorty Rogers in particular. On the other hand, he refused to think of asking his own band to play for "cheap stripper's wages." He wanted at least fifty dollars a night for himself. Then, only a month away from showtime, Lipton became embroiled in a territorial dispute with some of the local literati, and Rexroth wearily refused to take sides, insisting that he could take "no pleasure in a weekend of harassment & struggle."

Lipton took it for granted that Rexroth would be his house guest, but at the last minute that seemed uncertain, too, since the poet seemed to require assurances of more than shelter. After two "undomesticated" weeks away from home, he was going to want to meet "some nice quiet girl who lives near the beach & is *clean* & doesn't take dope. White will do, but colored preferred."

Lipton prevailed; Rexroth stayed at 20 Park Avenue. There he met Susan Weire, who did show traces of black ancestry in her perfectly symmetrical face. He fell in love with her like a sixteen-year-old, and when friends saw them together on the beach, they noticed that she had adopted Marthe Rexroth's walk. Rexroth was so shattered for a while that he actually considered moving to Los Angeles, which would have been rather like Billy Graham moving to hell.

The West Coast Poetry and Jazz Festival, staged for four nights running in the newly reopened Los Angeles Jazz Concert Hall, was a surprising success. Two local bands, which included Shorty Rogers, Fred Katz, Bud Shank, and Buddy Collette, played backup for Perkoff, Rexroth, Saul White, an amateur actor, and a professional disk jockey in the most improbable sellout event the Crenshaw district had ever seen. Poetry and jazz had broken out of the cellar bars and coffeehouses straight into show business, and Lipton had given it a new name: *jazz canto.* The term never quite caught on, but the critic from the *Times* had to admit that the new art form might "someday open up new horizons of public acceptance for both mediums," and even Anaïs Nin thought it had a future.

After Rexroth returned to San Francisco, Lipton wrote to ask him a special favor. New York University Press had approached him about expanding his article, "Youth Must Serve Itself," into a book. He had all the material he needed, including 48,000 feet of tape recorded readings, conversations, and soul sessions with the young barbarians of Venice West. The publisher's $300 advance was not enough. What did Rexroth think of his chances with the Guggenheim Foundation? Would he be willing to help?

There were no foundations, of course, for helping poets support new babies. The Perkoffs had fought every night before he left for the Poetry and Jazz Festival. He had wanted to read; she had wanted him to be there when she went into labor. Rachel Perkoff, a poet's daughter, had obligingly gone three weeks past term, but what had once been a critical situation was now almost preposterously desperate. There would never be enough money the way Stuart was used to making it, but he had a new idea. A hip coffeehouse and restaurant might attract locals and tourists alike; if the crowds at Lipton's jazz-and-poetry extravaganzas were any indication, the public's new fascination with the avant-garde might even last long enough to make them rich.

The Perkoffs borrowed money from their parents, rented the shell of an old bleach factory just off the Promenade, and took on a partner, Rudy Croswell, who had spent enough time as a waiter in the Village to know how successful coffeehouses were run. Perkoff and Tony Scibella peeled the walls of #7 Dudley back to the brick, restrung all the wiring, ran plumbing, built partitions, painted the walls, and somehow got rid of the chemical smell. They hung big light globes from the ceiling and installed an elaborate, New York-style copper espresso machine. Scibella painted the name in neat letters on the small picture window: "Venice West Café Expresso" (everybody pronounced it with an "x" anyway). The health department issued a permit effective the following Monday, but Perkoff refused to wait that long. Why waste the weekend? What was wrong with Friday night? What could go wrong?

It was too pristine, too perfect. Croswell knew a lot about hip coffeehouses, but Perkoff knew what he could live with—and what he could not. Minutes away from opening time, with people lined up outside, he opened a bottle of ink and attacked the walls, slashing at the antiseptic white with poems, names, incantations. As the first customers shuffled in, the words blazed from the east wall in savage, uneven letters:

ART IS LOVE IS GOD

The line was Wally Berman's, and Perkoff, always willing to acknowledge a debt, printed his name carefully underneath. When Croswell arrived and saw it he was beside himself, but it was too late. The words stayed up, soon to be joined by paintings, collages, drawings, and still more words. It was Stuart Perkoff's wall, and the words had won.

CHAPTER FOUR

"Begin with an individual," F. Scott Fitzgerald once wrote in "The Rich Boy," "and before you know it you find that you have created a type." For Lawrence Lipton, struggling through 1958 to finish his book about the young bohemians of Venice, the distinction was largely irrelevant. In his professional experience, a good character *was* a type—a reasonably original package of instantly recognizable character traits. More than that, a good character, like a good advertising slogan, had to have a "hook."

But not too sharp a hook. Since life among the "disaffiliated" had more than enough built-in shock value, he was going to have to soften his focus on the people. Their way of life might be perfectly outrageous, but they themselves must be likeable, good-hearted, and easy to tell apart. It was going to be a neat trick: making the "scene" seem a threat to the Republic and the people seem as harmless as rodeo clowns. The crusade against conformity demanded sacrifices of everyone, however, and just now, at any rate, it called for instant clichés.

Stuart Perkoff became "Angel Dan Davies," the "ecstatic, self-righteous mad" poet who came to the Liptons' every Sunday, played "little boy hungry" to get sandwiches from Nettie Lipton, and smeared the mayonnaise into his drawing when it happened to drip on the page. Charlie Newman became "Itchy Dave Gelden," scratching constantly "because he had no skin; he was as open to the world as a turtle without a shell." Suzan Perkoff became "Margot," and Bunny Bratton "Thelma." Those whose poetry Lipton planned to showcase ended up with two names, their own and an invented alias, while Tony Scibella, who avoided being interviewed only to turn up under his own name in the photo section, ultimately got his opinions cited as those of "everybody else." Like most mystery writers, Lipton emphasized detail—the odd habit, the physical anomaly, the memorable quirk. His characterizations were patronizing and occasionally insulting, but they were as real as he knew how to make them.

That was why Charlie Foster was such a windfall. When he first began to hang around Venice on the weekends in 1956, he was a stock character in transition—the Arrow Collar man, the man in the grey flannel suit, the congenital Man Most Likely to Succeed. Lipton knew a hot ideological property when he saw one. It was Foster, the voluntary failure, who could be used to make the case for "disaffiliation" better than Perkoff, Milton Bratton, Scibella, Saul White, or any of the others who had never had much to drop out from. If a ringer for Amory Blaine could renounce the world and grow happier, healthier, and more productive, then perhaps success was overrated after all.

That would have not have come as news to Charlie Foster. He already hated the world's idea of success with an intensity other men only affected. It was not his fault that he had always been most likely to be *voted* "most likely to succeed." He had the looks, the talent, and the social and educational advantages to shoulder other men aside gracefully. He seemed to be the sort of man who had fascinated Scott Fitzgerald—born to a status he had the ability to achieve on his own. It had thus been something of an achievement for Foster to fail so spectacularly at so many things by the age of thirty-five.

Born into a fair amount of New England money in 1922, Foster had grown up tall, blond, handsome, agreeable, and well-connected. His mother, Mildred Foster, raised him as a Christian Scientist, and while he careened off in his own spiritual directions after he went away to college, he retained the conviction that life, properly lived, called for the constant unmasking of error. A Sea Scout, an athlete, an honor student, and a man sought out by the right friends, he had won a scholarship to Colgate, done graduate work at Harvard and Boston University, and served honorably as an aerial gunner in World War II. With his parents' overwhelming approval, he had married his first wife, Eunice, in the Grace Episcopal Church in

Newton, Massachusetts. Several years, three children, and many disillusionments later, the same Eunice had flung his mother's engagement ring, with its big, square-cut diamond, through the window of their car into the Mexican night.

By that time, Foster was a confirmed drunk, a "blind hog with no self-control." Alcoholics Anonymous seemed to work for short periods, since there was no such thing as getting by on style alone at an AA meeting, but pulling himself together invariably meant going back to work—usually in the advertising industry, which for Foster meant plunging back into the realm of the false, the fabricated, the half-true. It was also a world that ran on ethyl alcohol, and unfortunately, it was always more than willing to take him back.

Even when Foster simply walked away from jobs without warning, excuses continued to be made for him. When he came to live in his mother's new home in Pacific Palisades, he found the LA advertising community to be just as soft a touch as any other. He was not all con, after all; he was as good as they came. Often hired to fill absurdly responsible positions, he always delivered the goods—right up to the moment he walked away.

It was not as though he never tried anything else. Filling out an application for unemployment insurance in Santa Monica in November 1957, he listed so many jobs that the interviewer demanded to know why he was so unstable. So Foster, who had only listed as many as the form would hold, obliged by giving him a crash course in instability. He told him about having been an assistant controller for a research-and-development company in New Mexico, about running his own mail-order business in Berkeley, about teaching school in North Carolina, and about working as an ordinary seaman on the Great Lakes. Afterwards, he realized he had left out working as a pipe welder in Emeryville, a toilet-bowl cleaner in Albuquerque, an onion topper in the Imperial Valley, a strawberry picker outside Santa Maria, a claims adjuster for the Liberty Mutual Insurance Company, a reporter for the Retail Credit Company, a special agent for the California State Compensation Fund, and a Good Humor truck driver in Los Angeles. He might also have mentioned teaching at a girls' school in Mexico City, writing stories for science fiction magazines, selling oranges door-to-door in the black section of Palm Beach, Florida, washing dishes in Chicago, and pouring soap through a funnel into little boxes in Boston—but the interviewer had clearly lost interest.

What Foster did best, and hated most, was writing advertising copy. It was bad enough to be paid ridiculous amounts of money for telling "lies, half-truths, evasions, for taking the positive point of view"; the worst part was having to use his own magic—his gift for teasing fine layers of reality into still finer layers of fantasy—to violate other people's imaginations. He hated it because it was effortless; it actually came more easily to him than telling a story to his friends.

Once, in Mexico, he had actually earned five hundred pesos in an hour—a fairly respectable sum in the mid-fifties—for helping his cousin's advertising agency save its biggest account. The client, a medical supply dealer, had demanded that something new and different be put in front of him by two o'clock that afternoon, but the copywriters seemed hopelessly stuck on "very faintly concealed variations of 'XYZ Syringes are the best goddamn syringes in the world.'" Since he needed the money to get to Puerto Vallarta, Foster volunteered, and after an hour of looking over both the client's past advertising and the current issue of his chosen medium, *Selecciónes del Reader's Digest*, he decided to resort to "that old standby, fear":

ARE YOU RISKING YOUR LIFE—
OR THE LIFE OF YOUR CHILD—
BY USING DIRTY SYRINGES?

He closed with "the moral injunction, 'It's just as important to have your own needle as your own toothbrush.' Signature of client, XYZ Syringes, best goddamn syringes in the world, etc." The manufacturer "went wild"—he knew the real thing when he saw it—and Foster used his five hundred pesos to drift a little deeper into that sad, rich, and outlandish subculture that a generation or two of American junkies, bohemians, remittance men, and GI Bill expatriates had created in the alternate universe that was Mexico.

Every conceivable kind of misfit seemed to thrive in that world, which Foster described fondly, realistically, and without romanticism in long, picaresque stories that he never bothered to publish. It was the same ground covered in the late forties by

Jack Kerouac, William Burroughs, Neil Cassady, and Allen Ginsberg. In only about a year or two, Kerouac's novels would inspire a new onslaught of gringo mystics and adventurers. Foster
had gotten there on his own, however, and unlike Kerouac and
his friends, he tried to accept it on its terms rather than his.

Kerouac, for example, built a whole fantasy of female saint-
hood around "Tristessa," a morphine-addicted prostitute he
barely knew. Foster, on the other hand, managed to write about
Herta, who might have been Tristessa's benzedrine-powered sister, without making her more or less than she was. As he described them, Herta and Jerry, the burnt-out jazzman she lived
with, were simply people Foster could have known anywhere.
Where Kerouac's mission was to offer "prayers to the world in
the form of novels," Foster had a different vocation: to learn to
write without any compromise at all, even if it meant stripping
his mind of every defense it had. He wanted to achieve a level of
truth from which nothing could be taken back.

Foster's writing, like his own ragged, complicated mind, was
full of tricks. His realistic short stories were long excursions into
self-consciousness, featuring endless digressions and stark ex-
aminations of his own confused sexuality. They seemed pointless, like the long, disconnected stories he told when he was
drunk. He would play out plotline after plotline until there
seemed to be no way back, and then, on the last page, he would
reel them all in. In the meantime, as a friend observed, "the road
forked without warning." Even his intentional fantasies, such as
"The Troubled Makers," focused on his own misgivings about
creating visions for others. He knew there was a difference between creating and lying, but he could never tell with any certainty what it was.

When Foster first started hanging around Venice in 1956, he
was still writing ad copy for the J. W. Christopher Company in
Los Angeles. Though still "all gray flannel" on the outside, he
caught Larry Lipton's eye immediately. Lipton made friends
with Foster, let him sleep overnight at 20 Park Avenue, and began to get his attitudes down on tape for the "youth book."
Sober, Foster could explain himself clearly in the terms Lipton
preferred: truth, phoniness, the rat race, the emptiness of working for money. In a sense, Foster's renunciation had been purer
than his own. Lipton had given up a six-figure income, but Fos-

ter had thrown away social advantages that no self-made Jewish writer of Lipton's generation would have had in the first place.

When Foster finally moved into a Venice storefront without lights, heat, or running water, Lipton was triumphant. Initially naming him "Matt Russell," then settling on "Chuck Bennison," Lipton plugged him straight into the main thesis of his "youth book." Here was the self-made misfit, the natural achiever whose defection had made him not only pure, but happy. There could hardly be a stronger testimony to the health-giving properties of Venice West. "Today," Lipton wrote, "Chuck Bennison is bearded and barefoot; he has shaken off John Barleycorn and taken on Mary Juana and burned all his gray flannel britches behind him." He had even grown a beard, which he called his "letter of resignation from the rat race."

Not everyone in Venice accepted him so readily. It was not that he was still too conventional, but that he was too strange even for Venice West. He always seemed to be trying too hard; his emotions lay so close to the surface as to frighten practically everybody. Even Lipton conceded that he put "more body English into his jazz-listening than the cool cats approve of." Tony Scibella, speaking for the beachfront regulars, considered him "obviously brilliant," but "probably insane." At best, he was "one of us in a different way"; at worst, he was "different," "a wack," a "nut" that nobody wanted around.

In spite of what Lipton was writing about him, Charlie Foster still drank. He thought it helped him "relax, talk to girls and be like other people." It certainly did help him talk—softly, laconically, and with the utmost care not to leave anything out. Most of those within earshot ended up shouting, "That's good, Charlie. Now, shut up!" The Perkoffs managed to accept him, and when Stuart crept into his pad one morning and wrote, "This is the face of God you see" on Foster's mirror, Charlie felt accepted in a way he had never experienced outside rural Mexico.

"I am from Venice," Foster declared finally in an unpublished memoir. "I died in Venice & I was born in Venice. & it is the world of Venice that I would know & love. & I would take the measure of its suffering."

So he stuck it out. He had affairs with Bunny Bratton and Julia Newman, went to work as a mail carrier in the neighborhood, and wrote long, strange diaristic stories he could never be persuaded to publish but sometimes read aloud to his friends. Suzan Perkoff had even considered him as the instrument of her revenge in January 1957, when her husband was having his affair with Susan Weire. But after talking him into borrowing Rod Alger's MG for a "fantastic death defying run" through the city, Suzan's conscience got the better of her, and she chose Danny Farber instead—because he was "a bastard and a cocksman and it would be ethical to use him." After Stuart's fling had played itself out, Foster fell shatteringly in love with Suzan Weire himself.

"How to form an extended kin group," he wrote not long after that, "or, how the incest tabu can be cultivated till it covers & practically hides all the women you know." The fact was that he needed a circle of friends much more than he needed the love of any particular person. His friends might be outcasts from society, but at least they fit in with each other. He fit in nowhere. That was what made their admittedly limited acceptance so important:

> When I have been so twisted & weird & sick that it was absolutely impossible to put up with me or tolerate me in any shape or fashion or by any known means whatsoever, the people in Venice . . . suffered me, they suffered the revulsion & literal & actual belly-turning, puking & brain-twisting sicknesses that I brought to them. In their love they made excuses for me that were only exceeded by the excuses I made for myself. I brought poison to them and they suffered me to come back & bring them more.
> That is to say, they gave me love.

Lipton, on the other hand, thought they babied him too much. He had little patience with alcoholics, and he always thought Foster came unstuck a bit too self-consciously. Besides, he wanted him to live long enough to do something with his talent, and if he was going to use him as a case in point, he needed him sane. Who would care what a drunken beach loony had given up?

It was also true that of all the poets in Venice West, no one came closer than Charlie Foster to writing the type of poetry Larry Lipton himself would have liked to create. As the bravest of his friends sometimes pointed out to him, Lipton was a born satirist with no particular gift for the metaphysical. According to Rexroth, he could have become "another Calverly, Belloc, Benson, Fogarty," but Lipton wanted to be Blake, Eliot, and Martial rolled into one. Unfortunately, his hard-working, overly civilized poems celebrated savage ecstasy better than they inspired it. Foster, on the other hand, was equal parts rationalist, satirist, and holy lunatic. Where Lipton wrote about the need for visions, Foster saw them—then wrote them up in the form of mad, infinitely detailed travelogues.

Normally as territorial as he was thin-skinned, Lipton went out of his way to encourage Foster, although he could never shake the habit of trying to be his teacher. For his part, Foster knew he needed someone to prod him. He might never have finished tinkering with "The Troubled Makers" had not Lipton snatched it away from him and sent it off to *Evergreen Review*. As the oldest and most intellectually secure of Lipton's initiates, he appreciated his help and forgave him most of his pretentions. He even dedicated poems to him. Lipton made a point of keeping the one about "Bwana Lawrence":

WHO RUN DIS HER COMPOUND NOW?
You can *ask*? Why, *he* do.
Who do?
BWANA LAWRENCE . . .
WHAT AN APPETITE THAT MAN GOT—WHAT MANA!

               . . . now
you know as well as i do a man
of THEM dimensions he don't need
to do nothin stupid like move his
legs to get exercise . . .

he's just doing it to keep up the
flagstone spirits of all these young,
dead-type 2nd string shamans.

all the time going around growing
beards or shaving them off &
   trying
to look wise & as if they knew the
inside story of what's up

        & that's better than working
        for an eatin-type living . . .

        & all the time these junior birdmen
            shamans
        think he's practically a fallen forest
            giant.

Not that he ridiculed Lipton's ideas about getting back to the roots of religion. He himself studied the I Ching, the Tarot, the Kabala, and the Egyptian Book of the Dead, along with Freud, Jung, the Old Testament, and Robert Graves's *King Jesus*. He spent much of the year 1958 trying to write an immensely long poem that would have made a system of all the incompatible spiritual insights he had ever had. Despite his freewheeling confusion, Foster was convinced of one thing: the literal existence of Moloch, the hungry god of the materialists. Where Allen Ginsberg had used Moloch metaphorically in "Howl," Foster saw his real presence lurking behind almost every human exchange. He was not quite sure of what to do about it, either, except to reject Moloch and all his works—which inevitably meant denying himself to a degree even Lipton thought extreme. Foster, in turn, sometimes thought of Lipton as an easy-chair shaman who never actually got down and struggled in the mud of the soul.

Lipton, like Robert Graves, was a neopagan out of intellectual necessity. He praised the old religion because it accepted human nature without censuring whole blocks of it, and because its rituals seemed to address real psychological needs. For similarly utilitarian reasons, Kenneth Rexroth continued to think of himself as a Catholic. Lipton, Rexroth, and Graves were all Enlightenment men; none of them meant to subordinate his will to any god, old or new. It was the "2nd string shamans" of Venice West who took their religious primitivism where they assumed it was meant to be taken, to heart.

Stuart Perkoff, for example, had come to believe in the Muse— not a metaphorical Muse who stood for creativity, but a literal female deity who visited him at night to bring him poems. He declared her to be his "Lady," consecrated his journals to her, and slowly began to relate to her as the principal female in his life. Throughout 1957 and 1958, as his marriage deteriorated, he steadily transformed his inner circle of friends into a ring of devotion to the Lady.

At roughly the same time, Venice West welcomed the arrival of yet another jealous god in the person of his self-anointed prophet. Alexander Trocchi—late of Paris and the expatriate review *Merlin*, late of New York City, late of some the most rarified circles in Western letters—came to Venice late in 1957, bearing impeccable avant-garde credentials and the manuscript of *Cain's Book*, a novel devoted to his personal relationship with heroin. He was having a difficult time with it, and Lipton, who had corresponded with him for years, may have persuaded him that Venice was the one place where he could finish it. At any rate, his presence certainly upgraded the value of the local literary real estate, and the younger writers were anxious to learn from him.

Despite his Italian name, Trocchi was a Scot from Glasgow who had already established himself as one of the two or three major voices of Celtic existentialism. Though still in his twenties, he was a graduate of literary scenes so esoteric that it was a mark of sophistication even to know about them. As editor of *Merlin*, he had published Samuel Beckett in English at a time when it was almost impossible to find him in any-thing but French. He liked to call Beckett his "virtual father" ("limerick & cork & glasgow-down-derry & up yr shellaigh-leagh," Charlie Foster called *that* connection), and those who had worked with him in Paris considered him the writer "most likely to become our generation's Joyce or Hemingway or—most likely—Orwell."

He wrote as cleanly and judged as harshly as Orwell, but there they parted company. Orwell had been nothing if not committed—to humanity, to socialism, to telling the world the truth. All of Trocchi's fiction, on the other hand, took the form of a lone man conspiring with himself. Trocchi recognized only the obligation to tell the truth to himself; if that meant telling it to others, so be it, but *so what*?

His still-unpublishable first novel, *Young Adam*, had gone Camus's *The Stranger* one better by making its existential hero's involvement in the story completely unknown to anyone but himself. The narrator, a young barge captain who spent most of his time passing the time, found himself in possession of enough knowledge about an accidental death to clear a man accused of murder. Coming forward, however, might have cast suspicion on himself, depending on how badly the local authorities wanted a murder conviction, so that, in a land of stupid officials and even stupider institutions, was that. While *Young Adam* seemed to center on the morality of telling or not telling, the real issue was whether or not Trocchi's hero had the strength of will to let a dim-witted and oddly trusting man go all the way to the gallows for his convenience. In the end, after weeks of following the case and savoring his own delicious reactions to it, he found that he could do just that. Better to let an innocent fool die than to allow a contemptible society take his own life into its brutal, stupid hands.

To support life while editing *Merlin*, Trocchi had translated novels from the French for Maurice Girodias, whose Olympia Press was helping to make "underground literature" an essential part of American intellectual life in the last, grudging years of literary censorship. The Olympia Traveller's Companion paperback series included the first English editions of Nabokov's *Lolita*, Donleavy's *The Ginger Man*, Beckett's *Watt* and *Molloy*, Genet's *Thief's Journal*, several of Henry Miller's novels, and those most banned of all books, the works of the Marquis de Sade. With Girodias, Trocchi had also brought off one of the better literary frauds of the decade.

Girodias had originally owned the rights to Frank Harris's *My Life and Loves*, a four-volume work which was still making nothing but money for the firm that had taken over the bits and pieces of his first publishing venture, Obelisk Press. Girodias knew that an uncompleted fifth volume was supposed to exist, and once Olympia Press was in the black, he made up his mind to track it down and publish it. One million francs later, not counting lawyers' fees, Girodias discovered that what he had bought from Harris' widow, sight unseen, was a packet of ragged yellow pages with practically nothing on them. A positive thinker to the end, he took them to Trocchi for an extraordinary bit of editing. In ten days the writer had fashioned a volume of first-rate, wickedly readable Harris out of thin air. It was a put-on worthy of Harris himself, and it was certainly Trocchi's kind of fun—a counterfeiting job that required as much brilliance to detect as to write, and that gleefully took advantage of those solemn supporters of the Olympia Press, most of them American, who assumed that what was suppressed was *bound* to be superior to what was allowed.

After acquiring a heroin habit in Paris, Trocchi had moved to New York City, which was a bit like moving to Riyadh to be an alcoholic—it could be done, but there were easier places to try it. His novel became a day-by-day account of the life of a cerebral addict who, unlike most of the city's junkies, managed to support his habit without stealing—by running yet another scow on yet another river outside yet another nightmarish city. By 1957, Trocchi had already spent at least one publisher's advance trying to get the book right. Perhaps the move to Venice would supply the necessary perspective. Larry Lipton, at least, was confident. Trocchi would finish his great novel, he predicted, "if he can kick the heroin habit." That was certainly not the way Trocchi saw it; he had no intention of kicking, since his habit and his book were virtually one.

Like *Young Adam, Cain's Book* was a diaristic novel. Trocchi believed that only the "defiantly first-person" novel had any claim to honesty. He thought the conventional novel forced the author to pretend to know things about his characters that he could barely hope to know about himself. *Cain's Book* would be the whole truth—a work created in, of, and for the ecstatic spiritual isolation that was heroin's gift to Alex Trocchi. After moving into Charlie Foster's old storefront pad with Lyn, a woman who had already backed more than one self-destructive artist, he worked tirelessly and obsessively. "A man can do anything if he's got the right woman to help him," Lyn told Lipton. "The Bible says love is stronger than death. I think it's even greater than heroin, and we're going to prove it."

Trocchi did kick—in fact, he spent most of his time kicking. There was no money and often no heroin. There was a fair amount of marijuana around, but Venice had not yet become serious junk territory. Tony Scibella and Stuart Perkoff tried to score for him, but when Trocchi himself failed to find junk, it usually meant there was none to find. His friends tried to keep him going on goofballs, dolophene (a.k.a. methadone), and anything else that seemed to cut his symptoms. Occasionally there would be a windfall—a stolen doctor's bag or an unguarded supply of prescription drugs, such as the ones Scibella found while he was helping his father paint a dentist's office:

People in the dentist's office, they couldn't stand the smell of paint, so they closed and left. And there was a box of those pharmaceutical samples—but it was all kind of gorilla pills like Thorazine, you know. So that's what we kept him on—tongue swollen up—ah, Trocchi. He was a good dude, man. And he worked *all* the time.

Trocchi sometimes found time to visit literary friends in the area, such as Christopher Isherwood, but for the most part he stayed in, tried to stay straight, and wrote. In the jargon of the time, however, staying straight meant staying loaded, or at least staying comfortably ahead of being sick. As long as Lyn could work to support both of them, *Cain's Book* continued to grow. But then Lyn began using herself, which meant that sooner or later, Trocchi's sabbatical would have to end. Still he could not finish.

Part of the problem was the book itself. Who could say when it was done? It had its technical aspects—characters, incidents, and a plot—but all of them, like the activity involved in obtaining a fix, tended to vanish from memory whenever the book's real dynamic asserted itself. Trocchi was writing about something that absorbed him completely, that ordered his life, that confirmed his sense of superiority. In all his experience, heroin was the only thing he had encountered that could withstand his intellect. It fascinated him, punished him, filled him with promise, and allowed him the luxury of obedience. As *Reader's Digest* might have put it, it gave him something to believe in. But when is a work of perfect devotion complete?

There was no more pretense of a fictional character in Joe, the central character in *Cain's Book*, than in the aw-shucks, all-American name the author had given him. He was Trocchi himself, floating in his scow on the East River and examining himself under the intellectual equivalent of hospital lighting. Though sensually and mentally alive, Joe was as detached from his fellow creatures as the need to make connections would permit him to be. He was not a narcissist; his self-absorption was unromantic. He simply accepted himself as the most interesting and accessible subject in the world. His isolation surpassed even the stark Martian aloneness of that better-known literary junkie, William Burroughs. It was the self-sufficiency of a man determined not to be affected by any experience but his own.

Heroin, of course, was the essential element. Its self-reflective shell encased him completely: "The perceiving turns inward, the eyelids droop, the blood is aware of itself . . . the organism has a sense of being intact and unbrittle, and, above all, *inviolable*."

Or, as American hipsters put it, "cool." Heroin was more than the chemical co-efficient of Trocchi's intellectual convictions; in every way, he *loved* it. Whether he was actually shooting up or only writing about it, his absorption was minute and complete. Every part of the routine—the arm tied up tight, the powder cooked up in the spoon, the liquid sucked up through the little ball of cotton, the blood filling up the eyedropper to prove that the needle was in the vein—seemed to be happening for the first time. His awe of the ritual even included a diehard romantic's faith in its higher significance. "All of this is not for nothing," he wrote. "It is born of respect for the whole chemistry of alienation."

According to Trocchi, no one who was not on junk had a right to express an opinion about it—while most people who *were* on junk had nothing interesting to say. He reserved his worst contempt for the junkie who broke faith with his habit, either by trying to kick it or by claiming it was only a physical need. "If you simply put heroin down," he insisted, "you are avoiding the issue. It isn't the horse, for all the melodramatic talk about withdrawal symptoms. It is the pale rider." Heroin was the modern mystic's way of knowing death. It was not a way of coping but of being, with its own clock, its own calendar, and its own exclusive brand of freedom: "That is one of the virtues of the drug, that it empties such questions of all anguish, transports them to another region, a painless theoretical region, a play region, surprising, fertile, and unmoral. One is no longer grotesquely involved in the becoming. One simply is."

William Burroughs would later put it even more succinctly: "NOTHING ever happens in the junk world." It was more accurate to say that only one thing ever happened. Junkies lived in a universe endlessly imploding upon a single event: the fix. Junk time was thus cyclical time, and cyclical time is, by definition, ritual time. For Trocchi, the fix was Alpha, Omega, and the Eternal Return compressed into one. In a lifetime of refusing to be impressed, the junk equation was the one *necessary* conclusion he had ever acknowledged.

He therefore refused to register even mock disgust at how low the drug made him bow. He insisted he was never anything but a man doing what he chose to do. He described his fellow junkies in terms of their lies, weaknesses, and physical deterioration, but that, as he saw it, was no more than the result of their doing what *they* chose to do. What really made life hell for heroin users in America was the great mass of people who knew nothing about the drug, but whose fears, neuroses, and need to dictate to others had been translated into "barbarous" laws. "These crude laws," he wrote, "and the social hysteria of which they are a symptom have from day to day placed me at the edge of the gallow's leap. *I demand that these laws be changed.*"

The one question he never attempted to answer was why a British subject who could have lived in peace as a licensed addict should have brought himself to America to subject himself to such laws—*if* the laws were the problem, rather than a large part of the attraction. Nor did Trocchi seem to notice how closely his outlaw moral judgments seemed to correspond to conventional ideas of right and wrong. The hero of *Young Adam* was not an "unmoral" man trying to preserve himself, but a man fascinated with his ability to do evil—evil, that is, as any Scottish Presbyterian might have understood it. The junkie protagonist of *Cain's Book* was equally beguiled by the vacant moral places in himself, so that each new triumph over the standards ordinary people lived by seemed to contain an element of revenge. Amorality is not, however, delight at what one can bring oneself to do; it is simply not caring. For Trocchi, that apparently took all the fun out of being wicked.

He was a proselytizer, with an answer to every faint-hearted objection. His editor at Grove Press, Richard Seaver, wanted him to cut the long passages of libertarian cant and "junkie-piety" out of *Cain's Book*; he thought they were a distraction that actually weakened Trocchi's case against the drug laws. Trocchi kept them in; like the Midnight Mission, his policy was no sermon, no meal. In the language of born-again evangelism, he was a soul-winner. He "converted" Saul White and others to heroin, and he even made the idea of shooting junk "intellectually possible" for Stuart Perkoff, who had always cultivated a sensible fear of the needle.

Though completed in New York City, *Cain's Book* would prove to be the only first-rate work of long fiction even partially written in Venice West. When Trocchi presented him with a carbon copy of the first 102 pages, Perkoff set it up in a spring binder like an icon in his home. Long after Trocchi had gone away, Venice poets and artists would continue to talk about his novel as if its existence lent validity to what they themselves were doing. The one thing never suggested was that it was possible to read *Cain's Book* not as a dark statement of freedom, but as a document of ultimate submission to the consumer ethic.

If junk were anything, it was a consumer product. The difference was that unlike cars, expensive Scotch, ranch-style homes, and all the other commodities commonly sold with the promise of heaven on earth, heroin actually delivered. The addict's need for heroin was only an exaggerated version of the relationship every good media director sought to establish between his client's product and the people to whom it was offered. Pushing other products usually meant resorting to fear, group pressure, sexual innuendo, and all the other manipulative devices known to a multi-billion-dollar industry, while the heroin trade prospered on the basis of word-of-mouth alone. Nor did most of its consumers suddenly wake up one morning to find themselves addicted; beneath it all, the whole point of using junk was to get a habit.

It was true that for a user, life consisted of doing whatever was necessary to obtain, consume, and find the money to pay for an illegal *thing* he could not live without. But in the late 1950s, not being able to live without *things* was being touted as the American Way, if not nature's way. For those who still clung to the freedom *not* to consume, ever more powerful means of persuasion were on the way.

If the junkie debased himself more than the ordinary citizen to obtain the product he needed, he also had fewer illusions about why he needed it. In that sense, *Cain's Book* was a statement of absolute freedom; but it was a vassal's freedom, a choice of idols. Trocchi had liberated himself from everything but the fundamental pattern of life in a consumer society. On the other hand, like any good pitchman, he had a gift for making irony vanish. One by one, the young disaffiliates of Venice West caved in to his reasoning; only Charlie Foster, the former adman, remained unimpressed. They might be immune to Cadillacs, pile carpeting, and ranch-style houses, but in a material culture, to twist a popular maxim just a bit, it hardly mattered what you worshiped, so long as you worshiped something.

Trocchi left Venice when Lyn, who was supporting them both, became too strung out to work. Besides, as his friends had already observed about him, he was "always waiting for the bus, whatever bus was coming." According to Lipton, he had already put himself "out of the pale" with the ferocity of his habit—although that conclusion probably said more about Lipton's ambivalence toward drugs than about Trocchi's "monkey." Lipton liked to shock the squares by talking as if he approved of pot and benzedrine, but he was always quick to add that his friends had "no desire for the heavy stuff." In any case, Trocchi had probably had enough of kicking every other day. He wanted to get back to New York. The problem was money, but he had hit upon a solution. He and Lyn would somehow get to Las Vegas, where he would write and shoot, and she would strip, shoot, and turn tricks. It was not much of a plan, but it was better than fencing stolen typewriters. Early in 1958, his novel still unfinished, the two of them left for Vegas. By midsummer Alex was back in New York. When Tony Scibella visited him there, Trocchi gave him his first fix.

Lipton had meant Trocchi to play an important role in his youth book. Under the name "Tom Draegen," Trocchi had appeared in the early chapters as a representative of the international hip scene who could even recall going pub-crawling with Dylan Thomas. Halfway into the first draft, Lipton had clearly lost his enthusiasm for Trocchi. He was going to have enough image problems as it was with his chapter on "The Euphoric Fix," and by that time Trocchi seems to have worn out his welcome with everybody. Besides, Lipton no longer felt the need to legitimize Venice West by linking it with any other scene. The more publicity he saw given to North Beach, the Village, and Kerouac's literary flying circus, the more inclined he felt to go for broke. If Lipton had his way, Venice West would become more than one beat enclave among many; as a Madison Avenue copywriter might have put it, it would be tomorrow's beat scene today.

To enlarge his case, Lipton enlarged his book. As originally written, it was a relatively modest study of the tiny community around him. By giving everyone at least two names, he had made that community seem far larger than it was, but at least he had let the people he interviewed speak for themselves. Now he began to write—or to dust off—long ideological chapters on the epochal significance of it all. The taped conversations stayed in the book, but through his preachy new chapters, he transformed Venice West into the proving ground for practically every serious idea he had ever entertained.

He knew he needed a hook, but for once the hook invented itself. He had realized that time was slipping away when *Evergreen Review* published a San Francisco issue in 1957, soon to be followed by a beat issue of one of his own outlets, *Chicago Review*. On the other hand, when his book appeared, it would have the benefit of two solid years of free publicity, much of it semi-hysterical. Since people were interested in "beatniks," that was what his young people would become. Even *Coastlines*, which tried not to ally itself with any literary faction, was devoting serious attention to the "issue" of beat-versus-square. What the readers of the highbrow journals debated today, *Time*, *Life*, *Look*, and *Newsweek* would take to the bank tomorrow.

So Lipton made the marketing decision of his life. None of the Venice bohemians called themselves "beat," but Lipton, who had had some success in getting them to see themselves as "disaffiliated," now concluded that the two words meant the same thing—which was very close to saying he had invented them both. As an old bohemian, he knew that such movements came and went; as an old advertising man, he knew that some opportunities came only once.

The "youth book" became a book about modern civilization itself, as challenged by the example of those who chose to live outside it. There was nothing new about Lipton's premise that the young were inherently wise and honest and their elders inherently blind and hypocritical. That idea had always gone over well among the young themselves, and just now it formed the main theme both of J. D. Salinger's *Catcher in the Rye* and of a whole new cycle of horror movies aimed at drive-in audiences (meteor falls to earth, teenagers see the monster crawl out of it but no one will listen, etc.). What *was* new was Lipton's contention not that enlightened youth would change the world, but that disaffected youth had changed it already—as though the mere existence of a counter-community such as Venice West were enough to prove the jig was up.

"I have chosen Venice, California," he wrote, "as the scene, as the laboratory as it were, because I live here and have seen it grow up around me.

Newer than the North Beach, San Francisco scene or the Greenwich Village scene, it has afforded me an opportunity to watch the formation of a community of disaffiliates from its inception. Seeing it take form I had a feeling of "this is where I came in," that I had seen it all happening before. But studying it closely, from the inside, and with a sympathy born of a kindred experience, I have come to the conclusion that this is not just another alienation. It is a deep-going change, a revolution under the ribs. These people are picking up where we—left off?—no, where we began. Began and lived it and wrote about it and waited for the world to catch up with us.

Who *were* they, if not just another crop of privileged dilettantes who would eventually join the system or find themselves blacklisted? They were none other than the very agents of change Lipton had written about in *Rainbow at Midnight*: the savages, the nonparticipants who sought to destroy civilization by defying its morality and rejecting its benefits. "When the barbarians appear on the frontiers of a civilization," he warned, "it is a sign of a crisis in that civilization. If the barbarians come, not with weapons of war but with the songs and ikons of peace, it is a sign that the crisis is one of a spiritual nature." The beats—or "beatniks," as Herb Caen, the columnist for the *San Francisco Chronicle*, had named them—were the new barbarians who, through their poverty, their "loveways" and their cult of the solitary artist, sought to give the world a new basis for living and thinking in the late twentieth century. They were destroyers, all right, but they were also spiritual builders: they were, as Lipton called them in a flash of inspiration, the *holy* barbarians.

He liked that term so much that he used it as the title of his book, which he turned over to his new publisher, Julian Messner, on 9 February 1959. Complete with a photographic essay by Austin Anton and a rather trashy cover showing two local artists getting into bed with a local coffeehouse waitress, *The Holy Barbarians* would become nothing less than the busy American's single-volume guide to the Beat Generation. That its appearance would also coincide with a massive onslaught of free publicity from the mass media proved to be fortunate, but incidental to Lipton's purpose. Besides, he had always thought that a good book was one that sold, and if *The Holy Barbarians* ended up getting the attention that should have been paid to *Brother, the Laugh Is Bitter*, it only meant that its author had been right—one way or another—all along. And *right* was what he meant to be. If the book made money, fine, but that was not why he had written it. *The Holy Barbarians* was, in fact, the statement Larry Lipton had been working up to all his life.

Like most who speak for movements, Lipton had a habit of exaggerating the size of his army. In his book and in his ever-more-frequent radio and TV appearances, he tended to give the impression that Venice West was full of beatniks, even though he was only talking about two or three dozen people, most of whom knew each other, none of whom called themselves beatniks, and all of whom could have crowded into the Venice West Café on a slow night.

The photo essay at the back of the book managed to say a great deal about the truth and falsity of the whole enterprise. First of all, there were the pictures of Henry Miller, Kenneth Rexroth, Robert Duncan, and Kenneth Patchen, none of whom lived anywhere near Southern California (Miller had lived in the Palisades for a while, but had gone back to Paris). There was even a shot of Lawrence Ferlinghetti at the City Lights Bookstore, standing in front of his famous window display of banned books—with only a tiny end note to advise the reader that the place was in San Francisco. "Jazz Canto in the Cosmo Alley coffee shop," one caption read, "is a listening experience of ritual, and religious intensity"—but Cosmo Alley was really in Hollywood, half a block away from Sunset and Vine. The Venice scenes were more like family snapshots, recording quiet, cluttered, unpretentious lives more or less centered around a brightly lit coffeehouse that looked like nothing so much as somebody's kitchen.

The photographs taken inside the Venice West Café, like the book itself, could be read on two distinctly different levels. Those who wished to see something dark and subversive in them could certainly find it. The café's patrons were rather shabby-looking, its furniture basic and primitive, its walls covered with slogans and abstract paintings, and its clientele, like its jazz combo, racially mixed. There were even beatific-looking little children present, a sign that things had already gone too

far. The most effective shot of all, taken from the outside looking in and soon to be reproduced on hundreds of postcards for
the tourists, showed dark human silhouettes huddling together
like conspirators behind the words Tony Scibella had painted
on the window: "Venice West Café Expresso."

Viewed as if in a family album, however, the same pictures
showed a handful of unpretentious-looking human beings en-
joying each other's company during a homey and very fragile
moment in the life of Venice West. It was still the only public
gathering place for the people who lived in the shacks and
storefronts of Venice, and it served them as a family restaurant,
a recital hall, a late-night hangout, and a kind of adult day-care
center. Tucked away on Dudley Avenue, in a red-brick storefront slot that had been an Orthodox *shul* before it was a bleach
factory, the tiny space now housed one of the least promising
commercial ventures in Los Angeles. The Venice West could not
have started off more awkwardly: Stuart Perkoff had opened its
doors three nights ahead of the date specified on the health permit, and two days later, on a Sunday morning, the health inspector himself had happened to come down to Venice for a bit
of sun. Naturally, he had written it up on the spot for every
violation he could think of, and from there things kept rolling
downhill. It was just what Lipton called it, "a real beat generation coffeehouse that tourists haven't discovered yet," but there
was still not enough of a Beat Generation in Venice to provide
a living for a man with a wife and three children.

The place had also evolved into just what Perkoff had secretly
wanted it to be, a "huge junk construction" with paintings, collages, and poems instead of wallpaper, and tiny, scattered oc-
tagonal tables instead of booths. Ball fixtures hung primly from
the ceiling, but the stove, fan, refrigerator, and other kitchen
fixtures stood as exposed behind the counter as they might have
been in anyone's apartment. It was a place to gather, to talk, to
think, to read aloud, and to feel a part of something secret that,
with any luck, would remain a secret a little longer. It was
everything, in fact, but a place to make money, and in trying to
make it work, Perkoff was pushing against himself. His friends
tried to help, but how often could anyone eat, how much coffee
could anyone drink, and how were *his* friends supposed to pay
for any of it?

By the time Lipton brought his photographer around, the

Venice West was already dying—but no one could have told that from the pictures. Paul Friedin, the white alto sax player (backed up by Rahmat Jamal on drums, Everett Evans on bass, and Abdul Karim on stand-up piano), looked moody enough to suit the narrative and photogenic enough to play in the Hollywood version, if there was going to be one, but everyone else, including the black jazzmen, looked thoroughly unremarkable. Only the occasional beard, along with Lipton's quirky, floppy golf cap, offered any hint of the strange social phenomenon that had begun to unsettle such serious observers as Norman Podhoretz and Paul Coates. With Wally Berman's creed, "Art is love is God," splashed across the far wall, the photographer captured a bearded, lanky Tony Scibella holding a friend's tiny, laughing daughter on his lap. Around him, people grinned at each other. Stuart Perkoff and Larry Lipton leaned rather knowingly on their chins at the chess table. Nettie Lipton and Suzan Perkoff, who got enough of their husbands' seriousness at home, shared a table up front near the musicians. The spell of live jazz had spread through the room, the friends and the night, and no matter how cool it was all supposed to be, the abiding quality of the evening was closeness and warmth. For one more off-season in Venice, at least, art was love *was* God.

The café failed, of course. On the third or fourth of January 1959, Perkoff sold it to John Kenevan for two hundred dollars. There was no short-term charade of a job to replace it, nor did he look for one. It was the time of year when the entire Ocean Front shut down—bad for business, good for poets. Perkoff felt released, as if his total failure had made a final point.

He began leaving home in the early mornings to walk the Promenade with Tony Scibella and Frank Rios, a young novice poet just in from New York City. A former stick-up man, a junkie at fourteen, Rios was the coolest and most accepting of the three. He wanted to become a poet the way Scibella had, by soaking up what Perkoff gave off. They "ran together" all spring, Perkoff and Scibella in their dungarees and t-shirts and Rios in his tight hipster's suit and shades. The looniness of the season seemed to bring out the voices in all three of them. Perkoff taught them to listen to their own minds, to speak the words that formed there without hesitation, and to take no thought for the morrow. Almost none of the poetry they shouted to each other along the Ocean Front survived the hour it was born—partly because they trusted the Muse to give more and partly because the day always began with a solid ritual belt of Tussar.

Tussar was not, strictly speaking, an illegal drug. It was, and still is, a registered trademark of the Armour Pharmaceutical Company, which includes ten milligrams of codeine phosphate, a natural opiate, in every five milliliters of its adult formula, Tussar-2. In 1959, however, Tussar was based on a "semi-synthetic" opiate then estimated to be twice as strong as codeine—dihydrocodeinone bitartrate—whose curious commercial history continues in a number of products under its revised generic name, hydrocodone bitartrate.

Why change the name of a profitable substance? The answer may be innocuous enough, but may also have to do with the drug's unpredictability, since after more than thirty years on the market, no one seems to know exactly how strong it is. The *Physicians Desk Reference* describes it as being "pharmacologically 2 to 8 times as potent as codeine," without explaining under what circumstances its strength may vary by a factor of four. The *PDR* also notes that in "equi-effective doses," hydrocodone has a greater "sedative effect" than codeine—in other words, it gets the user higher even though its pain-killing effect is the same. The recreational use of such a drug is therefore bound to include a surprise or two, and there is simply no way to predict how near or far the user may be from getting a habit.

In 1959, moreover, narcotic cough syrups could be bought by signing for them rather than presenting a prescription. The pharmacist's book was subject to inspection, but the inspectors tracked sales, not inventories. All it took to score Tussar illegally was a little imagination, and Perkoff, who had plenty of that, maintained a "drugstore connection" who was good for a standard six-ounce bottle of Tussar at the very reasonable price of $1.80. Split three ways, that gave each of them the equivalent of at least two grains of codeine, and possibly eight, for sixty cents a hit. Whether taken alone or combined with several other drugs, that was more than enough. Even a poet could afford it.

Although he thought it was "funny how sometimes it seems to affect me so much more than others," Perkoff was still not thinking in terms of having a habit. It was his wife who noticed the change in him, without, however, suspecting what it meant. There were no needle marks, after all, and Tussar was so cheap that she could hardly feel the money flowing to the pharmacy. But Perkoff had grown "cold"—not sexually cold, but "sealed off, encased in ice" (in Trocchi's word, *inviolable*). She endured his "hideous personality changes" until he was no longer "touchable" at all, and then she took stock.

Perkoff seldom laughed or even argued with her any more. When she demanded a human response from him, he simply closed in on himself. Scibella and Rios satisfied his need for friendship and respect. As for women, there were plenty of them around for sex, and that supreme woman, the Muse, the Lady, for love, inspiration, and rituals of forgiveness. The Perkoffs had always agreed to separate if they ever stopped communicating, and at the end of April 1959, only four months after the failure of the café, Perkoff agreed that he had better go. He moved into Milton Bratton's apartment on Hollister Street. When he dropped by three days later to visit his children, he declared to his wife with some pride that he had finally gone ahead and stuck a needle in his arm.

That same spring, on Park Avenue, Larry Lipton was awaiting the arrival of *The Holy Barbarians* in the bookstores. He was still taping poetry readings and planning a new long-playing record album of poetry and jazz—a project that called for many, many takes, since the poets never seemed to remember the need for performance discipline. Lipton felt he had discipline enough for all of them. As for getting Venice West the recognition it deserved from the non-book-buying public, he knew the local media were already in the habit of coming to Venice for lip-smacking tales of crime and degradation. And if Lipton knew how to do anything, he knew how to talk to the press.

A local civil liberties attorney, Al Mathews, was even talking about setting up an artists' colony in Venice—perhaps in an old hotel, where poets and artists could live and eat for free and show their work to the public in some local gallery. There might be some question as to who was an artist or a poet and who was merely an Ocean Front bum, but Mathews, who had plenty of money and faith, though no particular eye or ear, planned to leave that to the Shaman of the Tribe himself.

Only vaguely aware that their destiny was being plotted for them, Perkoff, Rios, and Scibella roamed the Ocean Front as the "Zen Zootists," the flying squad of the Muse, their pockets stuffed with pens, ink, glue, scissors, notebooks, journals, joints, pills, and six-ounce bottles of Tussar. It was a "magic time" of pure inspiration, pure comradeship, pure spontaneity. Wherever they were, art was:

> Wherever you'd go [Scibella later recalled], you'd sit down, take out all the shit & cut out pictures & write poems & then we'd be walking down the street & Frank'd say, "Listen to this!" He's got that one-man, "be-bop-bat hit the be-bop-bone," this whole thing, and the stuff I was writing 'cause I didn't know how to write, influenced by these two maniacs.

While Lipton was engineering one image, they were creating another: the myth of the time of purity, the time "before the media hit," and before the beatniks came to Venice. In only a few months, it was all going to seem like the time before the Flood. There was a let's-ditch-school quality to it, an off-with-the-boys, Huck Finn kind of freedom. Like all magic, it also entailed an eerie and uncomfortable sense of privilege. "I always thought that it wasn't mine," Scibella would later admit. "I was like the vessel. I was the tube—for the Lady, you know. It flowed through my hand and I couldn't explain it. Because we were *literally*—poetry."

It was a season for believers—but not for quite all of them. Charlie Foster, who believed in Moloch, the insatiable god of the materialists, took a good look around him, collected his thoughts and his worn-out clothes, and left.

CHAPTER FIVE

Lawrence Lipton relaxed grandly, "like a Pasha," in his Venice living room. His guest, Caroline Freud, had come all the way from London to interview him for *Encounter*, the influential little journal edited by Stephen Spender. Her article, "Portrait of the Beatnik," would share an issue with essays by Edmund Wilson, W. H. Auden, and C. P. Snow. While Lipton would later claim to have sensed that she was "out to do a hatchet job," he took the utmost care to see that she got her story.

"Beat, you will understand, my dear young woman, is far more than a religion," he explained. "Beat, my dear young lady, is a way of life." He closed his eyes and puffed thoughtfully on his cigar. "Here, down in Venice West," he went on, "we have a new kind of beat, the real beat, the Beat Generation of the future. I have called them by their true title, 'The Holy Barbarians,' and the report that I have just finished making about them will be called by that very name." He had already fielded inquiries about it from the Book-of-the-Month Club, the anthropology department at UCLA, and Metro-Goldwyn-Mayer—and that was just the beginning. "Already," he declared, "my poems are being scribbled on the lavatory walls of New York, already our Movement is spreading to Japan, Italy, France, Germany, and Great Britain. The Holy Barbarians, you will see, my dear young woman, will very soon be of world-wide interest!"

He waved his hand toward a stack of tapes on the floor. "I have probably made more tape-recordings of beatnik conversations than any living man," he said. "There you have one hundred hours' worth of authentic beat conversations, private philosophic conversations, you understand, taking place in simple pads, amongst young and simple people, but ones who are asking, more profoundly, more honestly than any previous generation, who they are, and where they are going."

None of this was particularly hard to follow; what puzzled the English journalist was why she distinctly heard him say, "*we*, the Holy Barbarians."

"I am the Mentor of the Holy Barbarians," he explained solemnly. "They call me *The Shaman of the Tribe*. I interpret their way of life to the public."

Interpret was too modest a word. When it went on sale in June 1959, *The Holy Barbarians* was an immediate success—though not necessarily for the right reasons. The author had intended it as a serious work of popular sociology; people bought it as a primer on a fad. With its case-study format, pulp-fiction style, and long, serious-sounding—but easily skipped—theoretical chapters, the book was easy to mistake for something either more or less substantial than it was. Its photo essay, verbatim conversations with "real beatniks," and handy glossary of hip jargon made it a kind of do-it-yourself guide to the Beat Generation, especially for those who had tried in vain to find any bearded, jive-talking hipsters in Kerouac's *On the Road*. If, in its corny, heavy-handed way, *The Holy Barbarians* also made a real contribution to knowledge, the screenwriters, sensation-mongers, and would-be bohemians who swallowed it whole for its worst qualities could hardly be blamed for that.

As if there were not enough selling points built into the book itself, Lipton promoted it with all of the energy he had once devoted in vain to *Brother, the Laugh Is Bitter*. Clearly, beatniks were a better draw than anti-Semitism ever was or would be. Kerouac's novels had already fired millions of young minds, appalled the literary establishment, and alerted the news and entertainment media to a popular mania of vast potential. The trouble was that most of the real beats were too unpredictable to show on television; Allen Ginsberg, for example, could hardly open his mouth in public without saying *something* objectionable, if not technically illegal. Larry Lipton, on the other hand, knew the rules. He had been saying daring things for years without making sponsors pull their ad schedules, and he did know how to seize a moment.

"The Holy Barbarians are the conscience of the world," he

told reporters from *The Saturday Review* while awaiting his cue backstage at the "Jack Paar Show." "The Beat pads are full of Holy Clowns who are out to shock the world out of its materialism. You've got to swing with that idea, or you're still in Squareville."

Reviewers tended to like *The Holy Barbarians*; it was the first book on the subject that many of them claimed to be able to understand. *Time*'s review, despite being full of gratuitous jokes about body odor ("There is a strong scent of social science in Venice West"), called it a "professionally written, well-documented report on this intriguing, if minor social phenomenon." Even the literary critic at *People's World*, an organ of the tired Old Left that Lipton affected to despise, allowed the book to persuade him that the beat phenomenon served the class struggle after all.

The literary establishment was far less kind to the beats themselves. Norman Podhoretz had already spoken for most of his colleagues in his essay, "The Know-Nothing Bohemians," in which he characterized Jack Kerouac's "primitivism" (his word, not Kerouac's) as a "cover for an anti-intellectualism so bitter that it makes the ordinary American's hatred of eggheads seem positively benign." Like most professional intellectuals, Podhoretz drew a distinction between older forms of bohemianism and this latest outrage. While the now-sainted rebels of the past had repudiated "the provinciality, philistinism, and moral hypocrisy of American life," the beats attacked intellectualism itself—and the danger only began there.

According to Podhoretz, the real problem was not what the beats had to say, but who was likely to be listening. The suburbs of America, he warned, were "filled to overflowing" with disenchanted people who were only too willing to see themselves as "conformists" and the beat way of life as "the heroic road." These uncritical souls might be easily swayed by false spontaneity, false ecstasy, and the claimed advantages of "feeling" over cold intellect. What could be worse than for the unlettered to be led by the unthinking?

Besides, he said, the beats' very obsession with *intense* feeling was a dead giveaway. If they lived their lives so intensely, why the emphasis on constant sensation, constant excitement, even constant "illumination"? Was it really so hard to feel anything in America?

Even Kenneth Rexroth had begun to repudiate the movement

the minute it had gotten away from him. He still liked and admired Ginsberg, but he attacked Kerouac and his novels at every opportunity. He even told Larry Lipton rather sniffily that in his opinion, the real Beat Generation had "stopped with us." The Beat Generation "may once have been human beings," he wrote. "Today they are simply comical bogies conjured up by the Luce publications."

Kenneth Patchen, who had helped found the poetry-and-jazz movement, agreed. The beats, he said, needed to be "housebroken." Curtis Zahn, the bearded, sandaled Malibu poet who had shocked Lipton in 1954 by lying on the floor during a poetry reading, rejected the whole notion of a great unwashed prophetic movement. "The Beat have already been ridiculed to death," he wrote in a letter to *Liberation*, "and, of course, deservedly so.

> By having been made into colorful clowns by the rich slick magazines, they have been rendered socially obnoxious and ridiculous ... the slicks have given the innocent reader the impression that a real Underground is being given an ear. It isn't. Only a harmless, crackpot, soapbox kind of character is being plugged.

Zahn was a regular contributor to *Coastlines*, the literary review Larry Lipton had first cultivated, then cast aside after Ginsberg's "naked reading." Mel Weisburd, the editor, still took that episode personally—he had struck back at the time with an editorial, "The Merchant of Venice"—and it had always seemed to him that the Beat Generation was a case of literature being used to sell a way of life. But he had continued to print Lipton's reports on the progress of the semi-mythical Venice West Poetry Center, along with Curtis Zahn's characterization of the Venice poets as "the Great Ungifted."

The Holy Barbarians changed all that. For one thing, it contained an insulting account of the Ginsberg reading which described the *Coastlines* group as a timid clique of post-McCarthy leftists. More important, it confirmed Weisburd's suspicion that Lipton no longer cared about literature at all. He responded by printing Gene Frumkin's essay, "The Great Promoter: A Hangnail Sketch of Lawrence Lipton," which was nothing less than a declaration of literary war.

Frumkin, who had also been present at the reading, denounced Lipton as a vicious huckster who would ultimately sell
out the beats, too:

> A most important weapon in the promoter's arsenal is distor-
> tion: making his own product seem splendid and the competi-
> tion's seem awful when really they are exactly the same. If a bit
> of the truth does ooze in between the lines, that's okay, provided
> it's on his side. But beware of treading on the corns of the pro-
> moter, for he will tread back on yours—with a steamroller.

Calling Lipton a "cold, dogmatic wind from the past," he predicted that he would use "all the tricks of the trade, including
the hatchet and TV appearances," to sell his product. At all
costs, the beats themselves must resist the temptation to let
him speak for them—although things might already have gone
too far. "There is no such thing," he concluded, "as beat vs.
square."

The Holy Barbarians had its enemies in Venice, too. Some of
Lipton's friends disliked the names he had given them; others
resented the money they assumed he was making. Ben Talbert,
the painter, even broke into his garage and stole many, and perhaps most, of the tapes on which the book had been based.
Others still admired the poet and literary arbiter, but resented
the inside-dopester who had cheapened and distorted their way
of life.

Stuart Perkoff, who thought Lipton should have called his
book *Holy Horseshit*, asked only that he not be drawn into any
of the author's publicity stunts. He had other things on his
mind, not the least of which were no income, no home, no
family, and a growing dependence on liquid codeine. Above all,
now he had left her, he was completely preoccupied with the
fact that his wife had let him go.

Suzan Perkoff had never had a serious emotional interest in
anyone but her husband, nor did she develop one now. She was
not, however, the first woman who ever tried to close an emotional chapter in her life by plunging into strictly physical relationships. It was not, as Stuart imagined, a game designed to
torment him; in fact, it had nothing to do with him at all. She
tried to explain that to him, but little of it got through. Fortu-
nately for her, the sexual etiquette of Venice West tended to

favor the woman in these matters. She might never be taken seriously as a poet or an artist, but her choice of lovers was her own concern.

Stuart, for his part, never embarrassed her in public. He did spend an entire morning composing a strange, rhyming curse ("and *I* don't rhyme!"), which he then delivered to all the men he assumed had been with Suzan. After slipping the last copy through her bedroom window at 3:00 AM, he began to pound on her front door in a "paroxysm of violence."

"Whatever it means," Suzan screamed, "It's past! Past! I haven't got it, whatever you want. That's the way it is. Who the fuck are you that you should have me?"

"Besides," she shouted after him, "you didn't get 'em all!"

The poet was not without options. There was always Susan Berman, a doctor's daughter who had more or less reconciled herself to being the second woman in his life, and there was also June, a married woman who was skeptical enough about his intentions to limit herself to sleeping with him once a week. Those were only the regulars. But Stuart remained so obsessed with the loss of Suzan and his family that he never quite caught the mad party spirit of Venice West in the "Magic Summer" of 1959.

Four months after he had sold it, the Venice West Café was suddenly booming. Its new owner, John Kenevan, often had to turn away customers for lack of seating space. It was not the only hip coffeehouse in Southern California—Long Beach and Hollywood were full of them, and the Lighthouse, down in Hermosa Beach, had Shelley Manne's combo as a house band—but it was the one depicted in "the book."

"One morning," Stuart Perkoff would later write, "we who lived in Venice woke up and walked out onto the Promenade and we saw hundreds of people who looked just like us." Some had come for the weekend, others for good. A few, like Art Richer, whose wife and family were also pictured in "the book," had brought artistic reputations with them. Others had decided to acquire reps by being in the right place at the right time. Venice, said the publicity machine, was where the future of the Beat Generation was being made. The hip migration was only the beginning.

On Sunday mornings Perkoff and Scibella still liked to take their Tussar ration up to the roof of the Grand Hotel, a fleabag establishment on Market Street where no one ever bothered them. At six or seven o'clock it was still quiet enough to hear the waves slapping on the beach, and with their feet propped up on the railing under a clear sky—and with the help of a joint or two—they could spend the whole day writing or drawing. It was in just that beatific state that they heard the first, alien noises of the great invasion. "What the hell's going on?" Scibella shouted, but both of them knew.

They looked down to see the early morning streets choked with cars—cars in the alleys, cars creeping down the narrow streets, cars hopelessly in orbit around the traffic circle at Windward and Main, cars full of kids, cars with license plates from places like Indiana, Iowa, and Ohio. It reminded Scibella of "being in Mexico when the American tourists came in":

> There was cars all down Market Street, all in the Speedway. And these people, like the typical—shorts, the Hawaiian shirt, and the camera . . .
> All the people were coming out for the summer to see the beatniks. You'd be sitting on the lawn, you know, smoking a cigarette, cooling it, and here'd come a family in shorts, camera & a straw hat to try & take yr picture: "Look, there's one!"

Along with the sightseers came the reporters and the television cameras. Some of them already knew their way around; they had come to Venice often for stories about drugs, crime, and illicit sex. Now they had orders to interview amusing people who *believed* in drugs, rebellion, and "free love." The tabloid types found themselves competing with front-page, prime-time journalists representing millions of readers and seven-figure advertising budgets. For all of them, and for most of the tourists as well, Venice West had become a half-mile-wide, open-air zoo—a place to observe the ridiculous, imagine the unspeakable, and never even have to leave the car for long.

On the other hand, the invaders, like *turistas* everywhere, were good for the economy. Some paid for autographs; others offered "two dollars to read a poem to my girl." The few who tried to buy their way into the scene with drugs were considered the fairest game of all.

"Hey, want to get high?"

"Sure, man. Thanks!"

"Know where any parties are, man?"

"You mean with free sex?"

"Yeah, man."

"Got a car?"

"Sure."

"Hey, Colorado plates, wow, that's great. Well, drive us up this way . . . park here . . . thanks, man."

Anyone whose picture had been printed in the photo section of *The Holy Barbarians* became a tourist attraction in spite of himself. That could be annoying, but it had its good points; the Tussar crowd, for example, found that many of the tourists were hip enough to provide free heroin when the pharmacist went on vacation.

The timing could not have been better or worse, depending on one's point of view, for the long-promised Gas House, a project that promised to put a real public face on Venice West. A converted bingo parlor at the corner of Market Street and Ocean Front Walk, the Gas House, with its Kinney-era arches and columns and its never-ending paint job, would serve as an art gallery, a members-only coffeehouse, a glorified flophouse for artists and poets, and an all-purpose hip community center, with the public invited in on specified evenings for poetry readings, jazz, deep conversation, and dazzling, pre-"psychedelic" light shows. Al Mathews, one of the earlier hip lawyers in Los Angeles, had put up the money; Lipton, as director of "entertainment," would supply the rhetoric and the style.

It would be an exercise in art and community, but it would also be much more. The painters and poets would be on display right along with their works, and that made public relations too important to leave to chance. Accordingly, the Gas House acquired not only an official spokesman, but an official greeter: Harry Hilmuth Pastor, better known as Eric Nord. Nord, already famous in North Beach as the owner of the Co-Existence Bagel Shop (which billed itself as the "Gateway to Beatland"), stood six feet seven inches, weighed three hundred pounds, wore sandals, tent-like sport shirts, and a modest red beard with no mustache. He had inevitably acquired the nickname "Big Daddy," after the Burl Ives character in *Cat on a Hot Tin Roof* (and with the help of the San Francisco gossip columnists). Although, at this point, he seems to have been strictly an added attraction, he cheerfully allowed himself to be described as its "co-owner" and "founder." With his glad-handing manner and surprisingly gentle voice, he could hardly have made a better front man. But did an artists' colony really need a front man?

From a practical standpoint, it probably did. With hordes of tourists, reporters, and photographers in Venice—and scores, if not hundreds, of would-be beatniks sleeping on the beach—*someone* had to appear to be in charge. Why not someone big enough to deal with troublemakers *and* glib enough to handle the tricky questions? For over a year in San Francisco, Nord had gotten away with operating the legendary dollar-a-head, bring-your-own-bottle "Party Pad," a warehouse packed with couches which was just what its name implied. He had even lived down the scandal when a distraught poet had thrown himself off the Party Pad's roof—and when the same poet's girlfriend had come out from Chicago to investigate, only to be strangled by a drunken, drug-addicted black seaman (who swore he had never heard of the Beat Generation). If nothing else, Eric Nord was "image insurance"—and the Gas House was going to need it.

It was important to remember, as Mathews and Lipton certainly did, that the Gas House would not be so much an art gallery as an art *showroom* with the artists attached. To survive as a shelter for creativity, it would have to be operated, and probably fought for, as an act.

Some of the artists refused to be made into an arcade attraction. Stuart Perkoff had told Lipton, "I don't care about your book; that's fine. But don't *use* me." Nevertheless, he came home late one night to find a copy of *The Holy Barbarians* propped open to his picture in one of the Gas House windows. He smashed the window with his bike lock, stole the book, and never apologized to anyone.

It soon became apparent that while Eric Nord was good at meeting the public, he was neither energetic nor interested enough to manage its day-by-day operations. For that, Al Mathews shrewdly chose John Thomas, a bulky new arrival who looked like a cut-down version of Paul Bunyan—huge bones, huge rib cage, menacing brow, and beard. Had he come to Venice a year earlier, Thomas would certainly have found his way into *The Holy Barbarians*. A computer programmer from Baltimore who had quit his job rather than shave off his beard, he was also a family man who had abandoned wife, home, kids, and future to hitchhike three thousand miles into the blazing

sunset. Thomas had still been working for UNIVAC when he
read "the book"—and it was fair to say he had come to Venice
in spite of it. "It was a silly book," he later wrote,

> All about the beat scene in Venice, all about how glorious,
> how secret and beautiful and important and glorious, etc. It was
> one of those books. I riffled the pages. I wasn't interested. At
> the back of the book there was a selection of photographs—of
> Kinney's pseudo-Italian buildings, of some people being cool in
> a coffeehouse, of (for no discernable reason) some eminent poets
> who lived elsewhere. . . .
>
> Later that year I set out for San Francisco but I didn't get there.
> I got as far as Venice and stayed. I met most of the people in the
> book. I went to the coffeehouse of the cool-being people. I came
> to know the man who had written the silly book and he was just
> what I expected him to be.

Thomas, like Jack Kerouac and James Jones, had been "poi-
soned by Thomas Wolfe at an early age," and he had frankly
run away from Baltimore to be rid of his responsibilities. Since
leaving the Air Force in 1954, he had worked at the usual young
novelist's jobs—taxi driver, recreation department worker, mental ward orderly at the Phipps Clinic of The Johns Hopkins University Medical School. By a fluke, he had gotten into computer
programming in the UNIVAC division of Remington Rand,
from which, in turn, he had been rented out to Bethlehem Steel
to write its automation procedures. That had meant a better
standard of living for his wife and two children, but it had also
made it impossible to write, and the frustration—dozens of novels started, none finished—put a fatal strain on his marriage.

He resolved that dilemma by getting run over by a car. When
he returned to work in April 1959, he had grown a beard, and
rather than shave it off, he had let himself be fired. Then as now,
getting fired "for cause" meant no unemployment compensation. His wife's new love interest, a lawyer, had hired him to
work in his paint factory, but after three weeks of mixing pow-
dered paint and cleaning out vats with thinner—and upon
receiving some legal papers he barely understood—he had decided to quit. While his wife was visiting friends in Pittsburgh,
he sold his library for twenty dollars' traveling money, hiked up
to North Avenue, then part of US Route 40, and stuck out his
thumb.

He meant to go to San Francisco, but in Pennsylvania he was offered the ride every hitchhiker dreams of: the one that takes him all the way across the country, even though it ends up in the wrong place. Johnny Johnson, a well-connected show business figure who made his actual living betting on golf, stopped his Cadillac just outside of Pittsburgh and offered to take John to Beverly Hills. Johnson paid for everything—meals, lodging, gasoline—with one-dollar bills from the trunk of his car. He insisted on sending Thomas out of sight before opening the trunk, but except for that charade, he never demanded anything but conversation.

At the end of the ride, Thomas opted for a short hop to Venice rather than another long and uncertain ride to San Francisco. The transcontinental getaway had been adventure enough for him. It was immediately obvious that if he stayed in Venice, he could get away with doing absolutely nothing but what he wanted to do. Quite by accident, he even acquired a new artistic persona. He had always described himself as a writer, but when his new friend, the poet Maurice Lacy, asked him, "What do you *write*?" he answered without thinking, "I'm a poet." Since he knew the word would get around, especially among those few people whose respect he really wanted to have, Thomas had no choice but to write some poetry.

Stuart Perkoff taught him a great deal by example. It was obvious that Perkoff wrote for the love of writing—which, in turn, forced Thomas to confront the fact that he had never given the *writing* part of being a writer much thought. He had always wanted to be a man who *had written* things, whose thick, acclaimed novels were already on the shelf. Now he was forced to admit that "the novel-writing ambition was just sheer, vulgar pretense, wanting to be a great man." On the other hand, once he tried his hand at it, he discovered that he really was a poet, albeit a lonely one in his belief that poetry was words, not sounds, and that it came from various sources within the poet, not from some untouchable woman hovering overhead.

Unlike practically everyone in Venice West, especially the newcomers, John Thomas had done enough reading to know that most of the art being produced around him was neither particularly good nor particularly innovative, except in the sense of blissfully reinventing the wheel. Was an idea original if the artist was completely unaware that Tristan Tzara had thought of it fifty years before? John had to watch his mouth when it came to that sort of thing; he knew that in this crowd, his standards were unfairly high. While the scene might be nothing to compare with Montmartre at the turn of the century, it certainly gave him what *he* wanted, which was a total immunity from what the unimaginative liked to call real life. He did have to endure one social handicap, however: he never learned to like marijuana.

The American entertainment industry, meanwhile, seemed to have settled on beatniks as its latest substitute for creativity. Bearded, "poetry-spouting" characters appeared on television, in the movies, and even in such long-running comic strips as "Popeye" and Ernie Bushmiller's "Nancy." Everyone knew what a beatnik looked like; the beard, the sunglasses, the sandals, and the cigarette on the lower lip were instantly recognizable symbols. They were even easy to draw. To these was added a new prop, the beret, which was apparently unique to beatniks from Central Casting. One of the most unorthodox comic strips, Gus Arriola's "Gordo," also featured the most unusual beatnik, a six-legged spider named Bug Rogers, while the fall television season's funniest show, "The Many Loves of Dobie Gillis," introduced the funniest media beatnik of them all, Maynard G. Krebs.

Beatniks were such box-office insurance that the producers of *The Hypnotic Eye*, a low-budget horror movie aimed at drive-in theaters, invited Larry Lipton and Eric Nord to play in the film's obligatory coffeehouse scene. After being driven by studio limousine to the set in Culver City, Lipton read "Confessions of a Movie Addict," a poem he had written for the occasion, while "Big Daddy" beat out time on Tony Scibella's conga drum. "How can we lose," the director explained, "with blood, sweat, and beards?"

One long-running radio soap opera, "The Romance of Helen Trent," even added a regular beatnik character—"bearded, sandal-shod Pete Ridgeway," the "black sheep of the Ridgeway family." Pete hung out in "West Venice" and spent most of his time "in a strange mood," trying to persuade Helen to run away with him. It was difficult to see why Helen indulged this long-winded, cynical young man who was *obviously* going to attack her before the summer was over, but whenever he announced himself with such lines as, "Mind if I sit on the floor? I'm used to it," he was usually good for at least ten more minutes of air time.

HELEN: Look, Pete, I told you I have guests coming, and I have to pick things up a little. . . . Gil Whitney is bringing his sister out.

PETE: Would I approve of her?

HELEN: It really doesn't matter.

PETE: It matters what I think of all your friends, Helen. Don't you know I'm the last barrier between you and total surrender?

HELEN: Surrender? What are you talking about?

PETE: Surrender to mediocrity—to security—middle-class, gray-flannel security—in other words, marriage to Gil Whitney. Let me show you *my* world, where nothing matters but being yourself. It's not too late, Helen; *be* somebody, not for what the world thinks but for your own sake.

HELEN: Pete, let go of me! Have you lost your mind?

PETE: [Ominously] Yeah . . . I think so. I'm *far out*, Helen. *Come* with me!

HELEN: Pete—get out of here!

Living alone in her secluded beach house, Helen was obviously out of touch. On the other hand, Gil Whitney's sister Claire, a naive but well-intentioned young modern, had read all about "West Venice."

CLAIRE: [Helen] knows a real beatnik? Oh, how exciting! Gil, everybody back East is fascinated by that place.

GIL: They're a bunch of bums! Spongers! They don't work, they don't—

CLAIRE: But they do! They get a "gig"—

GIL: A—"gig?"

CLAIRE: I read about it. It means just—*any* job to support themselves until they can afford to stop working for a while. It has its points!

GIL: *Points?* It's anarchy! It's—against everything sound, stable—against everything—

CLAIRE: Against "everything this country stands for."

GIL: Are you making fun of me?

CLAIRE: No. But I *must* ask Helen.

The publicity and the assorted foolishness brought mobs of the curious to the gallery in the Gas House, which was fine with its entertainment director, Larry Lipton. He and Mathews were making plans to open its light shows and jazz-and-poetry performances to the general public. The property owners of Venice, who had begun to realize, belatedly, that it *was* possible for rental values to fall even lower, would have none of it. When it was only a matter of a few oddballs living in substandard buildings down near beach, no one had been particularly alarmed; now that they were dealing with beatniks, and hundreds of them at that, it was quite a different story. Accordingly, a local realtor, Alfred S. (Stan) Roberts, organized a protest group, the Venice Civic Union, with the declared intention of shutting down the Gas House and forcing *these people* out of town. The organization found a natural ally in the Los Angeles Police Department. It should not have come as a surprise to anyone that the reaction followed the publicity straight to the Gas House.

For the sake of community relations, beat artists, who had already covered the sidewalks in front of the Gas House with abstract designs, went to work painting the neighborhood's garbage cans. Roberts and the "realestateniks" were not impressed; all the campaign proved to them was that the beats were even stranger than anyone had imagined. When the Gas House tried to hold an open house, two thousand people turned up—but the police were on hand to prevent anyone from going inside. Poetry readings, the officers explained, were "entertainment," which could not be presented without an entertainment license issued by the police commission. It would be all right, they said, for the Gas House regulars to hold a private meeting, but the minute anyone stood up to read a poem, that would be the end of it.

Larry Lipton's foresight saved the evening. Suspecting that he might be barred from reading his poem, "A Funkie Blues for All Squares, Creeps and Cornballs," he had brought along a tape-recorded version, and somehow he persuaded the police to let him play it. It was not one of his best; in fact, it was one of his worst—an ugly, self-righteous little poem that accurately expressed all that was unlovely in Lawrence Lipton. On the other hand, this was a confrontation with the power of the state, not a faculty tea:

Their arms are knives, their fingers all nails.
When they try to make love they hurt each other.
When their lips close, smiling, it is
Like the maw of some poisonous flower closing.
They torture themselves with shame and pride,
With time clocks and unattainable ambitions.
They get so they believe their own hired liars.
They bug themselves with their own advertising slogans.
They drag themselves over miles of broken glass
And stone themselves with false confessions.
They seem to be atoning everlastingly
For some nameless long-forgotten crime.
If I knew what it was they had done
I would talk to God about it.
I can't promise I could get them off
But I'd feel duty bound to use my influence.
As it is, all I can do is feel sorry for them,
And for this they will never forgive me.

Since the LAPD was serious about keeping the Gas House closed to the public, Al Mathews decided to fight. Unfortunately, the only body empowered to issue an entertainment license was the Board of Police Commissioners, and in that light, it was probably less than politic to retain as his attorney the well-known civil libertarian, Abraham Lincoln Wirin. Wirin, who had defended Caryl Chessman and Barbara Graham, was nothing if not resourceful, and the case drew wide coverage in the local and national news media.

Lipton did his part by generating as much publicity as humanly possible. He even persuaded Sydney Omarr, of CBS Radio, to stage a nationwide broadcast, "The Beatniks," which consisted largely of the shaman himself interviewing his friends. An old radio hand, even if his style was becoming a bit dated, Lipton took the microphone right into the Gas House:

LIPTON: We're gathered around a table at the Gas House, on
            the Ocean Front in Venice West. . . . Among us here
            . . . is Eric Nord, who is by way of being the leader
            of this group, and he should tell us a little bit about
            the hassle we've been having here with the heat.
            What is the trouble here, Eric?
NORD: Really, the trouble, Larry, is that it should not be any

> trouble at all. But there are a few people in this
> neighborhood that we have not had the pleasure to
> have in our group, and who've been wondering
> what's been going on, who've been worried about
> us. And this worry has led them to call the police to
> investigate us.

Included in the broadcast was a "typical" Gas House discussion of sex, chaired by Lipton and ending with his admonition, "OK, now, let's not talk about it. Let's *do* it!" Since "free love in the Gas House" was one of the Venice Civic Union's favorite nightmares, the wisdom of that emphasis was questionable.

The Gas House actually received some "responsible" support of its own from a counter-protest group, Bob Chatterton's Venice Citizens and Property Owners Committee for Cultural Advancement; among the signatures on its petition was that of an old resident, Stan Laurel. When the hearings began on 12 August 1959, there was no getting around the fact that the police held all the cards, and that to win it would be necessary tò persuade the bureaucrats who had closed the Gas House to overrule themselves. The only way to do that was to convince the public that it was silly to view the Gas House as a menace to the Republic. Police testimony emphasized noise, weird goings-on, and lowered property values, and it was soon clear that Larry Lipton was not the only one who knew how to exploit the media.

"They're a dirty bunch of people," Millie Rieber, a Venice hotel manager, told *Newsweek*. "They drink and every night is debauchery. They make free love practically in the streets, play bongo drums, and none of us can get any sleep at all after 2 a.m." To counter the charge that art was being suppressed, the Venice Civic Union and its supporters insisted they were objecting to a form of behavior, not to artistic expression as such. Stan Roberts told CBS Radio: "I believe that for every six artists the Gas House attracts, it attracts sixty or seventy bums—what I call "hoodniks"—that roam the streets from 11:30 till four and five in the morning . . . breaking in vacant buildings and just raising commotion in general all over the area."

Mrs. Robert Swan, who lived directly across the street from the Gas House at 9 Market Street, told the police commissioners that the sound of beatniks pounding away on their bongo drums in the Gas House cellar carried through the storm drains to the streets outside. She also produced a journal she had been keeping on the "goings-on" next door, which included "kissing and messing around" and other "immoral actions" in addition to all the noise.

The Venice Civic Union even produced an undercover witness, Michael S. Kelly, who testified that he had regularly visited the Gas House, "posing as a beatnik," at the behest of Stan Roberts. More than five hundred spectators were on hand to hear his testimony. No, he had never seen any entertainment, but he had seen beatniks passing a jug of wine around, and he was sure some of the wine had been drunk by juveniles. How did he know it was wine? Well, he had tried some. At least once, he had seen artists' models posing in the nude.

"How long did you stay on this occasion?" Officer Mulhern asked him.

"About one-and-a-half months," Kelly replied, to the vast delight of the audience. After a moment's thought, he realized the questioning officer had wanted to know how long he was there on that particular day, not the total length of time he had spied for the Venice Civic Union. No, he explained, he had only watched the models for fifteen minutes.

Larry Lipton, as "director of entertainment" for the Gas House, seemed torn between wanting to win and wanting to be right. Shortly after one of the police commissioners told him he had a responsibility to keep "undesirables" out of the Gas House, Lipton returned with an extraordinary contraption which he solemnly described as an "electronic doorman." Built to his specifications by the Gas House light crew and decorated by Bill Riola, it was a primitive but functioning robot with a little pop-eyed face, a built-in tape recorder, and an incredible array of sirens, whistles, bells, and flashing red lights. "Duhab"—short for "Detector of Undesirable Habitués"—was described as being able to sense the approach of "teenage werewolves, dope addicts, sex fiends, subversives, alcoholics, and homosexuals (male and female)," and members of the Venice Civic Union—in which event, all of its alarms were set to go off at once. Duhab made good theater, but bad hearing strategy; it helped make Lipton himself the issue, and gave the hearing examiner,

Officer Thomas Mulhern, the opportunity to focus on the "moral character" of those who would be directing "the proposed entertainment."

Expressing doubt that Lipton "knew the meaning of the word 'moral,' " Officer Mulhern went so far as to accuse him of wanting to "pit race against race"—even though the racial issue had been injected, and rather belatedly at that, by a witness for the Venice Civic Union, Mabel Hardy (who claimed that "half of the men there are colored and white beats are walking around with them arm in arm"). Predictably, Lipton lost his temper, and he, Mathews, and the rest of the Gas House party walked out. Al Wirin moved to have Mulhern disqualified, but there was no way to force the issue. The outcome was a foregone conclusion. Mulhern's final report, submitted at the end of December 1959, stressed the morality issue, adding, for good measure, that "issuance of an entertainment license would increase the problems of the police department."

The Gas House art gallery was allowed to stay open, so long as no one performed there and only a single person ever slept there at night. For once, Mathews had beaten the city to the punch. While his clerk, the wily but disbarred lawyer Kimball Fletcher, became the building's only legal resident, Mathews was already implementing phase two of his plan: the establishment of a subsidized colony of creative disaffiliates on the upper story of one of the better-known Venice landmarks, the old Grand Hotel. In one sense, it would be a poor artist or poet's dream, a kind of beat monastery; in another, it would be like living in a glass box on top of a billboard on Sunset Boulevard. It was ironic that most of the original beats had come to Venice seeking absolute obscurity, but there was nothing to be done about that.

CHAPTER SIX

"Venice getting dimmer in distance," Stuart Perkoff wrote hopefully in his journal as the bus neared San Francisco. "Let Lipton have his war."

He had come north to get away, to duck the big issues, to simply be a poet in a place where that was considered an admirable, but not an especially remarkable, thing to be. There were plenty of gawkers in North Beach—Gray Line Tours brought busloads of them through every day—but there were also plenty of creative people, some of whom had been writing good poetry for a long, long time. Still essentially an old Italian residential neighborhood, the Beach considered itself the creative heart of the city in which Lawrence Ferlinghetti had won the right to publish *Howl and Other Poems* in open court. The beat scene was concentrated on Grant Street, a couple of blocks from the City Lights Bookstore. Poetry readings were held regularly at the Bread and Wine Mission, the Coffee Gallery, and the Cellar, which also maintained its own house band to back up the poets. At the center of it all was the Coexistence Bagel Shop, which Eric Nord, reportedly on the advice of his lawyers, had forsaken for Los Angeles and a new notoriety as the manager and founder of the Gas House.

"I hope I can read here tomorrow nite, to poets, like," Perkoff wrote in his journal. "A measure of my weight, heavy or not."

The Beach was also full of drugs—and police. As early as August 1958, Grant Street had been assigned two foot patrolmen, one precinct sergeant, one two-man prowl car, a perpetually cruising paddywagon, and, representing Sixth U.S. Army, two MPs in a jeep. It had also been designated a problem area by the State of California's Alcoholic Beverage Control Department, which meant that no more liquor licenses would be issued there. It was essentially an amphetamine scene—San Francisco's hypes tended to shoot speed rather than heroin—but there was more than enough of everything, most of it of better quality than Perkoff had ever experienced. To celebrate after his first reading, he smoked Tangiers hash with Wally Berman and Bruce Boyd and shot up a quarter-grain of high-grade morphine. "Gorgeous high," he wrote, meaning both the drug and the reading. "Think will move." New friends also introduced him to such advanced practices as mainlining coke and heroin together. Each high seemed more profound than the one before it, and most of the highs came free.

"Sitting waiting for Bruce to show," he wrote in the artsy dimness of a North Beach coffeehouse.

> Paintings all on walls beatniks in chairs dark beer in steins pretty high pot tussar wine beer (dark black goody) jazz session abt to begin. . . . God I got to get to work again. Let that manna flow thru the hands . . . Everything does seem clearer here, but the excitement grows & I have to be careful abt that.

It had taken him no time at all to fall into a self-defeating routine that never seemed to involve writing anything. He also managed to bungle a long-standing and extemely complicated affair involving two women who had followed him to San Francisco, each knowing that the other would be there. At least, there was still Susan Berman, as "warm & sweet & loving" as ever. Anything he did was apparently all right with her. But the grand getaway was clearly a failure. No poems came to him, and nothing in his life had been resolved but the question of whether or not the cells of his body needed junk. Need it they did. He spent his last night in the city vomiting, screaming, writhing in convulsions on the floor, and fighting off absolute terror by smashing himself against the wall. He refused to recognize it as withdrawal, but it was the worst night of his life. He shivered miserably all the way back to Los Angeles, propped up in his seat and scribbling in an enormous, road-distorted hand about fear, confusion, poetry, and his hopes of finding a way to live purely and simply *somewhere*.

Back in Venice, the media games had been taken over by the

really serious players. Thanks to an incident that should have remained innocuous, *Life* had come to town. Three high school students from Hutchinson, Kansas—Kathryn Vannaman, Anne Gardner, and Luetta Peters—had written to Larry Lipton, inviting him to speak before their class, and, of course, to bring his beat friends with him. The town was "Squaresville itself," they explained, and as its future citizens, they wanted "to be cooled in." When Lipton actually accepted, their parents made them take back the invitation—but not before the facts of the story, such as they were, had somehow found their way to the Time-Life Building in New York City.

Suddenly photographers with Leicas and Nikons were swarming over both places—Hutchinson, Kansas (population, 38,000) and Venice (population, 40,000). The result was a splashy feature article, "Squareville U.S.A. vs. Beatville U.S.A.," which appeared in *Life* on 21 September 1959, positioned just after the letters to the editor and right among the expensive far-forward ads. The story even rated a cover blurb, "Kansas Squares vs. Coast Beats," which appeared just above the group portrait of the Mercury Astronauts' wives.

"On the following pages," editors promised without a trace of irony, "*Life* matches pictures taken in Hutchinson with those taken in Venice, and brings the homey pleasures of Squareville face-to-face with the far-out freedom of Beatville." They meant this literally: the layout devoted the top half of each page to Hutchinson and the bottom half to Venice, with stodgy block type used for the former and jagged, "far-out" lettering employed below. The story proved to be no story at all. Like the jig that Hitler never really danced in Paris, it was a deliberate manipulation of images, a nonevent created in the lab, the boardroom, and the production department.

"The clash between the squares and beats," the copywriters insisted, "is taking place in many small ways all over the U.S." Since no such clash had actually been captured on Tri-X film (the photojournalist's friend) in either of *these* places, the paste-up boys had been obliged to stage one by juxtaposing down-home shots of daily life in Hutchinson with scenes of silliness and squalor in Venice. On the upper half of one two-page spread, for example, the Hastons (Ruby, Jim, their teenaged daughters Cindy and Patty, and their little dog), an apparently happy, middle-class Kansas family, were shown watching television together and flipping through the family album (a source

of "unfailing fun"), while directly below them, Art Richer and
his wife sat discussing "art philosophy" in their stark, mattress-
strewn "cool pad" in Venice. Richer was bearded and barefoot,
his wife young and pretty, and both of them showed a lot of
skin. The Hastons looked like practically any white, middle-
class family on either side of the television screen. Ruby and Jim
Haston had gone steady for ten years and actually lived abroad
(courtesy of International Harvester, a full-page, four-color advertiser on page 27), only to settle down in "the nicest small
town in the whole world."

In Hutchinson, the text went on, "when people are looking
for something to do, they may drift down to Sylvan Park."

> There, on warm evenings, the Hutchinson Municipal Band
> plays. . . . Sometime or other, everybody in town goes out to visit
> the half-mile-long Co-op grain elevator, one of the biggest in the
> world. There are regular tours of the salt mine and of the state
> reformatory. . . . For the youngsters there is a municipal pool,
> bowling, roller skating, movies, and a Friday night record dance
> at Convention Hall. The rest of the week they gather at the
> A & W root beer bar.

Hot times in Hutchinson apparently consisted of whittling
with the good old boys in the park and watching the girls of
the American Legion drum and bugle corps work out in full
regalia—boots, shakos, dummy Springfields, and all. The only
thing left to say was that for *real* excitement, folks gathered to
watch the highway department paint lines in the street. By contrast, a shot taken outside the Gas House showed "Mad Mike"
Magdalani decorating garbage cans while "Tex Kleen," nautical
cap on head, sat nearby in his hand-painted bathtub reading
poetry.

A kind of resolution was implied in the article's closing pages,
where Hutchinson High students—mostly girls, mostly pretty,
and many wearing black mesh stockings—were shown performing "Shady Sadie and Her Swinging Seven," a hip parody
of *Snow White* ("Draw closer, cats, I'll give this Sophie a buzz
. . . I'm the coolest ever was"). The only thing missing from the
piece was an interview with even one of the three girls who had
innocently launched the whole exercise by writing to Larry Lipton. According to *Life*, they had been "whisked away to seclu-
sion by their distressed parents"—in other words, their mothers

and fathers had refused to let them be exploited. As one of them had told a reporter over the phone, "All we did was send a letter. We know beatniks aren't good, but we thought they just dressed sloppy and talked funny. Now we know that they get married without licenses and things like that."

Beatniks, the article seemed to be saying, were only a funny, harmless manifestation of the childish in all of us—an expression of that longing for complete freedom that kept all of us sane, but which the sane ones among us recognized for the fantasy it was. As one Hutchinson High student told *Life*, "I'd like to be one for a week. I'd like to do what I want to do and say what I want to say and have no worries, and know it wouldn't affect me in the future."

Period, end of story, back to reality, buy the deodorants and the life insurance, etc. On the other hand, *Life* was prepared to let its six-and-a-half million readers have it either way—or both. In spite of its deceptively trivializing tone, "Squaresville vs. Beatsville" was not a piece of fluff. It was a major feature in the most important weekly picture magazine in America— expensively produced, prominently positioned, and surrounded by advertisements costing between fifteen and twenty thousand dollars per page, not counting what the advertisers may have paid to have their ads placed within or near it. (It would be interesting to know how many had insisted on *not* having their ads placed near it.) Beatniks were even considered a strong enough draw to share the cover with one of Henry Luce's favorite causes, Project Mercury—after the publisher had paid half a million dollars for the exclusive right to publish the astronauts' life stories.

Three issues later, the editors also devoted an unbelievable twenty column inches to the letters generated by "Squaresville vs. Beatsville." Most of those letters—or at least most of the ones selected for publication—were surprisingly positive. Almost everyone seemed to find *something* to approve of in the beats, or to ridicule in the people of Hutchinson, Kansas. "If the values of a Kansas town are so uncannily excellent," asked one reader, "why have they not satisfied everyone? Why have the beatniks, with all their admitted mediocrities, sprung into existence?"

"Obviously," one reader wrote, "the one has produced the other. The distortions of beatnik society are almost a direct mirror image of the intellectual, artistic, and spiritual poverty of

American life." There it was—"the spiritual poverty of American life." It was the classic American intellectual's complaint
about the country—but what was it doing in one of the great
"wish books" of the postwar consumer culture? Had the editors
judged the time right to start bestowing a new status on *some*
of their readers—those who had presumably achieved enough
standing in the affluent society to start feeling superior to it?

Even those who found the story slanted objected only to the
angle of the slant. None seemed to mind the publicity it had
given to bohemianism, although one twenty-two-year Venice
resident did insist that life would return to normal once "these
screwy beatniks" had gone. A Hutchinson woman maintained
that there was *plenty* to do in her community, namely: "Several
lakes within a 50-mile radius where we can boat, water-ski or
swim, an impressive sports arena which is used for national
basketball tournaments, concerts, and rodeos, an excellent city
recreation program where you may learn anything from ceramic
art to ballet."

What? Ceramics and ballet in Kansas? But real life in either
place was beside the point. In the interests of social theater, both
communities had been used with equal cynicism. Most readers
obligingly took sides, although some took the opportunity to
attack both ways of life. No one at all—no one, that is, whose
letter made it into print—seemed to be willing to entertain the
notion that life was equally valid no matter how it was lived. In
short, the article had worked. Its only discernable purpose had
been to create a large controversy where a little one had existed
before, and to make sure Americans were properly divided on
the subject—a goal it had managed to accomplish even though
the "event" on which it was based had never even happened.

A magazine of *Life*'s stature, of course, could hardly endorse
bohemianism without alienating millions of squares. On the
other hand, coverage *is* promotion, and the editors certainly
knew it. It was hard to say where they really stood. Like the
French revolutionary in the old story, they seemed to want to
find out where the people were going so that they could lead
them there. In the end, it hardly mattered. Their bets were safely
hedged, and as long as the beat horse was willing to run, they
were willing to ride.

One immediate result was that millions of Americans—far
more than would ever read *The Holy Barbarians*—now knew
the name and face of "Lawrence Lipton, the leader of the Beat-

niks." He had been pictured on the very first page (opposite an ad for New York Life), reading poetry to jazz before a rapt and youthful audience in his own living room. Displayed above him were the typically dreadful yearbook photos (the only ones they could get) of the three girls who had long since regretted writing to him. It was hard to resist the conclusion that the call to *Life* had come from the telephone at 20 Park Avenue.

It was certainly Lipton who had sent the photographers up to Suzan Perkoff's, where they were upset to find her house clean and her children clothed. They had taken some pictures anyway, but the photo editor had apparently discarded them. The article had even contained a plea for the survival of the Gas House, quoting Al Mathews: "Sure, bongo drums are loud, but my friends tell me that a bongo is a way of dissolving your antagonisms toward other people." That was Lipton's kind of argument. The Venice half of the story was a showcase for his places, his current friends, and his now-standard message that beat was just like real life, only better and more exciting.

Despite growing resentment against him, the Shaman of the Tribe was both busier and bossier than ever. Al Mathews had left it to him to screen applicants for free rooms at the Grand Hotel, which also included free meals in the Gas House. The Grand was big enough to hold a fair number of poets and artists, but not quite everyone. The project was going to depend, to some extent, on revenue from the paying customers on the first two floors.

After the exterminators had killed the rats and roaches, the poets rewired the building, patched the plaster, painted the walls, got rid of the rendering-plant smell (the last residents had boiled their own soap on the premises), and took over the entire third floor. One artist-in-residence even wired the third floor for sound, so that every room had a little speaker connected to his hi-fi set. Of course that meant everyone had to accept his taste in music, but what did they want for free?

There was never any question that Perkoff would get a room; besides, he had nowhere else to go. Tony Scibella got in too. Even though he and his wife Sam were still on good terms, he had had to "disappear" so that she could draw county assistance. Frankie Rios, for one reason or another, failed to qualify, but he slept most nights on Scibella's or Perkoff's floor and ate with them twice a day for free in the Gas House.

"It is a strange experiment," Perkoff wrote, "The Gas House

& the hotel & the support. Having a room & 2 meals a day provided to me makes me feel rather giddy & light-headed. Night-wedded. Tight-bedded. Perhaps Al Mathews is really concerned to bring peace & love into the world. . . . I think it's going to be cool."

It was a bit like like being sponsored by the Huntington Hartford Foundation. In obedience to Allen Ginsberg's admonition to "dig prosody," Perkoff laid in a supply of drugs, locked his door, and read Herbert Reid's *London Book of English Verse* all the way through. Nothing broke the spell. There were no struggles with the squares, no tourists, no scavenging reporters. There was no Beat Generation, only poetry and his own place in its tradition. The first thing that struck him was a feeling of "not being very good. . . . You know—of *not knowing*. It's a wonderful feeling of how much there is. The whole road . . . like, there's William Butler Yeats, and here I am. And you know, I *know* I have the right to call myself a poet."

From a strictly bureaucratic standpoint, of course, only Larry Lipton had the right to call anyone a poet. The project could not afford to feed every beatnik on the beach, and distinctions had to be made. Food money came from a gallon jug set up for the tourists in the Gas House; John Thomas, who doubled as the cook, emptied it every day at four o'clock and made his plans from there. If the take was too small for dinner and the next day's breakfast, Mathews or Lipton would throw in five or ten dollars—enough to put a foundation of Spanish rice under whatever else Thomas could come up with. And he was resourceful. There was always free fish for chowder on the pier, because there were always things the fishing boats caught unintentionally. There was even a pet food store in Santa Monica that sold filet mignon for fifty-nine cents a pound, and John Thomas simply never told anyone it was horse meat.

Lines did have to be drawn, and one of them ended up being drawn against Frankie Rios. Friend or not, poet or not, he was not an official resident of the hotel, so he was not entitled to eat in the Gas House. When some of the newcomers who did live there complained about it with all the self-righteousness of paying customers, John Thomas was forced to turn him away; he was "not on the list."

"If Frankie can't sit down with us," the old guard declared, "*none* of us will eat here." By evening the revolt had spread up the Promenade to the Venice West Café, where John Kenevan grandly proposed to hold daily free spaghetti feeds for poets. By dinner time the next day, the parade of "poets" ran all the way down the beach. After a nasty confrontation with Rios, Lipton pulled strings to get him into the hotel, but the basic problem remained. What made a poet different from any other hungry man? How could one human being authenticate another? What ever happened to "just blowing?"

There was certainly nothing infallible about "Bwana Lawrence's" judgment—or perhaps the bardic revolution simply needed more recruits than it could find. The Perkoff/Scibella/Rios party considered Lipton's roster "at least eighty percent lame"—nonwriters, nonpainters, people who really did think anyone could do *anything* and call it art.

"These local beatniks are too much," Perkoff wrote in his journal. "It's the non-doers who have all the personality of a used condom that really are a drag. So many of them consider themselves comedians, too." He and his friends grew ever more fervent and exclusive in their cult of the Muse; there could be irreverence about anything else, but not about poetry or the Lady. It was partly reverence for the words, partly awe of "the magic," and partly fear that if they failed to keep the Lady's trust, she would simply take it all away. Perkoff, for one, combined his love for her with a deep distrust for himself. He knew he was becoming a totem; he saw it in the faces of his more slavish admirers.

> I know that look; I've had stars in my eyes, and I recognize it, and it's not right. It's—*not—right.*
> I dig to be dug, probably more than I ought to, but this . . . this is such a straight and ego-feeding thing . . . I can sense it coming in and feeding that part of me. That's just not—that's *got* to stop.

It did not stop. His stature rose even higher when several of his poems were chosen for Donald Allen's anthology, *American Poetry in the Twentieth Century*. "Wow!" Perkoff wrote. "To have several poems in a respectable anthology—Grove Press! Important haps in Amer. verse since WWII! It really shakes me." A Gas House patron even paid twenty-five dollars for one of his paintings. "Very dangerous," he cautioned himself. "I certainly ain't that good at anything. Forgive me, O Muse. I don't mean to take yr credit."

He did accept an invitation to appear on network television—not as a "spokesman" but as a contestant on Groucho Marx's game show, "You Bet Your Life." Before he rode with Suzan to the NBC Studios in Burbank, he fortified himself with pot and Tussar. He had also taken to shaving his head, and the combination of bare skull and thick black mustache made his eyes seem bigger and more luminous than ever. The other contestants worried him because they looked "so American & clean cut." One of them asked what he was doing with his pen and old-fashioned composition book.

"Writing."

"Poetry?"

"No, just scribbling."

"Well, *why*?"

After Perkoff and the scriptwriters had worked out the lines he was to trade with Groucho Marx, he found himself paired with a tall blonde, and the two of them shuffled out to meet Groucho.

"You know, you have a really interesting mustache there," Groucho said. "Any special reason for wearing it?"

"Well, in reality, I think I look good in it," Perkoff answered, hands clasped nervously behind his back.

"So does a walrus. Why do you shave your skull?"

"It's much more comfortable."

"Are you what is, uh, usually called a 'beatnik?'"

Perkoff rolled his eyes. He looked like a skinny little bald imp in his out-at-the-knee dungarees, but he was a born performer. "No, I'm not," he said thoughtfully, as if no one had ever asked him that question before. "I'm a poet and a painter and a sculptor."

"In other words, you're out of work?"

Stuart seemed to enjoy that line even more than the audience did. Marx turned to his fellow contestant: "Doesn't he look like a beatnik to you?"

"Kind of," she answered shyly, "except he doesn't have the beard."

"Tell me, then—if you're not a beatnik, what *is* a beatnik?"

"Well, I think a beatnik is a person who lives a certain way, believes in certain things . . . their way of life implies getting along on a minimum of money, and a belief in their ability to work out their own problems without external coercion, so long as they don't harm anyone."

"Do you believe in this philosophy?

"Yes, I do."

"But you're not a beatnik?"

"No, I'm not."

"Well, how do you differ from the beatniks?"

"I work."

The audience laughed harder than the script seemed to call for. Marx waited, then pursued the point: "I thought you said you were out of work."

"Well, I work all the time—writing, painting. It's hard work, even if there's not much money in it."

When it was time to play "You Bet Your Life," Perkoff actually won three hundred dollars. Then he used the word "name" in a sentence, and with the usual race-track fanfare, the most famous stuffed duck in America dropped down from the top of the set to announce that he had said the Secret Word. That meant another fifty dollars for each of them, for a total of nearly twice what John Kenevan had paid him for the Venice West Café. Perkoff was already translating his take into practical terms—a pound of pot, a thousand pills—though he expected to give most of the money to Suzan, Benny, Sasha, and Rachel. Before he sent them away, however, Marx had one more question.

"How do you eke out a living?"

"I guess I don't."

"Don't you ever feel tempted to occasionally write for money?"

"Well," Perkoff replied with perfect timing, "sometimes I write home to my father. *He* sends me money."

Groucho Marx, of course, had deliberately given him a forum, and soon he would even donate a little money to the Gas House. The network took nearly two weeks to cut a check for Perkoff, and when it finally came through, he took all but seventy-five dollars of it, along with a gift of pot, to Suzan. But he had done so well before the cameras that Paul Coates, the hard-boiled local newscaster, soon asked him to appear on his popular late-night expose, "Confidential File." Perkoff and bass player Leonard Salman arrived wearing three-piece suits, which alarmed their host.

"Well, wait a minute. *You* guys aren't beatniks!"

"Sure we are," Perkoff replied, and proceeded to summarize his beliefs so compellingly that one viewer later wrote both to applaud him and to denounce the world "normal" people had made:

> A world with a phenomenal rise in crime, juvenile delinquency, alcoholism, narcotics addiction, insanity, divorce, broken homes, resorts to tranquilizers, and—last but not least—the poisoning of the earth's atmosphere by nuclear explosions. . . . It is the "beat" generation that has taken on the responsibility of protest that we shirk. . . . Let us give honor where honor is due—to the protestants to our collective insanity. *We are the bums—* not they!

Perkoff had no real interest in becoming a television personality. He was having enough trouble coping with his newfound stature on the beach. It was "very good for the old ego" when John Kenevan told him he was the "major talent on the scene," but he hated what publicity, fantasy, glory-hunger, and "snob-shitting snotnose adolescent" poets were doing to Venice West. "Jesus!" he wrote one evening in October 1959. "This is the revolutionary free generation, wow! I mean, forget it. . . . What do I have in common with these people? Sometimes it just seems ridiculous. They blab fountains of bullshit, everything they say is a guarded wall, a deceptive weapon—game game."

They were even taking the magic out of using drugs.

Nor was Perkoff the only beat celebrity who now felt inclined to disown the movement. One evening, word spread up the Promenade that Kerouac himself was on the beach; Steve Allen, the television star, had brought him down to see the local "scene." Suzan Perkoff heard about it all the way up in Ocean Park; Bill Riola dashed into the Grand Hotel to tell John Thomas, "Kerouac's on the beach, man, he's got the whole gang, they're all after him!" Thomas was too proud to gawk at any celebrity, and those who did rush off to see Kerouac—at Larry Lipton's house, naturally—found him drunk, morose, haunted.

"Aw, *come* on, Jack," said Steve Allen, who had actually invited Kerouac to read passages from *On the Road* on his Sunday night TV show—despite the timidity of the networks and

Allen's own ratings war with Ed Sullivan. There was nothing in
Venice to please Kerouac. Now thirty-seven, he was a sad old
falling-down Tokay drinker, and just about everything made
him sadder. He hated all the posturing and negativism that had
come to characterize the beat scene:

> The cool girls with long thin legs in slacks, the men with
> goatees, all an enormous drag. . . . Nothing can be more dreary
> than "coolness" . . . postured, actually secretly *rigid* coolness
> that covers up the fact that the character is unable to convey
> anything of force or interest, a kind of sociological coolness soon
> to become a fad up into the mass of middleclass youth for a
> while. . . . All I could do was sit on the edge of the bed in despair
> like Lazarus listening to their awful "likes" and "like you know"
> and "wow crazy" and "a wig, man," "a real gas"—all this was
> about to sprout out all over America even down to High School
> level and be attributed in part to my doing!

As Larry Lipton had maintained in *The Holy Barbarians*,
Kerouac's novels described "the beatniks of the forties, not the
fifties." Lipton himself had a better grasp of what was going on
in the big-city beat enclaves of the late Eisenhower era, and he
had probably done more to shape it. It was he who had told the
would-be dropout what to wear, what expressions to use, and
why it was sociologically important that he do so. Accordingly,
the bearded, sandaled, code-talking young middle-class hipsters
who made the headlines probably owed more to his gift for
making things simple than to any example Kerouac had set.

Nevertheless, when Lipton invited him to the recording session for his new poetry-and-jazz LP, the successor album to *Jazz
Canto*, Perkoff decided to go and take his chances. Instead of
the old friends and warmth, he found the Liptons' house taken
over by "a mob of people & lots of bad vibrations," with Larry
himself dashing around giving orders. Stoned on Tussar, Perkoff
wanted only to read his poems and leave. "Lipton's voice grates
my ear," he scribbled into his diary. "His guests grate my
eye. . . . Now Lipton comes out on the tape, reading that bad
jazz. . . . If I just stay uninvolved, I'll make it thru the evening
without any difficulty." When his turn came he smoked a quick
joint, read three poems with "knees trembling through the
whole scene," and retreated to the hotel—only to be awakened

at two in the morning by "a chick screaming crying smashing things, in the hall loud voice evil saying 'we can't have it the police were here we don't want them again take a walk work it out yrself if I have to do something I will.'"

Only a few nights later, after a bitter argument, Tony Scibella, suddenly transformed into an outraged husband, charged into Perkoff's room, beat his friend senseless, and left him lying on the floor in a bloody clutter of torn poems. That same week, the county of Los Angeles forced Suzan Perkoff to swear out a warrant against her husband for nonsupport. "O my beautiful sons, my beautiful daughter," Perkoff wrote, "Now I think they are going to put me in jail for not bringing you money to feed you & clothe yr sweet bodies. I can't touch it without getting dirty . . . Sasha, Benny, Rachel, true loves of my real life."

His answer was to burrow ever deeper into the bowling-alley comradeship of the Grand Hotel—and, despite himself, into the belief that as a poet, he was somehow a great cosmic exception to the ordinary dynamics of human life. In fact, he was becoming one of a type. Most of the poets and artists who had holed themselves up on the third floor of the Grand Hotel had wives they no longer lived with, plus one or more adoring girlfriends whose separate existence they barely thought about. Some had obligingly left home so that their wives could draw welfare, but others, like John Thomas, had simply lit out for the territories and never looked back. They lived in a sealed world of male ritual and friendship not vastly different from an Edwardian gentleman's club, except, perhaps, for the quality of the upholstery. They counted art as a man's province, like statecraft, railroad-building, or empire. Along with getting high, it offered a way of feeling good and whole together. For quite a long time, being high and being creative had seemed to mean the same thing, and the needs of the high now asserted themselves as if they were the demands of the Muse herself.

Perkoff's old friend James Ryan Morris told him he could feel himself getting strung out. Stuart still preferred to think of himself as a cough syrup junkie, but when his drugstore connection went on vacation, he and Tony Scibella had "schmecked"—shot heroin—for seven straight days. Even after drinking six ounces of Tussar, he still could think of little but "bad naughty black soul beautiful white goddess heroin."

He still used other people's needles and let his friends do his scoring for him. Occasionally he would help steal a doctor's bag, deal a little pantopon (synthetic morphine) on consignment, and lose days at a time to goofballs and liquid Seconal. There were too many burns, too many missed opportunities, too many five- and ten-dollar deals that never went down, so he started scoring for himself—only to find that the "Narc heat" had the power to shut down all transactions in Venice for days at a time.

At the start of the summer, he would have been capable of waiting. Now he had no choice but to ride with his connection to the source itself—the great open-air dope exchange of Los Angeles, which was to be found, more often than not, in the same part of town as the garment, produce, flower, and financial districts. On this particular night, it was happening on Broadway between Second and Third streets, on broad, surreally lit sidewalks in front of the Grand Central Market. To Perkoff, it looked like "a junkscene in a dream . . . hundreds of cats, waiting for the man, looking for the man, scoring, selling," all right out in the open under the lights of City Hall, the building transformed in recent years by the popular television show, "Dragnet," into the nation's best-known symbol of justice.

"A truly wondrous scene," Perkoff wrote admiringly in his journal, which he then left on the car seat while he went out to take care of business. He had forgotten entirely about the "strange chick" who was still sitting silently in the back seat. But she had noticed him. While he was out scoring, she opened his book, with its invocation to the Lady, and wrote in neat, square capital letters:

THE EDGE IS COMING CLOSER AND NAUSEA WRACKS MY MIND . . . LOOK AT WHAT LIES BELOW THE EVER-INCREASING SPINNING THAT NEVER STOPS, THE BLURRING OF REALITY ONCE SO CLEAR, THE SUDDEN JOLTS OF WARNING BY THE BODY THAT TIME IS SHORT. AND THE DECISION HAS TO BE MADE SOON.

YOU KNOW YET DISBELIEVE. YOU ACCEPT WHILE REJECTING. SMOKE DREAMS WON'T SOLVE THE PROBLEM, ONLY TAKE AWAY MUCH-NEEDED MINUTES, HOURS & DAYS. DON'T PLAY HIDE-AND-GO-SEEK, PLANNING ON NEVER FINDING.

SOMEDAY YOU'LL HAVE REACHED THE WHOLE. ALL THE MISSING PARTS WILL SLIDE INTO PLACE. IT WAS SO DIFFICULT TO EVEN SEE BEFORE, NOW THE SEEING IS ONE AND WHOLE. BUT WILL THE FINAL WHOLE BE RE-ALITY OR ILLUSION? COMPLETE ILLUMINATION OR THE FANTASTIC DREAM OF A LUNATIC?

CHAPTER SEVEN

Considering its drawing power in the media, the Beat Generation was not, in the strictest sense, a merchandising success. Beat themes were used to sell all sorts of products, but none of them had much to do with the beat way of life itself. A few bright entrepreneurs made money selling stick-on beards, "rent-a-beatnik" services, and "beat but neat" sweaters, but these were fast-buck items, not serious contenders in the consumer product wars. Despite the fact that Americans were spending more money than ever before on nonessential goods, the only fast-moving plaything that owed much of its popularity to the beat image was the bongo drum.

Sold in pairs and played with the whole tandem unit wedged between the knees, the cheap little drums were everywhere. Miniature bongos dangled from rear-view mirrors; bigger bongos adorned coffee tables, woke up neighbors, annoyed parents, and helped get thirteen- and twenty-year-olds thrown out of school. Bongos turned square apartments into pads, weenie roasts into swinging beach parties, and after-hours get-togethers into occasions for calling the police. Often given as gifts, they would be kept for a variety of reasons—as jokes, as assertions of hipness, or as souvenirs of Disneyland, Coral Gables, or Tijuana. Few of their owners ever tried to play them more than once or twice, but that, in a way, was the whole idea. Like hip talk, heavy eye makeup, and faded dungarees, bongos were safe, trendy symbols of a rebellion that almost anyone could enjoy in small, harmless doses. The point was not to take them too seriously, and few imagined that they did.

In Venice, drums were still a serious matter in the spring of 1960, especially in the hands of Curtis J. Smith, a.k.a. Tamboo. A tall, muscular black former Marine who had come in with the first wave of hip invaders in the summer of 1959, he and a squad-sized army of disciples played bongos and congas on the beach every day, rain or shine, tourists or no tourists, heat or no heat, and despite his status as a latecomer, "Tamboo blowing drums on the beach" had become a symbol of assurance and continuity for those who remembered the "old days"—by which they meant last year.

When Tamboo's mother died in April 1960, Stuart Perkoff kept a night-long vigil with him out on the sand, watching in fascination as "this huge cat, a mtn of lite, a fountain of being alive,"

> Placed his graceful hugeness against the huge ocean, & mixed his blood with its blood, mourned in his own way, this man of all the juice & fire of being a man, alive, a real person in our strange world, black against the black sky, pure against the pure sea, whole against the broken earth, sang against the dying blood . . . not questioning himself, because he is surrounded on all sides by him, the air & the nostril, the blood & the piss & the ocean that birthed us all, the head & the drum & the face & the heart, carved from the same tree of itself.

There could not have been a purer description of how the beat artist saw himself in the world. For Perkoff, however, life had become a jumble of distractions. Still, he had solved at least one problem that morning. His only bottle of ink was up at Suzan's, but he had found that if he filled his fountain pen with water, the dissolved residue flowed rather elegantly onto the page in pale shades of grey. Writing that way took a bit of practice, but it was no more difficult, after all, than learning to eat with a mouthful of unfamiliar teeth.

His own teeth had crumbled away so badly that his mother paid to have them pulled. While he was in Santa Barbara for the extractions, real life had intervened in still another way: "some fucking druggist" had actually had the nerve to charge him $2.75 for what he considered a one-dollar bottle of Tussar. Life was getting tougher in Venice, too. There was less of everything now but trouble. The narc heat was everywhere, and so were the "outlaws"—bikers, pushers, burn artists, people looking for a fight, and the usual contingent of thugs, thieves, derelicts, and rapists. Junkie poets could hardly demand protection from the police, and few of them knew how to protect themselves, either. They were lawbreakers, all right, but as criminals, they were a joke. In short, they were completely on their own.

Frank Rios, the only one of them with any street instincts, had gone back to jail. When the police had rousted Perkoff, Rios, and a sometime connection named Eddie, Rios, who had the Tussar in his pocket, had taken the fall. As a known addict and habitual offender, there had never been any question of where he was going. "How can that be?" Perkoff wrote. "O Lady, are you letting him escape?" His break with the other "dooge stooge," Tony Scibella, still seemed irreparable, leaving Perkoff more or less at the mercy of his admirers. He kept "forgetting" to pick up the bottle of ink from Suzan's. It meant he had to keep writing with water, but it gave him an excuse to keep going back.

After the Grand Hotel folded, Perkoff moved into a garage pad near the Venice West Café. The rent was seven dollars a month, but even that had had to be guaranteed by John Kenevan. His new plan, like all the old ones, was to "stay high, be alone, think, *work*." But staying high seemed to leave very little energy for anything else. He had finally suffered his first undeniable withdrawal symptom—a pain that felt "like a hideous tickling in the core of the bone"—and his life seemed to be dissolving into an endless round of schemes, risks, conjectures, promises, betrayals, irregular ecstasies, and agonizing waits. Heroin was still relatively cheap, but four dollars a cap was a lot of money to a man with only one bottle of ink.

There was another problem, too. Susan Berman, who was pregnant, wanted him to marry her. They could go to Mexico, she said, and live happily and simply. Perkoff refused to consider marriage—he was *already* married—but Mexico sounded like a possibility. There he could write, think, be alone—Susan Berman was always good about that—and, of course, stay high. There was certainly nothing in Venice to hold him. John Thomas and the other members of the "Venice West Foot Stomping & Poem Eating Society" kept talking about putting out a magazine, but as usual, there was no money. The others thought Larry Lipton might be good for a touch, and Perkoff,

who seemed to have the strongest immunity to "Liptonitis,"
was the logical one to approach him. "Ha!" he wrote. "Little
do they know I have a hypersensitivity to the scene. To him."

In the meantime, Perkoff got his coffee free at the Venice West
Café. "How funny," he confided to his journal. "Here I sit in
the cafe, nite after nite, something I never used to do, & write,
& look at things & people & I am so *in* & *hip* I sort of make
myself sick." If Venice were really such a free, vital subversive
place, he reasoned, *"wdn't you think there'd be some jazz musicians on the scene?"*

In the meantime, Perkoff was trying to juggle several sexual
affairs at once. ("If you had honor," a woman told him one
night in the Venice West, "you'd be a beautiful cat.") The most
important one, with a weekend beatnik from Pasadena named
Maxine, had already gotten him beaten senseless with a stick.
That was only a minor complication, and it certainly made
things more intense. Perkoff rejoiced in the "leaping growth of
two relationships in my life—the one with Maxine, the other
with junk"—which had wakened him out of his "1/2 life stu-
por, the coma of non-response." It was only after Susan Berman
outmaneuvered him by taking the issue to his mother that he
agreed to go to Mexico, with his parents subsidizing the trip.

The night before their departure, Perkoff was sitting in the
Venice West Café when he saw what seemed to be a parody of
"Mad Mike" Magdalani—"fat, with hair," and wearing a suit—
come in and take a seat. "What have you *done* to yourself?" he
demanded, after making sure it was really Mad Mike.

What Magdalani had done was to sign himself into Camarillo
for treatment. Desperate for acceptance and barely understood
even in Venice, the frantic painter who had once tried to ap-
pease the community by decorating its garbage cans had simply
had enough. Before coming to Venice, he had worked as a
butcher and occasionally as "trade," that is, paid companion-
ship for older homosexuals. He had only discovered his true
vocation by accident, when a doctor who was treating him for
acute anxiety had admired his doodling. With his shaved head,
his Marx Brothers solemnity, and his absolute belief in his own
greatness, Magdalani had become a beach character, a real-life
stereotype of the earnest, benighted beatnik. *Life* had considered him eccentric enough to include in its photo spread on

Venice two summers before. But he was serious about his work, and no Venice artist had ever worked harder.

Mad Mike painted all the time and on every available surface—walls, canvas, ceilings, momentarily stationary objects. Every square inch of every hovel he lived in was covered with pictures. "There's two types of beatniks," he had once told a radio interviewer: "One whose life is art, in some field or other, and whose life is sacred, and whose art is sacred—and the other whose life is nothing but laziness . . . more or less like any type of hoodlum's who has no purpose in life." He still believed all that, but he thought that a stay at "The Place" might help him become more normal. Why did an artist have to be unhappy? Perkoff was skeptical, but wished him well. The next day he was off for Guadalajara.

"To be high & alive!" he scribbled in October 1960. "If I stayed in Venice I wd have died." He was shooting a phenomenal amount of junk, but in Mexico, 99 percent pure heroin cost $14 a gram. The only drawback was where he had to go to get it; his new connection was actually *inside* the Guadalajara penitentiary. He was writing every day now, and when he and Berman moved into a five-room house that gave him a cell of his own to work in, he felt unstoppable. "Changes & growth too much," he wrote. "I feel it bursting from me."

He actually started work on a novel; except for Alex Trocchi, no one from the Venice scene had ever completed one. Like Trocchi, Perkoff had his doubts about fiction. He had always made it a point "not to pretend to know where I do not know," and he agreed with Trocchi that a writer could scarcely claim to know all of his own thoughts, let alone anyone else's. But he even felt confident enough to risk using that ancient deceiver of authors, the straight third-person narrative.

While he made a good start, he never finished the novel. Shortly after the birth of his daughter, Eva, on the first of November, he was arrested. It took a great deal of effort, and probably quite a bit of money, for his father to secure his release. When he limped across the border the following spring, the San Diego police were waiting to pick him up. The Mexican authorities had even given them his journal, with its characteristically precise record of fixes, names, prices, dosages, and deals. All of that had happened in Mexico, however, so the most they could do was roust him a bit and let him go. Somehow he dragged himself to Suzan's new apartment in Inglewood, where she had moved to escape the drugs, the heat, and the beatniks.

When he arrived at his parents' ranch in Santa Barbara, he was like a mummy of himself. In a Mexican jail, as every California schoolboy knew, most of the necessities of life were for sale, and he had gone in broke. They had even cracked his new dental plate. When he was strong enough to argue with her again, his mother tried to persuade him to rethink his priorities in life.

"You're so much like you used to be when you were young," she said. "So clean. When you haven't been taking *anything*."

"Maybe I don't want to be like I was when I was young," Perkoff snapped at her. To him, being young meant being frightened, confused, and "bored to screaming." He was now utterly convinced that drugs were the key to his visions. "I get a little high," he wrote, "& things begin to bubble up & swarm in my hand. So hard to tell that to Mom, impossible to tell it to Dad. Maxine knows. Su Berman knows." He would not have been interested in hearing that this was junk, the great ventriloquist, talking with the voice of the Muse.

Every addict had *one* withdrawal symptom which was insurmountable, *one* custom-tailored horror that made death easier to face than kicking. For most it was a physical horror, a cold burn or an unbearable sensation in some part of the body that was not supposed to contain any nerve endings. For Perkoff, it was loss of creativity. He was convinced of it, so it was true. As soon as he was fit enough to sneak away from the house, he bought a bottle of Tussar, drank it, and was rewarded almost instantly with twenty drawings—one of them, he noted proudly, "quite wild & dadaist."

When he got back to Venice, he learned that John Thomas had fled to San Francisco to avoid arrest on a nonsupport warrant, and that Mad Mike Magdalani, the painter of garbage cans, had killed himself.

Larry Lipton had a theory, as always, about Mad Mike's suicide. "He didn't destroy *himself*," he assured Perkoff. "He destroyed it—*it*—that thing that was in the mirror." Instead of making him normal, his last stay in Camarillo had finished the job of making him feel like no one at all. So he had "killed that image in the mirror," knowing that "that image, that man, *can't paint.*" He had gone out to his garage, locked the door, hanged himself from one of the crossbeams, and remained that way, swaying, for seventeen days—"surrounded by his work," as Perkoff envisioned it, "and, I presume, no longer surrounded by his problems."

Death seemed to be the ultimate tourist, the ultimate police-man, the ultimate sociologist in the summer of 1961. "The killers swarm the city," Perkoff wrote:

> it is a summer madness
> they look thru faces of mirror
> they call my name

It was a mean-spirited time in which the police, the thugs, the career criminals, and the solid citizens of Venice all seemed to have banded together against a ridiculously peaceful common enemy. Two years before, Venice had been on the fringes of the serious drug world. Now it was known throughout the city as the place to go for an easy score, an easy bust, an easy roll, and, for those so inclined, an easy rape. The gaudy hulk of Pacific Ocean Park, which had been built to challenge Disneyland, now stood rotting on long black pilings over the water; instead of saving the economy of the Ocean Front, it had hastened its dissolution. Tourists, sun-worshipers, and bodybuilders (con-sidered members of a bizarre subculture in 1961) still crowded the beach by day, but the night belonged to the muggers, the drunks, and the psychopaths.

There were suicides, too. Rod Alger, the gallery owner, had killed himself at roughly the same time as Mad Mike. Up in Berkeley, Bill Margolis, formerly of Venice West, had jumped from a third-story window, crippling himself on a parking meter. If Margolis could do it, Perkoff reasoned, he could do it. Of course, he was still "very Jewish" when it came to suicide— it was "not permitted," and that, he hoped, was that. On the other hand, there were other ways of getting to hell.

Intellectually as well as physically addicted to junk, he had returned to find Venice in the grip of a junk famine. It was un-doubtedly an artificial one, the product of hard work by the police or, more likely, deliberate engineering by the suppliers, but either way, the result was the same:

great monkeymouth sucking leech like on my throat, sucks
down to bone core of junk yen ... monkey can't have it all
the time got to not kill me o great beautiful hungry monkey
wants his junk wants it bad tries to suck the memory of its taste
from me ...
      & maybe tomorrow he'll feed, & maybe
not but he's hungry
h
  u
    n
      g
        r
          y

Perkoff stayed in Venice. Kicking, after all, was only kicking.
The intolerable thing was not to write, and the words now
flowed from his hand, as he always liked to describe it, in spite
of everything. Friends were dead, Rios was in prison, Scibella
and Milton Bratton had moved to Hollywood, and his wife and
children were getting ready to move to San Francisco to be near
his brother Simon (better a deputy father than none at all). The
police, who knew a gold mine when they saw one, were watching all the known users and their hangouts more or less constantly. The received wisdom was to shoot all the heroin before
going out. Once the junk was in the body, a possession charge
was out of the question. The only possible charge was "marks,"
i.e., showing physical signs of having injected drugs. None of
this was enough to drive Perkoff away. Like Charlie Foster, he
had "died and been reborn in Venice"; unlike Foster, he was
determined to stay.

Mexico became his other home, and he spent part of the summer of 1961 covering the walls of his rented house in Guadalajara with a record of his "debts"—the names and particulars of
every poet, friend, and avatar who had ever helped shape his
thought. He always returned to Venice, where, with his tight
little retinue of poets and hangers-on, he evolved into an institution in spite of himself.

The following summer, Charlie Foster returned to Venice.
There was nothing calculated about it; as always, he simply appeared. Gaunt and shabby in his flapping, castoff clothes, he
looked as if he had never been away. He had, in fact, been gone
for nearly three years.

Most of the time, Foster had been wandering and writing in Mexico. He had lived for a while in Guadalajara, where someone had thought he would make a good business manager for an English-language magazine, *Mexico This Month*. It was pleasant work for easy money, but after two months he had simply decided he "didn't want a job anymore." Shoving on into rural Mexico, he had made friends easily with the *Indios*, taken their ego-shattering natural drugs, and seen visions that had made him think it was really possible to carve a way to the collective unconscious through the stubborn walls of his own. His ultimate aim, as ever, was to overcome the "curse of self-consciousness that we all carry—self-analysis, self-observation, the acute opinions of our friends." To that end he made his life with strangers, served strange gods, and tried to remind himself,

> man, you can't live clean
> you got your fingers caught
> in that sticky machine!

He really did believe in spiritual progress, and he was equally certain that the human mind contained all the maps it needed to find the way out of its misery. He had searched for them in the Tarot, the I Ching, the Zen texts, the Celtic myths, the Golden Treatise of Hermes, the novels of Hermann Hesse and Robert Graves, the poetry of Eliot, Duncan, and Lipton, the prophecies of Spengler, the legend of Arthur, and the Second Law of Thermodynamics. To the same end he had eaten peyote with the *brujos*, drunk *mescal* with the good old boys in the Mexican night, starved himself, stayed sick much of the time, hid from sex and friendship, and wandered in ever wider circles over the unpaved regions of his mind.

At last, half-dead, three-quarters starved, and without a home to go to, Foster had hitchhiked back to California and checked himself into Camarillo. As soon as he was well enough to travel, he had gone over the wall again. It was nearly Christmas, and he thought it might be pleasant to wrap packages in a department store in New York. If they caught him, at least he would end up with new doctors and a second opinion of what was "wrong" with him. The police grabbed him in Rhode Island, and when his mother refused to come and get him, the doctors had shipped him back to Camarillo for fifty days' observation.

Foster had gotten the point, and since he really did want to get out, he had started to do the things that were commonly considered signs of progress, such as signing himself out on pass and going into town to look for advertising work. It was a ridiculous thing to try without a resumé and samples of his writing, but it had impressed the doctors, and in due time they had let him go.

He had missed just about everything—the Gas House, the Grand Hotel, the media, the outlaws, the heat. The Venice West was still much the same, but Charlie had never exactly been a regular. In general, Venice seemed to have deteriorated—it seemed baser, warier, less alive, more depressing. On the other hand, perhaps there was not more decay than he remembered; perhaps there were only more carrion feeders.

Inevitably, word of Foster's return reached Larry Lipton—who had been trying for some time to find *him*. Alex Trocchi, Terry Southern, and Richard Seaver wanted very badly to include his fantasy, "The Troubled Makers," in their anthology, *Writers in Revolt*. Having no idea of how to find him, they had sent the release to Lipton, who knew Foster would care less about the small amount of money they were offering than about the chance to be anthologized with Allen Ginsberg, Jean Genet, Henry Miller, and the Marquis de Sade.

Foster was on his way to the Liptons' new home, which was some distance from the beach, when a complete stranger came out of his house and handed him several pairs of old trousers. "I don't know why," Foster shrugged when he told the story to Lipton, who had switched on the old Wollensak tape recorder the moment he walked in the door.

Larry and Nettie Lipton had given up the Park Avenue house and moved to a newer, smaller home on Burrell Street, near the tar sands and spent oil fields which were in the final stages of being transformed into that miracle of space-age real estate promotion, Marina Del Rey. *The Holy Barbarians* had never even come close to making them rich, and instead of writing the expected screenplay about the Beat Generation, Larry had turned to other projects, such as a preachy, unsellable script about Paul Gauguin ("You say I am a barbarian. It is true. I am a barbarian who is searching for a savage source . . . the *original* source, from which all religion springs"). The ideas were the same as ever, but when it came to selling them to the public, he seemed to be losing his touch.

The fact was that even his wilder ideas were becoming increasingly commonplace. While he expected to generate some controversy with his next book, *The Erotic Revolution: An Affirmative Statement,* there was almost nothing in it that could not have been found in Hugh Hefner's monthly installments of "The Playboy Philosophy." Lipton's case-study methodology and trite, leering vocabulary—"shackup" and "open secret" were two of his favorite expressions—made his arguments seem sleazy without being especially provocative. He could still get a rise out of the Goldwater conservatives, but as a sexual frontiersman, he was fast becoming rather dated. It was not enough to have been "right" about the sexual revolution; he wanted to be *new,* which only made what he wrote about it seem cheaper and more opportunistic than ever. In his search for fresh notoriety, it was easy to forget that he had refused to cash in fully on the hottest commercial property of his life—and that he went on saying these increasingly ordinary things because he believed in them.

"I am prepared to go beyond the Beat Generation, if need be," he had told two English professors who had come to interview him for the Living History Program at the University of Southern California. "I believe there is always a new front, a new frontier, in everything." That made it all the more frustrating to be identified with an exhausted rebellion. He still welcomed—and helped—the young poets who came to his door; "this could be the very one," he would say. Yet all too many of his angry young men could now be described as "professional" young people—the beat equivalent of professional Irishmen. The real Southern California "youth scene" had long since begun to transfer itself to that slender, overpublicized, and underpoliced sliver of County jurisdiction known as the Sunset Strip.

At forty, Charlie Foster might only have been described as "young" if he had sat in the United States Senate. Like his prose, Foster's body concealed nothing; the wrinkles in his face and the dry deadness of his hair offered hard but unmistakable testimony to the state of his liver, kidneys, and heart. He came to the Liptons now for the old acceptance and warmth, not for the money. They had never turned him away—not even after he had raided their medicine cabinet and gulped down all of Nettie's estrogen pills (asked about it later, he would only say, "Oh, it was a high").

He found Lipton reproving, sarcastic, and impatient to begin taping their "discussion." As the old Wollensak cranked away, Lipton allowed Foster to ramble on as usual, waiting for the chance to turn the characteristically shapeless monologue into a full-blown airing of the concept of "dedicated poverty." At last, when Foster mentioned the job he had abandoned at *Mexico This Month,* Lipton pounced. So! Walking away from money and security again! What was the *real* reason Foster kept doing this?

"I just needed to make a complete change in the way I was living."

This sounded too "casual" for Lipton. Had it "just happened?" Or had there been some deliberation to it? Instead of steering Foster into the desired exchange about "dedicated poverty," he only set him off an another round of long, complicated stories. Foster recalled a tragic couple up in San Francisco who had had a real problem with ether—first *he* had flipped out and disappeared for three days, showing up finally at his mother's "without any memory of how he got there"—then *she* had done up some ether with some cat in a car, both of them getting so high that they forgot about the ether and lit cigarettes.

"Ah!" Lipton shouted. "Self-destruction! I wrote a piece on that." Some people, he said, upon finding themselves close to psychosis, used pain to "reassure themselves." Did Foster understand?

Foster understood, but what did that have to do with his story? He picked up the copy of Perkoff's *Venice Poems* from Lipton's table. "Like the business in this book here," he said: "'Hit me, beat me, rape me, do anything, just prove to me it's real.'"

"'Prove to me it's real.' Well, you know, when she was going psychotic, Suzan Perkoff also had that kind of reaction, you remember?"

Yes, Foster remembered. After Suzan Perkoff's return from Camarillo, he had lived for a while on the Perkoffs' couch. "Suzan's passage through that seems so beautiful," he said to Lipton. "I mean, the way she's turned out." He began to talk about his own most recent stay at Camarillo, and about his escape, his capture in Rhode Island, and his disillusioning return to Venice.

"It's changed," he said. "The whole situation with regard to the police has gotten a lot worse; the attitude of the police has gotten a lot more of what I would think of as fascist, and much more pathological. The scene with the people I've seen around the beach here is much sicker, more cynical, and it has been less productive."

This was too much for Lipton. *Who* was "sick"? *Who* was "unproductive"? Tony Scibella and Stuart Perkoff were writing good things, and many new people had come into the "scene" and were producing paintings, sculpture, poems, and novels.

"But I don't think you care," Lipton added brutally. "It wouldn't even occur to me to introduce you to them, because I don't think you'd care what they're doing. What they're doing is of no interest to you. . . . You are very much wound up in your own work, and what transpires every minute of the day and night, you don't think much about."

Foster said nothing, although, as a believer in Lipton's own doctrines, he might have protested that an artist was *supposed* to be caught up in his work, that the creative act was all that mattered. But his old mentor was going for blood.

"You never look at television," Lipton said. "You don't look at the newspapers. When was the last time you read a newspaper?

Foster allowed that he *might* have read one "a couple of days ago." Lipton pressed on. Had he read any of the "new poets?" Well, no. Had Foster had any recent emotional affairs? Well, no.

"I get a pretty bleak picture about your trip to Mexico—sort of living in a fog, as it were. I get the same picture from some of the others, too . . . one person came back and said he'd visited with Stu and Maxine, and they were lying on the floor, stoned out of their minds, laughing and giggling at nothing . . . he said, 'I couldn't even establish that I was around, so I just walked out and went away.'"

Foster was reeling. "I usually got up early," he said quietly. "Around sunrise—"

Lipton now had his man on the ropes. "How come you can get up at sunrise on *those* occasions, and you can't make a gig by eight o'clock?" It was exactly the kind of question a square employer might have put to any of the "Holy Barbarians," just before he fired him.

The tape recorder, seemingly forgotten by everyone, kept on cranking.

"Well, that's *writing*," Foster tried to explain. Lipton himself had drawn the distinction often enough, especially when there were reporters listening.

"You say you had a gig there for three weeks. And you couldn't make the hours, you couldn't make the scene at all."

"Well, it was *meaningless* to me."

"Well, where do you expect to find meaningful work that's gainful at the same time?"

"Who said I was *expecting* to find it?"

Lipton seemed to realize he had stung Foster once too often—and that he, "Bwana Lawrence," was starting to argue against his own revealed wisdom.

"*Who* said I was expecting to find it?" Charlie repeated.

Larry laughed nervously. "That's just it," he stammered.

"Why go out and commit evil when you *know* it's evil?"

"You know," Larry said, chuckling, "anybody looking at you as a prospective employee would say you didn't have the energy to work—and yet, look at the amount of energy you expend on the things you *do* want to do!"

"Well, where do you *want* me to put it—where it belongs, or where it doesn't belong? *Do you believe in the reality of Moloch, or not?*"

Of course Lipton believed in it; he had spent the last two decades denouncing materialism, both as a system and as a faith. Along the way, he had also acquired fame, notoriety, influential friends, and instant recognizability on the street—all normally associated with material success, and all obtained without selling his soul. Think of the price he could have gotten for it! Who was Charlie Foster to play "dedicated poverty" with him?

"He's just trying to establish communication with you, Charlie," Nettie Lipton said.

"Well, I'm trying to establish communication with *you*, too!"

"Mail your letter," Lipton said finally. "Because the sooner you get it off to New York—and be *sure* to get it off tonight—the sooner you get it off to New York, the better, Charlie, because you'll get your money from it."

"Yeah," Charlie whispered. "*Money.*"

Larry handed him a five-dollar bill—no trivial amount for the Liptons, either—and crinkled it hard, for posterity's sake, next to the microphone.

"Listen," Nettie said. "You did it for love, and it's being published for love, and—"

"What do you mean?" Larry corrected her. "This guy chose it—he and his fellow editor—chose it because it's a damned good piece. And you'll remember I had a hell of a time getting it out of his hands! He wanted to improve on it, and I had to practically steal it out of his hands. Do you remember that?" he challenged Charlie. "You *don't* remember. He's forgotten everything."

"I haven't forgotten everything, Larry," Foster whispered sadly.

"I'll let you go now—it's getting late, and Nettie has to go to bed, too. You know how to find your way back? If you go straight down this street—"

"I *know*, Larry, I *know!*"

"I forget that you were a mailman around here! OK . . . let's be seeing you while you're around town. And tell the boys I'd like to have them come up some evening," he added hopefully, "and we can record some more poetry and have some more discussions."

It had been a close call for Lipton; he had actually caught himself siding with what was generally regarded as common sense. The fact was that in Foster, he had more than met his match. Where he was satisfied with not making make money, Foster had virtually no material life at all. He had cheated Moloch, all right, but at the cost of devouring his own substance. His writing meant so much to him that he shared it with almost no one. His visions were so important that he first stripped his mind bare to face them, then battered himself with chemicals to forget them. He demanded so much honesty of himself in love and friendship that he had had few friends and almost no loves at all. And he drank. Self-destruction was part of the old cult of the solitary artist, too—how many worshipful poems had been offered up to Charlie Parker?

The trouble with Charlie Foster's life was that he had actually made his bed on the cliff-edge of his ideals. It was hardly surprising that he looked so unnaturally old. As the personal embodiment of a myth, a set of aspirations that was always understood by those who shared it to represent a direction rather than a destination, he could hardly be expected to look like an ordinary human being. He had faced down the great false god of his time: the belief in salvation through material gain. Only Foster's definition of "material" had come to embrace every form of nonspiritual advantage. It was a tall order for a secular holy man with tendencies toward self-immolation. On the other hand, if a man's grasp could not sometimes equal his reach, what was a hell for?

It was always possible that he had never been anything but a "nut," or for those who prefer clinical terms, a sociopath. That was the reasoning most doubters used to dismiss the Beat Generation out of hand, and more than a few members of the Beat Generation had used it to dismiss Charlie Foster. Where were his books, his poems, his disciples? Did a solitary bum's inner landscape make him any less of a bum? What did he have to say to people less beguiled by their own confusion? Could he not have left one ordinary trace of himself behind?

When Foster was gone, Lipton turned angrily on his wife. He had apparently forgotten that the tape recorder was still running. "You should learn to let these people answer for *themselves*," he said. "Don't try to anticipate."

"I was just trying to draw him out."

"No, no, you weren't!" Larry thundered. "You were making answers. You were answering *me*!"

"Oh," Nettie said quietly.

CHAPTER EIGHT

On a Thursday morning in September 1962, a small crowd watched a crew of wreckers dismantle the Gas House. Its last legal resident, artist William Garrett, had left to seek "artistic asylum" in Mexico a couple of days before, and the tiny contingent of squatters who had tried to take his place had been awakened by the sound of sledgehammers.

The man who actually owned the building, Edward D. Higgins, had pleaded for months with city health and building safety officials, but they were determined to have their way. The Gas House was an "unsafe structure," and that was that. Four nights before the demolition began, more than a hundred people, described by one reporter as "bearded, sandaled, painted, drunk, sober, curious and . . . even sad," had held a noisy wake on the premises, beating drums, drinking wine, and dancing around a "dark, tall statue" of a man playing a bongo.

Larry Lipton watched quietly as the wreckers pounded the old sanctuary to rubble. He had not been a part of the effort to save it, which was probably just as well, but some of his fellow onlookers complained loudly about the destruction of "part of the history of Venice." In its fifty-seven-year lifetime it had served, at one time or another, as a quasi-legal gambling den, a respectable drugstore, a refuge for winos, and a wide-open saloon employing twenty full-time bartenders. It was only in its three-year-old incarnation as a "beatnik Mecca" that it had attracted any attention from the city at all.

"I wish they could find all the money I lost in there," one woman sighed to a reporter. Although he managed to get his picture taken for the papers, Larry Lipton, for once, had nothing special to say.

He had not *quite* given up on the Beat Generation. Early the following year he lugged his old tape recorder up to San Francisco to gather material for a projected book about poets and poetry, *The Growing Edge.* John Montgomery, the prototype of Henry Morley in Jack Kerouac's novel about Zen Buddhism, *The Dharma Bums,* did his best to steer him to the right people, but it was obvious that even in San Francisco, where the "West Coast renaissance" had been launched only eight years before, poetry had diminished as an independent force for change. The creative act was no longer sufficient in itself; now it had to be overtly political or otherwise committed—it had to *do* something. ("What we need now is political stuff," Lawrence Ferlinghetti had told John Thomas. "You got anything on Castro?") When poetry needed to justify itself on utilitarian grounds, it was clearly time for those who had made it a way of life to decide whether it was poetry or influence that they really believed in.

This was not to say that the working poets no longer believed in what they were doing, or that the revolution in awareness they had helped to launch had lost any of its momentum. The movement had broadened its basis for membership and would soon open its ranks still wider. Largely through the astonishing popular success of a handful of folk singers, links were being forged to the most powerful engine of persuasion ever directed at the youth of America: the mainstream music industry.

The people who ran the business hardly cared what they offered the public, but there was certainly an enormous appetite out there for strong, simple, earnest lyrics that actually meant something. In the high-tide years of the Civil Rights movement, when it seemed possible to destroy evil institutions by simply exposing their wickedness, there could hardly be any doubt that for the moment, at least, sincerity was the best policy. With the exception of "We Shall Overcome," for example, the anthems most young Americans associated with the drive for civil justice were composed not in the South, but in the great urban centers of the East and West. In another year or two, when Bob Dylan (whose adopted name represented a stroke of genius on many levels) judged the time right to incorporate rock-and-roll idioms into his music, the transfer of authority would be more or less complete.

None of this was particularly troubling to Allen Ginsberg, Gary Snyder, or any of the other founding members of the Beat Generation—except, of course, for Jack Kerouac. Though still dedicated to their art, they welcomed what they saw as an impending change in the way ordinary Americans perceived themselves. Ginsberg, in particular, expected only good things from the more liberal attitudes toward consciousness-altering drugs which he himself had helped to foster. While still taboo in some circles—and marijuana itself was still hugely illegal—pot and the more powerful psychedelics were becoming increasingly acceptable and even fashionable. Their intellectual snob value owed a great deal to Ginsberg and his friends, and to the fact that, for the most part, they seemed to offer the user plenty of exciting, effortless, profoundly sensual fun. For those so inclined, there was even the promise of spiritual enlightenment—in other words, there was something for everyone. There was also the danger that a liberation movement predicated on passive experience, and tied to the ingestion of specific chemicals, would end up leading its true believers by a short route back to consumerism. Charlie Foster might have been less than optimistic, but Allen Ginsberg was more than willing to take a politician's chance.

There was another danger as well. Where the Beat Generation had always expected to remain a minority, the emerging second phase of the "revolt of the young" could count on real numbers. Soon the "under 25s" would constitute more than half of the population. The only trouble was that, as with all mass movements, the greater the participation, the lower the standards for membership. Not everyone could be a poet or even an appreciator of poetry, but anyone could change dressing habits, switch from alcohol to pot, listen to the right music, and buy the right products. On the other hand, in the America of the early sixties, infinite progress seemed to be an article of faith no matter where one cared to look.

In Los Angeles, it was now accurate to speak of a concentrated youth culture with enormous spending power and an alarming but hardly surprising disdain for authority. Broadly speaking, it was composed of middle-class sons and daughters who had been conditioned by their parents to think of themselves as precious—and by the advertising and entertainment industries to think of themselves as unique. These were the younger brothers and sisters of the high-school kids who had laughed at the media image of the beatnik, but had admired his defiant attitude and sometimes envied his freedom from responsibility. Their much-discussed alienation was usually more pose than substance, but it came more or less naturally to anyone who absorbed the message that he or she was special—and that was the message that had been beamed toward them from all directions since the day they were born. The society they were being "prepared" for worshiped the very principle of youth, and they were more than happy to accept the compliment. It was especially hard for them not to agree with all the talk about their being the nation's most important resource. It would be two or three more years before a war conceived by old ideologues and young efficiency experts would remind them of what America was accustomed to doing with its resources.

These were the earnest but cocky young minds Larry Lipton wanted desperately to engage. As resourceful as ever, he managed to parlay a speech on "avant-garde writing" at the 1963 Pacific Coast Writer's Conference into a contract to teach an extension course at UCLA on the same subject. He also quietly abandoned *The Growing Edge* in order to join the staff of the first underground newspaper of the sixties, Art Kunkin's *Los Angeles Free Press*.

Through his weekly column, "The Wasp" (so named in honor of Ambrose Bierce's column of fifty years before), Lipton immediately became the *Freep*'s all-purpose anti-establishment nay-sayer. His favorite targets were "Moneytheism"—his all-embracing term for the consumer ethic—and "Murder, Inc.," as he now chose to refer to all manifestations of government. Nobody in power could do *anything* to please him; on the other hand, though vaguely leftist in tone, his column embraced no specific ideology. Uninterested in converting anyone on the right, Lipton was too unsystematic to be counted as part of the real left—except, perhaps, by those who had difficulty understanding what the left was saying, and that turned out to be readership enough.

Lipton's column had a powerful appeal for those would-be rebels who considered themselves as alienated as anyone, but lacked the academic orientation to feel a part of the New Left—or, for that matter, to be taken very seriously by it. While the younger left-wing ideologues seemed to care very little, except in a broad theoretical sense, about the problems of working-class white people, Lipton had grown up in the slums of Chicago at a time when "ghetto" had meant a place where poor Jews lived, not poor blacks. Though often shrill and shallow, his arguments helped attract draft-age mechanics, unemployed teenagers, and politically conscious high school students to a cause that was still easier to "feel" than to understand. It represented a strictly entry-level kind of revolution, but everyone had to start somewhere.

Although he was often accused of trading on the reputation of Venice West, Lipton seldom mentioned it in his contributions to the *Freep*. He made an exception when John and Anna Haag established the Venice Music and Arts Center in storefront slot next door to the Venice West Café.

Though rather bravely named for a gallery measuring only fifteen feet wide, the center promised to combine all the most irritating qualities of the Venice West Café and the Gas House. It had been conceived as a showcase for painting, sculpture, folk singing, spoken poetry, and the way of life that went along with them. When the time came to open it to the public, the Haags, who believed in nothing so much as the power of creative confrontation, shrewdly invited Larry Lipton to organize the first show.

The shaman certainly rose to the occasion. He managed to find a classic example of Mad Mike Magdalani's garbage-can art for the exhibit, and he even pulled his little saucer-eyed robot, Duhab, out of mothballs. Every Saturday night, he told the *Freep*'s readers, Duhab would recite passages of scatological and otherwise rebellious literature. At the first sign of a police raid, he would claim immunity from prosecution on the grounds that since he was not human, he was incapable of "obscenity." The police were always free to disagree, but taking such an act to court would probably have the same effect as moving a show from New Haven to Broadway.

Lipton had come prepared to fight the last war. It had never occurred to him that many of the people who now considered themselves hip might resent the suggestion that they owed a cultural debt to Venice West. In a *Free Press* review entitled "Op, Pop and Slop," Paul Jay Robbins, whose usual beat was the Sunset Strip, dismissed Venice as "East L.A. with sandflies," an overrated beachfront slum whose lingering, never-deserved reputation kept newer, more creative, and infinitely hipper scenes from being recognized. Robbins seemed to despise the Center and all the "tradition" it stood for, but he saved his worst attacks for the old Merchant of Venice himself:

> Since Lipton (an unlettered Philip Wylie with his blither of insights which we achieve at sixteen) does so little to me under the best of circumstances, I have forgotten his endless explanations of Duhab. I do, however, recall that Duhab bore a cunning resemblance to his creator in the fragmented blare with which it tried to pass itself off as profoundly significant.

Predictably, Lipton was beside himself. He threatened to quit the paper, then made the publisher, Art Kunkin, crawl a bit before accepting—and publishing—an apology. *Freep* readers, especially those who lived in Venice, lined up on both sides. "If you don't like Venice," one of the artists in the show advised Robbins, "don't come back. . . . Venice doesn't like anybody that wears a Beatle haircut *and* a beard so that he will be sure to be hip wherever he goes." Another longtime resident wrote:

> This nonsense in Venice (this supposed art exhibit being the latest example) was first whipped up by Mr. Lipton in 1959, and it has been kept up by him, and by some miscellaneous poseurs and apostate gas station attendants. A lot of writers and painters have lived in Venice, but most of them have stayed home to write and paint, however inconvenient this has been to Mr. Lipton and his pre-fab beat scenes.

Harlan Ellison, the science fiction writer, was particularly disappointed in Kunkin's performance, which struck him as "midway between pathetic and ludicrous. God forbid you should ever have any real pressure put on you." Lipton sniffed that such attacks should be reserved for "The Enemy," adding that his readers would "know what I mean by The Enemy." He stopped short of reminding everyone that he had been hip before they were born, but he never repeated the mistake of assuming that Venice West "lived."

Only John Haag, as owner of the Venice West Café, still soldiered on under the same banner. A thirty-three-year-old Harvard man, technical writer, and poet, he was also an incomparable joiner. His list of affiliations seemed calculated to make up for all the years that politics had been considered an obscenity at the Venice West Café. A former Communist, Haag had also served as founding president of the Venice Chapter of the ACLU, chairman of the Venice Forum, publicity chairman of the Venice/Santa Monica chapter of CORE, "action chairman" of the Westside United Civil Rights Committee, rally chairman of the Congress of Unrepresented People (COUP), chairman of the International Days of Protest Committee, arrangements committee chairman of the Southern California Conference on Vietnam, and Westside head of the Ad Hoc Committee to End Police Malpractice—a cause very near his heart, since his agitation in its behalf had cost him both his job in the aerospace industry and his security clearance. In the summer of 1964, he was still chairman of the Los Angeles Area Council of the W.E.B. DuBois Clubs of America, co-chairman of the Los Angeles Committee to End the War in Vietnam, associate of the New Left School, and co-chairman of the Freedom Now Committee. A believer in revolution by peaceful means, he had tried to run for the California Assembly as a Democrat in 1963, was about to try for the nomination again, and would serve as a perennial Peace and Freedom Party candidate for one office or another right into the mid-eighties.

Haag had been coming to poetry readings in Venice since 1959, and when John Kenevan had given up on the Café in 1962, he and his wife Anna had bought it. Too political to command much respect on the original scene, Haag had waited for the scene to come to him, and now, more or less by default, it had.

On a hot Saturday evening in September 1964, Haag rang a cowbell behind the counter of the Venice West; moments later, Richard Hoffman, a Café regular, stood up to give a live reading of his poem, "The Bullfighter." Immediately, four plainclothes vice squad members signaled to four uniformed policemen posted outside. Confronted by no fewer than eight arresting officers, Haag, undoubtedly the best-prepared martyr in Los Angeles, surrendered. The charge was a familiar one: violation of LAMC Section 103.102, to wit, "providing entertainment without a police permit." When Haag refused to sign the citation, they took him in and booked him.

According to the police, if the poet had been drunk and started ranting on his own, no offense would have been committed. The vice detail had seen an announcement of the reading in the Café window on Friday—that was advertising—and by ringing the cowbell, Haag had made the reading a performance within the meaning of the law. It seemed that everyone had written off what was left of Venice West except the Los Angeles Police Department.

The next day, Haag posted a new announcement in the front window of the Café:

NO MORE POETRY
Due to the anti-intellectual yahoos of the LAPD
POETS ARISE!

To fight the case, Haag retained a prominent civil rights attorney, Herbert M. Porter. Haag's political activities had taught him a great deal more about fighting City Hall than Al Mathews had ever known. He recognized the exceptional weakness of the case against him, which rested, at best, on a questionable application of a questionable reading of the law. The entertainment issue was, as usual, a cover for harassment—in this case, political harassment, since poetry readings had always been tolerated at the Café, even with policemen present, until a radical had taken it over. Even before Haag's case could come to trial, the Los Angeles City Council opened another front in the war against bohemianism in Venice West. It was a little late in coming, but these things always took time.

On 30 November 1964, citing three years' worth of complaints from the Venice Ocean Front Improvement Association, Karl Rundberg, whose improbably drawn district included both Venice and Pacific Palisades, introduced a resolution calling for a ban on "the beating of drums and playing of other instruments on beaches and recreational areas under city control." Translation: no more bongos on the beach. The issue was not music, he said, but noise, particularly along the stretch of beach where Dudley Avenue met Ocean Front Walk—in other words, the immediate neighborhood of the Venice West Café.

"I want to get rid of all these beatniks who beat on garbage cans," he told reporters. "Those beatniks sleep all day. They start out in their beards about 10 pm and get all ginned up on beer and raise hell all night long. They have already spread," he added ominously, "to the Pacific Palisades."

"All these kids aren't beatniks," Councilman Ernani Bernardi, a former big-band musician, protested. "Some of them are very sensible."

Councilman Tom Bradley tried to point out that such an ordinance could not be applied selectively; if the Council banned bongo drumming on Venice beach, it would have to ban guitar strumming in Griffith Park. One member even professed to be worried that the law might discriminate "against American Indians," who often staged "tom-tom" events in the city's parks. Despite the most obvious objection—that disturbing the peace was already as illegal as it needed to be—the Council, with Mayor Sam Yorty's endorsement, directed the city attorney to prepare appropriate legislation.

"There is little enough joy in today's world," John Haag wrote in an open letter to the city fathers. "Let us not stifle what is left. Let us not make our city known as the city that outlawed music." As he himself knew perfectly well, however, there were other stakes involved in the battle of the Ocean Front.

At the urging of the area's congressman, James Roosevelt, Councilman Rundberg—along with Stan Roberts and Millie Rieber, representing that old nemesis of the Gas House, the Venice Civic Union—had recently met with officials of the Federal Housing Administration. Under an amendment to the Housing Act of 1964, the Federal Housing Authority had been granted the right to underwrite long-term, low-cost rehabilitation loans for city property owners. To the local business community, that meant the dawn of a new day for Venice; Mayor Yorty was even talking about bulldozing the place and starting over. But the agency had refused to allocate funds for Venice "in its present status." To the FHA, that meant the submission of a real plan for urban renewal; to the Venice Civic Union, it meant cleaning up the area's act.

The Gas House, of course, had already been demolished, as had the magnificent old St. Mark's Hotel, whose owners had spent $20,000 in a vain attempt to bring it up to standard. In his weekly *Freep* column, Larry Lipton warned that renewal would ultimately betray the Venice homeowners, too—a case of the "little realestateniks being gobbled up by the big realestateniks. . . . When their Venice goes," he predicted, "the names of the artists they harassed and execrated in the name of Law, Decency and the Four Square Gospel will be all Venice is remembered for in the class rooms and history books."

It was not quite the end for the Venice West Café. When the case actually went to trial, Judge Robert S. Thompson, who had hoped to write an opinion about its constitutional aspects, threw it out of court on the grounds that no advertisement had been seen in the Café window on the night of the reading—no advertisement, no entertainment. In the meantime, of course, the readings had gone on, and Bob Chatterton had even gotten away with a screening of his film, *Echoes of Venice West*. It was a victory, but like so many victories in Vietnam, nothing was won by it but the chance to fight again.

On 2 July 1965, after eight months of political wrangling, the City Council approved the final version of the antibongo ordinance by a vote of 11 to 2, only Councilmen Bernardi and Bradley dissenting. Before departing on a twenty-five-stop fact-finding tour of the world, Mayor Yorty hailed it as a victory for law and order.

"It's absolutely ridiculous, this beating of drums all night keeping respectable citizens alive."

"Freudian slip!" shouted a reporter.

"I mean, keeping them awake."

The mayor also announced the appointment of Councilman Rundberg, a lame duck in his own district, to the City Harbor Commission. John Haag and his supporters immediately filed out of the council chamber to begin a noon-hour demonstration on the steps of City Hall. Television cameras were already in place; so were the demonstrators' speakers, amps, and instruments. As the dancers began to do the "Rundberg Bounce," Haag announced that he and his supporters would test both laws—the one just passed, and a similar statute already in effect in Santa Monica. Thus far, they had obeyed the Santa Monica ordinance because "we still had Venice." One reporter asked a pretty, barefoot dancer in blue jeans if it was true, as Rundberg and the homeowners seemed to think, that at beatnik parties, "youths drank wine from the navels of young women."

"Yes, we do drink from navels," she answered sweetly, "and these people ought to do the same."

"Maybe they have small navels."

"They have small minds."

Larry Lipton had had nothing to do with the demonstration, but two weeks after this resurrection of the specter of Venice West, his popular UCLA Extension class was canceled without warning. But while he was predictably furious, it soon became obvious that his enemies, whoever they were, had actually thrown him right back into the briar patch.

Since the official University of California no longer served the people, he declared, the people must be offered an alternative. He began his offensive with a "teach-out" on the UCLA campus, but soon expanded the concept into something called the "Free University of California," situated first at the Pot-Pourri, a coffeehouse on the Venice/Marina Del Rey line, and then at a far more accessible location, the Ash Grove coffeehouse on Melrose Avenue. John Thomas, who had returned from San Francisco, and who was starting to revise his opinion of Lipton, helped him teach the first few classes. Over the next year, Anaïs Nin, David Ossman, Paul Sawyer, Gary Snyder, Charlie Foster, Julie Meredith (singing Lipton's poems set to music), Saul White, and even Stuart Perkoff participated in his workshops, read for his students, or taught his classes. It was a belated gift to the youth of the sixties from Venice West, and it expanded the old concept of poetry and jazz to include new dimensions of sight, imagery, and sound. Lipton was happy again; renaming his *Freep* column "Radio Free America," he was even starting to talk about establishing an offshore pirate radio station, which would, of course, bear the same name.

In Venice, however, the last stand of the Venice West Café had begun. After outraging the local conservatives by subletting 5 Dudley to a chapter of the W.E.B. du Bois Club, the Haags received notice on 23 January 1966 that Eugene del Genio, who owned the entire building, intended to put them out on the street.

A Chicago advertising executive, del Genio seldom saw his Venice properties, which were managed by his mother. He hated un-American activities, however, and from what he had heard, it was only the beatniks and the radicals who now stood between the Venice Ocean Front and its rightful state of prosperity. John Haag "hardly made two quarters off that café," and its clientele was making it impossible to rent the adjoining spaces to real businessmen.

Predictably, Haag promised new demonstrations. A flyer issued in his behalf appealed for

> ... a gathering immediately in Venice of all concerned persons: poets, artists, folk-singers, jazzmen, bongo-players, all who have benefited from the Venice West, personal friends, friends

of free speech, friends of political freedom, friends of racial equality, friends of peace, friends of socialism and all who support the coffeehouse concept.

A major rallying point was the collage Stuart Perkoff had just completed on the Café's east wall, where he had once written "Art Is Love Is God." Even though the landlord planned to scrape it back to the brickwork, Perkoff, the one-time anarchist, refused to become involved. The important thing, as he saw it, was not to preserve but to *do*, to create and keep on creating. He had been a poet in 1957, and he was a poet now; if Haag and his supporters wanted more than that, they wanted somebody else.

Perkoff was more ambivalent about the Free University of California. He wanted desperately to teach his own class, but he hated the idea of getting sucked into another of Lipton's project. How soon would the old man's ego spoil everything? He had even tried to write a play about Lipton, "a sort of negative or underbelly Faust," to be entitled "The Triumph of Clarence Clopton: Or, How to Make Nothing Out of Something in the Land of Opportunity." It seemed to him that the closer one got to Lipton, the farther he ended up straying from himself; he could see it happening to Saul White all over again.

Although he accepted a few of Lipton's invitations to read his poetry, Perkoff was essentially through with letting other people twist his fantasies to suit their own. In the end, like so many populist projects of the sixties, the Free University, unable to sustain its own momentum, more or less evaporated after Lipton, tired, overextended, and completely absorbed in his plan for a pirate radio station, lost interest in it.

John Haag won the struggle for the Venice West Café when a judge invalidated Eugene del Genio's eviction order. The struggle had taken a lot out of him, and apparently he, too, believed the point was to do, not to preserve. Or perhaps he simply could not face another battle over the Venice West Café, no matter how much he and Anna loved it. Shortly after his last victory in its behalf, he closed its doors and let it die, murals, collages, words, and all.

For Stuart Perkoff, on the other hand, life had begun all over again. He had married his lady of two years, Jana de la Fuega Baragan, and while it was technically a bigamous situation for both of them, he was positively solemn about it. An off-again, on-again junkie since the age of fourteen, Baragan was pretty, mysterious, and fey. She was pale and quiet, with quick black eyes and glossy black hair cut close to her face. Perkoff infuriated his daughter Rachel by bringing her up with him to San Francisco for the holidays, but he saw no reason not to share his happiness. They fixed heroin, shot speed, and floated through barbiturate fantasies together. They also shared a devotion to the Lady—although her Lady was Astarte, the Semitic goddess now revered under several names by the priestesses of Wicca, and his was still the Olympian deity who had sung through Homer. "Good verse good life," Perkoff wrote. "Jana & I refer to our relationship as 'The Great Miracle.'"

While Perkoff retreated into his own brand of domesticity, the social phenomenon he had helped to found was coming into full, rampant bloom in San Francisco. It was there that Kerouac, Ginsberg, Snyder, and Rexroth had announced its coming in 1955, and it was there, not quite twelve years later, that Ginsberg, Snyder, Michael McClure, and Timothy Leary (the Peter the Hermit of LSD), publicly blessed the acid-enhanced, fully electrified second phase of the movement for a new consciousness.

On 14 January 1967, thirty thousand people responded to their call for a "Gathering of the Tribes for a Human Be-In" in Golden Gate Park. It was almost literally a torch-passing ceremony. The day began with a poetry reading and closed with a free concert by the most exciting new properties in the music business, including Quicksilver, Big Brother, and the Grateful Dead, all of which were still neighborhood bands. The six perpetually feuding members of Jefferson Airplane, who had arrived separately, were eventually persuaded to get up and jam with another band's instruments. Security for the main power cable was provided by the Hell's Angels, who could not resist beating at least one party-goer senseless, but for all the electrified weaponry on stage, the most authoritative sound that day was the gentle tinging of Allen Ginsberg's Indian finger cymbals. The television cameras caught it all, and for a few hours, at least, as the crowd got higher and higher, the incense grew thicker, and the police stayed away, conventional reality seemed to collapse like a wilted balloon.

The immediate result, first in San Francisco and then in other cities, was an influx of adventurers, hip pilgrims, and runaways that recalled the invasion of Venice West eight years earlier, but dwarfed it. Three months later, only a few days before his death, Henry Luce, who was visiting San Francisco, insisted on being taken to the Haight-Ashbury district to see the beatniks. His reaction was not recorded, but it was clear from the copy in his magazines that he had judged this new development to be a winner. His editors were not sure quite what to call it, but they certainly knew better than to take it less than seriously.

For one article entitled "The Other Culture," *Life* reporter Barry Farrell sought out an expert only a *real* member of the avant garde could fully appreciate: Alexander Trocchi. Trocchi, his legal battles over *Cain's Book* long since won, had virtually given up writing. Now, as an international underground celebrity, he was totally immersed on work on something called Project Sigma, which was intended to give the world something it had never had before: a single, universal, *coordinated* avant-garde movement.

As a licensed addict living in London, Trocchi no longer had to fear the police. Young rebels knocked reverently on his door at all hours, and no tour of the hip scenes of Europe was really complete without a pilgrimage to his Kensington flat. In behalf of Project Sigma, he spent nearly all his waking hours in contact with writers, artists, and psychiatrists around the world—although he did seem to be able to find time for the odd visiting journalist. With his Holmesian pipe, hand-tooled Moroccan leather cap, and air of complete certainty, he projected the image of a hip elder statesman—or, as he liked to put it, a "cosmonaut of inner space."

"We're coming along at a perfect time," he assured *Life* reporter Farrell.

> Society is declining in its energies, falling off from its old mastery. It is now completely unable to control the quality of people's lives, and there is great discomfort in conventional circles everywhere. People don't know how to cope with the kind of life we're approaching. What Sigma has put together is a thin veneer of people all over the world, people who up to now haven't realized their vital contemporaneousness.

Trocchi had originally envisioned Sigma as an "academy of consciousness," a clearing house for research on the "connection between drugs and awareness." The thing had gotten away from him. He was trying to coordinate the ideas and activities of all avant-garde movements everywhere, and there were simply too many to keep track of in his head. One wall of his study was covered with what appeared to be an enormous military situation map; in fact, it was a map of Greater London, with arrows running in all directions and such cryptic notations as "Topolski Kernal Outpost" and "Ego-Optik Mk 2." Alongside it, he had taped the dust jacket of the first edition of *Cain's Book*. But fiction was a thing of the past.

"Time! Time!" he exclaimed to the man from *Life*. "I never have any time now that Sigma is going like it is." He paused to give himself a fix that the reporter found "oddly exhibitionistic." Although Trocchi was undoubtedly the world's "second most famous junkie," his habit seemed like an anachronism. With all the wild talk about LSD, which he had tried back in the fifties, heroin was yesterday's vice. Everyone *knew* about junk; there was hardly any horror in it left to exploit. Acid, on the other hand, with its mystical associations, its intellectual snob appeal and its campaign promise to turn every user's mind into a self-receiving television set, seemed to offer endless possibilities.

So, for that matter, did the underground. Having ridiculed the Beat Generation, *Life* and the other slicks seemed determined not to repeat the mistake. Besides, the new movement made for color photo spreads that were as eye-catching as any of the ad copy. In effect, it was a nonstop advertisement for itself, and it was going to get all the publicity it could handle—and perhaps a little more.

"*The Underground*," Barry Farrell mused. "The name carries a nice romantic ring."

> A vast mosaic of Underground friendships reaches around the world, linking intentions and ideas, putting distant people in touch with each other. Since many Underground obsessions are illegal, or at least officially immoral, the movement reveals itself slowly—you approach it like an artichoke. But what it amounts to is a culture unto itself, the Other Culture, all over the world.

In due course, an even better, more sociologically flavored term evolved: the *counterculture*. It was usually presented as something new, even something that had emerged in stark contrast, if not outright reaction, to the Beat Generation. The beats had been so cool, so solemn, so black-and-white. Even their music was cool and cerebral, while the electric music of the "hippies" was hot, visceral, and accessible to anyone who had a pulse. It may have been significant that the beats, who represented the last American generation raised on radio, had practically worshiped the sound of the human voice, while the hippies, drawn from the first generation raised on television, preferred the sheer, overwhelming power of the electric guitar. The most important difference was the one no one seemed to care about: that the beat approach to life had emphasized do-ing, striving, sacrificing, creating, while the hippies—in theory, at least—looked forward to a world of endless, strife-free, es-sentially passive "experience."

In Venice, meanwhile, one of the beat ethic's more seasoned practitioners, Stuart Perkoff, was making yet another subsidized attempt to lead an orderly, productive life. His father had set him up in a house in Ocean Park; there he and Jana Baragan would live quietly, write poetry, draw pictures, make collages, and learn to live without drugs. Or so the plan went, at any rate. Like all the other plans, it demanded more concessions than he was able to make.

To sustain his heroin habit, Perkoff had put together a modest scam. His role was to be the man who knew the connection; drug trafficking had become so hazardous in Venice that most reputable dealers worked only through third parties. When a customer wanted to buy, he would take the money and score. He earned himself a "taste" that way, but he also assumed the risk for both parties. With a steady stream of customers flowing through his house, it was only a matter of time before the police realized what he was doing. When they did, they decided to set him up for his connection. There was no hurry about it; they waited three months to issue the warrants.

Perkoff hardly remembered the specific buys they arrested him for, let alone the phony customers. The warrants were Federal, and although he ended up being convicted of "transporting marijuana" rather than selling heroin, he drew the maximum penalty of five years, to be served on Terminal Island, in the man-made Harbor of Los Angeles.

After his son's trial, Nat Perkoff drove down from Santa Bar-bara to clear out the house in Ocean Park. He and the landlord worked all day. There was no time to sort through the mountain of clutter. Since it all looked like trash anyway, they told the workman they had hired to throw it all out. At precisely the moment Stuart Perkoff's entire literary estate was being rolled out the door in a barrel, Larry Lipton, the man with the perfect sense of timing, happened to be strolling up the front walk. Once he realized what was happening, he refused to stop shouting until the police arrived and agreed to impound everything until Perkoff was released.

Alone, Jana Baragan was completely helpless, so Suzan Perkoff decided to take her in. Soon both of Perkoff's wives and three of his four children were all living together in a shotgun flat in the Tenderloin district of San Francisco. While Suzan worked days as a bookkeeper, Jana worked nights as a witch, burning candles, swallowing pills, and casting obscure spells at her tiny altar.

Although Perkoff could not have been more grateful, his daughter, Rachel, thought it was an awfully strange way to live, crammed into a succession of tiny apartments full of incense, music, pot smoke, posters, beads, and incantations with her brothers, their runaway friends, and her father's spooky, dreamy, childlike second wife. She accepted it all, though; it was simply her people, doing what they did. She spent her own time playing at the free school, tagging along after her brothers, and wandering through the shifting scenes of the Summer of Love with stars painted on her cheeks.

Charlie Foster, who had fled the Magic Summer of 1959, missed the Summer of Love as well. Having left Venice more or less for good in 1964, he had finally settled in Marysville, married again, started a new family, and completed the premature destruction of his body. At the end of July 1967, his body was found washed up on the beach at Fort Ross. It had probably been in the water for ten days.

He left behind some five thousand pages of poetry and prose, most of which, according to his editor, Charles Potts, "shd have bin thrown out by th author." Foster had once predicted that his biographer would "show up some time in the 31st century;" in the meantime, not even the City Lights Bookstore—now a cultural landmark surrounded by neon signs and nude bars, including the world's only topless shoeshine parlor—carried any editions of his work. That was because there *were* no editions of his work, just a few scattered fragments here and there, chiefly in science fiction magazines that even his friends had never read.

On the other hand, he had told the truth to himself, and there was nothing that a literary reputation or a profile in *Look* could have done to make it any truer. "My neurosis i found out," he had once written.

> my delusions i have acted out, worried at, spat upon,
>   cracked up over & been sorry when they went away.
> my hallucinations i have delighted in.
> my visions have troubled and enthralled me.

As 1967 ended, Larry Lipton, despite hundreds of letters and a great many contributions from his admirers ("I can not wait till you get on the air. In a few weeks you will get some bread from me to help"), finally gave up on the idea of launching a pirate radio station. There was just too much work to be done, and he was just too old. As if to make up for the defeat, his column in the *Freep* grew more strident and combative than ever. Completely overwhelmed by his own rhetoric, he imagined himself besieged, persecuted, conspired against—everything but ignored—by the racist, moneygrubbing, warmongering forces of "Murder, Inc." "Radio Free America" had become less a feature *by* Lawrence Lipton than *about* him, and every time the rhetoric of the student radicals or the Black Panthers seemed to be catching up with his own, he responded by upping the ante. There had to be a ceiling to it all. He had already made it clear that he despised the society he lived in; where was he to go from total rejection?

There was the Democratic National Convention in Chicago. Chicago was where Lipton had started out, and it seemed appropriate for the *Freep*—as well as *Cavalier*, the skin magazine which also carried Paul Krassner's column—to assign the story to him. *Esquire*, after all, was sending Terry Southern, William Burroughs, and Jean Genet, and Allen Ginsberg would be there along with hundreds, if not thousands of demonstrators. It was Larry Lipton, however, who had grown up in cold-water Chicago tenements when there was no guarantee that even white working-class people would ever get their rights. The copy Lipton initially filed from Chicago was full of the now-obligatory references to pigs, paranoia, and Mayor Daley's "police state." It was also full an old man's private anger:

> The smells are all the way I remember them: the stench of shit, piss and corruption in the precinct stations ... the smell of poverty—dry rot and wet rot in the slumlord ghettos, Black and White; the beer-slop smell of the old corner saloons and stink of human misery and political/mafia greed and corruption in the ward-heeler's headquarters and hang-outs; the sickening mixture of chemical antiseptics and pain, sweat and misery in the County hospital—and everywhere, now, the added stink of fear and paranoia in Daley's Concentration Camp Chicago.

On the night of the very worst rioting, Lipton headed for Lincoln Park to join Ginsberg and the other demonstrators. By the time he arrived, the area was already cordoned off by the police. When he showed his press card from *Cavalier*, a plainclothes policeman smiled agreeably and waved him through the lines. He had only taken a few steps when a uniformed officer without a badge aimed a long, low, full-bodied swing at his kidneys. The nightstick cracked Lipton across the hips, and the old agitator, now in his seventieth year and in precisely the right place, as always, went down.

Late in 1968, after more than a year on Terminal Island, Stuart Perkoff, Prisoner #12368, was coming up for parole. He had stayed out of trouble in prison, but the parole board official, who was a thorough man, had checked into his past and learned that, unlikely as it might seem, the sad, defeated-looking little convict before him was a charismatic figure, a man of influence, a leader. To his way of thinking, there were enough false prophets on the streets already. "I'm a little afraid to put you out there among all those impressionable young people," the parole officer said. True to his word, he did not.

Friends who encountered Perkoff in prison remembered him as a man with "no tip"—that is, no idea of how to form the connections and power alliances other men in prison used to make their lives bearable. Instead he kept to himself, watched, waited, and grew old.

"The people are here because the machine is hungry," he wrote.

tho they know no more of this than do their guardians
not knowing, they must, as tho they knew,
survive. or not survive. it is known some survive . . .

in all its history of unbroken feeding
no portion of that flow has discovered
& passed on any awareness
of what they bring to that machine
the humans in their rhythms feed, but do not remember

not knowing they are machine-food
they blame the priests & guardians
who, not knowing they are only machine-feeders no matter
what they name their rituals
blame the animals they herd

the machine knows no concern with definition
its only interest is that its needs be met
a constant flow of humans is ingested

CHAPTER NINE

In January 1987, more than seventeen years after his death, the city government of Lowell, Massachusetts, announced plans to dedicate a children's park to the memory of Jack Kerouac. It was an exceptionally fitting gesture; no American had ever written more lovingly or evocatively of his childhood in a working-class town. In *Doctor Sax*, *The Town and the City*, *Vanity of Duluoz*, *Visions of Gerard*, and especially *Maggie Cassidy*, Kerouac had made it clear to anyone who cared to look that in spite of his reputation as the "Bloody King of the Beatniks," he had nothing but affection and a kind of holy awe for the details and rituals of growing up in America.

Yet to at least one observer, the idea of dedicating a park to Kerouac seemed unfathomably perverse. Twenty-nine years after ridiculing Jack in "The Know-Nothing Bohemians," Norman Podhoretz, editor of *Commentary* and a major contributor to "Neo-Conservative" (i.e., post-liberal) thought, was alarmed enough to have another bash at him. "Though born in Lowell," he wrote, "Kerouac was not just a local boy who made good."

> As the leading novelist of the Beat Generation, he "spit forth" (to borrow a phrase from the leading Beat poet, Allen Ginsberg) a series of books heaping abuse on the way of life lived in places like Lowell. That way of life he represented as hardly better than no life at all. It was, he said—most famously in *On the Road* and then again and again and yet again—a form of spiritual death.

Podhoretz did acknowledge that in his later years, Kerouac "got off the road, settled down in a suburb with his wife and mother, and returned to the Roman Catholic Church." He had also become a knee-jerk political conservative, as well as a rather unwelcome admirer of William F. Buckley, Jr. As Podhoretz rightly pointed out, however, that was "not the Kerouac the world remembers." The world remembered a cult hero who had glorified the aberrant, permanently alienated the young from "the system," and raised irresponsibility to the status of a new religion. To Podhoretz, that made him an enemy of civilization, and to honor him by putting his name on a playground for children expressed nothing so much as a national death-wish.

Those who considered that an overwrought assessment, Podhoretz went on, had only to review the cultural history of the past three decades. In the beginning, the Beat Generation had been a literary clown act that only a few had taken seriously; "within a short time," however,

> The values celebrated by Kerouac, Ginsberg and all the other Beat writers had established themselves as the orthodox dogma of what came to be known as the "counterculture." Dropping out, hitting the road, taking drugs, hopping from bed to bed with partners of either sex or both—all in the name of liberation from the death-dealing embrace of middle-class conventions—came to be as "in" among the middle-class young of the '60s as early marriage and the pursuit of a career had been 10 years before.

One Lowell city councilman had voted against the resolution because he was "worried about the role model for the kids"— and rightly so, said Podhoretz. After all, Kerouac and his friends had helped to ruin "a great many young people who were influenced by their distaste for normal life and common decency." His syndicated article took its closing text from George Orwell: "The fact to which we have got to cling, as to a lifebelt, is that it is possible to be a normal decent person and yet to be fully alive." And yet, Podhoretz observed bitterly,

> We memorialize Ginsberg and Kerouac, thereby further weakening our already tenuous grasp on Orwell's saving fact and abandoning the field once again to these latter-day pied pipers and their current successors who keep telling our children that the life being lived around them is not worth living at all.

He had misread Kerouac, who had always preached the duty to live humbly, to perform simple, comprehensible acts, to seek and practice wisdom, and to "pray for all living creatures." He was right in the sense that most of Kerouac's admirers had misread him in just the same way. If it seemed a bit preposterous to blame "old sweet Jack" for the spiritual downfall of an entire generation (or two, or even three, depending on who was counting), it was certainly fair to say that a radical change had swept over American civilization in the past thirty years, and that Kerouac's name, with or without his consent, had been stamped all over it.

Long before his death, Kerouac had come up with an even simpler explanation: the communists had done it. Looking, as always, for a "youth movement to exploit," they had seized his movement and turned it into a "Beat insurrection." It was true, of course, that his twenty-two books had been filled with enthusiasm for drugs, unfamiliar religions, unconventional sex, and ways of life that any good Party member, like any good liberal, would have condemned as rootless and irresponsible. As far back as the very early sixties, Kerouac had felt completely out of place in the counterculture. Slumping into a numbing life of drink, self-isolation, and mean-tempered resentment, he had continued to write his novels, but few of them had attracted much attention among a generation of rebels who had largely forsaken the written word in favor of passive "experience" and an exuberant counter-consumerism.

Loathing what his movement had become, yet resentful at being left out of it, Jack Kerouac lived obscurely in a succession of middle-class neighborhoods with his third wife and cranky invalid mother. He ignored or attacked his old friends, drank poisonous quantities of alcohol, watched stupefying amounts of television, and never missed an issue of *National Review*.

"I'm not a beatnik," he liked to say, "I'm a Catholic." Having once failed rather heroically to reconcile the Christianity of Saint Theresa with the Zen of D. T. Suzuki, he now sat for hours in front of the TV set painting portraits of Pope Paul VI. His Greek in-laws did their best to show him love and keep him from harming himself, but every now and then he would stumble into a black bar, start "talking nigger," as he called it, and get himself pounded senseless. Too patriotic to condemn the

Vietnam war, he was also too much of a pacifist to support it. When Ken Kesey and Allen Ginsberg draped a flag over his shoulders at a New York publishing party, he took it off and folded it up into a triangular bundle, declaring that "the flag is not a rag."

He snorted when he saw a picture of Ginsberg and Peter Orlovsky demonstrating for the legalization of marijuana. "That's all this guy ever does now," he told a friend. "He doesn't work anymore." He himself worked in short bursts of prodigious industry followed by long weeks of drunkenness and exhaustion. A week and a half before his death he finished *Pic*, a novel about a twelve-year-old black boy in the South. Was it a "story of prejudice," a reporter wanted to know?

"Shit," Kerouac answered. "It's a story of life. Of people living."

Simple categories had always been his undoing. How else should a society choked on information be expected to defend itself? It all seemed inescapably tied to a process of inundation and eventual oversaturation. How much familiarity could the individual consciousness stand before either abruptly changing loyalties or simply cancelling further thought on the matter? How much did the actual content of an issue count against the accumulated weight of trivialization? In the fifties, the image of poetry read to jazz in late-night coffeehouses carried considerable shock value. By 1969, a three-day concert attended by half a million hippies was nothing less—but also, in a sense, nothing more—than an occasion for a full-color pullout section (also sold separately) in *Life*.

The same issue of *Life* contained Norman Mailer's essay on the flight of Apollo 11, a shining review of the "counterculture" movie *Alice's Restaurant*, and a mock-scandalized profile of Barney Rossett, the millionaire president of Grove Press. Underground literature had certainly been good to Rossett. The value of his company's stock had tripled in the decade since he had dared to accept *Cain's Book* for publication. In fiscal year 1969 alone, he expected to net three million dollars as his personal share of the distribution income from a single motion picture, *I Am Curious (Yellow)*.

Someone like Larry Lipton might have understood how strange new empires of money and influence could be built in the name of spontaneity and holy poverty, but Jack Kerouac, now a sad, pot-bellied drunk with a Kennedy half-dollar taped over his herniated navel, simply never would. On Dizzy Gillespie's birthday, 29 October 1969, while planning a new novel about his childhood and watching "The Galloping Gourmet," he suffered a fatal esophageal hemorrhage. His funeral, a state occasion for the counterculture, drew such old friends as Allen Ginsberg, Peter Orlovsky, Gregory Corso, and John Clellon Holmes, the novelist who had first used Kerouac's expression, the Beat Generation, in print. Since none of the working-class Greeks who had actually been his day-to-day friends were asked to participate in the ceremony, they decided not to follow the casket to the churchyard, knowing that after the interment the hip celebrities would go away and they would have Kerouac to themselves again.

Ironically, as thousands of young wanderers streamed into San Francisco to escape their parents, Suzan Perkoff continued to live there for the sake of her children. She had moved to the Bay Area to be near Stuart's brother Simon, the jazz pianist, who had a stable life and a strong sense of family. Her household still included her husband's fey, spacey second wife. She sometimes thought that her older son, Sasha, was shooting heroin with Jana Baragan, and that suspicion, along with Jana's witchcraft and Sasha's increasingly odd behavior, made life more than a little freaky in the succession of tiny apartments she managed to rent.

Even after Jana drifted back to Venice—where she would eventually kill herself with the wrong combination of pills and alcohol—Sasha's brooding strangeness continued. He grew quieter, but more agitated; he would pace up and down the apartment, laughing to himself and refusing to speak to anyone. When he sat down one evening to draw pictures, everyone felt relieved, but later the same night he broke through Suzan's bedroom door and stood threatening to kill her with a broom handle.

"Sash', you're scaring me!" Rachel screamed.

"I'm sorry. But leave me alone. I'm *doing what I'm doing.*"

When he began to smash things, Suzan and Rachel, still dressed only for bed, dashed out the door. They ran two blocks to the local precinct house, but the desk sergeant refused to intervene. Did Sasha have a gun? No? Had he ever threatened anyone before?

It was just a domestic problem, after all, and Suzan was going to have to deal with it. But first, Rachel had to be gotten completely away from San Francisco. Suzan arranged for her to stay with some of Stuart's relatives, who lived a safe, completely unremarkable middle-class life in Santa Barbara.

Compared with anything Rachel Perkoff had ever known, they might as well have lived on the moon. They all sat down to meals together. Their house was big, tidy, and well organized, and the very same people tended to sleep in it every night. They were far from rich, but to anyone raised in dedicated poverty, they seemed as rich as Croesus. Rachel missed her mother, but it was like a vacation in a foreign country. She entered public school, cut her hair, dressed "straight," played with Barbie dolls, and even began to wear a bra. She also refused to entertain the thought of going back to San Francisco unless she were allowed to live with her uncle Simon and her aunt Sarah in Mill Valley.

It took Suzan about six months to arrange that, and shortly afterwards she found an apartment for the two of them right across the street. It meant hitching a ride over the Golden Gate Bridge every morning to go to work, but it was worth it. She had failed, however, to get Sasha committed—the one violent episode was apparently all he had in him—and now he simply drifted in and out of wherever she chose to live.

Early in 1971, Jana warned Suzan that Stuart was about to be released. "I can't love him," she wrote. "You have to love him; I can't do it. Take care of yourself."

There was really nowhere else for him to go. Staying off heroin was an absolute condition of his parole, and Venice was no place for a junkie on remission. Besides, he wanted to go home. Though not quite forty-one, Stuart Perkoff was sad, subdued, and tired. They had let him grow his hair and beard on Terminal Island, but he still looked like what he was, a prematurely old man whose heavy body seemed to fit him as poorly as anything else issued in prison. Rachel hardly knew how to respond when he came for a visit—or when she realized he was going to stay.

It was a panicky situation. Stuart had always been a far-away proposition, a half-realized part of her life. When her parents told her they had decided to try to live together again, she began to cry hysterically. This *stranger* was taking away the friend who had cried on her shoulder when she was only five years old. After failing to fit Rachel into his own life, he now proposed to invade hers. It took her forty-eight hours, at most, to decide that she liked the idea very much.

Stuart got a job at a textile mill, running an enormous machine and commuting back across the bridge every night. He hated the work, but it paid enough to make it possible to rent a house in Mill Valley, with fireplace, carport, swing set, and all. There was a bedroom for everyone, even Sasha, who had wandered home with his head shaved from a stint at Camarillo, and Ben, who had started back to high school and was learning to play soprano sax. When Perkoff's daughter by Susan Berman, Eva, had a falling out with her mother, she, too, joined the family. They acquired dogs, cats, new friends, and a car; Suzan even learned to drive. Stuart even became something of a disciplinarian, and Rachel came to enjoy having some structure to complain about. If the Perkoff household was still a bit too chaotic to qualify for a spread in *Good Housekeeping*, it was the closest thing to that fantasy of a normal life that Rachel had ever experienced as her own.

It was partly the landlord and partly Tony Scibella who cut it short. In the mid-sixties, Scibella had moved to Denver and opened a bookstore; Frankie Rios had eventually joined him. According to Scibella, the two of them were making nothing but money. With the hippie thing at its high-water mark, they were even minor celebrities—present at the creation, so to speak. Tony was offering Perkoff a place to live and a one-third interest in the store. The Three Stooges of the Promenade would now become the new-and-used-book tycoons of Colfax Avenue. With the landlord preparing to sell the Mill Valley house out from under him, there was no way Perkoff could have turned the propostion down.

As a Federal parolee, Perkoff needed permission to leave the state. He also needed permission to enter Colorado, and obtaining both would take a long time. So as soon as he had submitted the paperwork, he decided to go immediately. Ben and Sasha refused to move, so he, Rachel, and Suzan packed everything worth keeping into a big Ryder truck and set out for Denver. Scibella settled them in his basement. He and Rios were still shooting heroin, but there was no reason for that to become an issue.

They celebrated Stuart's arrival by staging a poetry reading for him in the bookstore. A picture taken that evening shows Perkoff reading at a lecturn made of old soap crates, long hair pressed flat under a beaded headband, beard full and shaggy as a biker's, the tension showing in his short, half-locked arms, hunched shoulders, and deeply creased forehead. He was uncomfortable in the role of visiting celebrity, but it was good to know the magic still worked.

When word filtered through the Federal bureaucracy that Perkoff had moved without permission, it was the incident of the Venice West Café and the health inspector all over again. They *had* to send him back. The official explanation was that a bookstore was not a fit environment for a convicted drug offender; "young people" might wander in off Colfax Boulevard and fall under his spell.

In one sense it was just as well. On a trip with Scibella and Rios, he had shot some heroin—not enough to get a habit, but enough to frighten him. After he and his family set up housekeeping in yet another one-bedroom apartment in Marin County, he stayed clean. *Relatively* clean, that is. He and Suzan smoked a lot of grass and dropped a lot of acid, but he stayed away from heroin, kept out of trouble, and saved enough money first to trade up to a three-bedroom place, then to open his own bookstore, Wolf River Books, in Larkspur.

Perkoff also began a new cycle of poems centering on the Hebrew alphabet—tight, confident poems of knowledge and acceptance, one poem for each letter, each poem concluding with its letter's numerical significance. The new book he was planning, to be called *Alphabet*, would have a unity and a completeness that he had never achieved before.

The Perkoffs' marriage, however, was disintegrating for the last time. Suzan found Stuart increasingly sealed off, closed in, "untouchable." It had nothing to do with drugs. It probably had a lot to do with prison, but the net effect was the same. He even refused to fight with her any more. Late in the spring of 1973, he told Rachel that he was leaving, and that there would even be a divorce.

At the end of May, he took the long bus ride down to Venice. Jana Baragan was dead, but Bob and Anita Alexander had offered him food and shelter until he could establish himself. As founder and chief sage of something called the Temple of Man,

Bob ("Baza") took his vocation seriously, and a steady stream of proselytes, runaways, visionaries, and completely unclassifiable people flowed through his house on Cabrillo Avenue.

New journal in hand, Stuart Perkoff sat down at a bus bench at Santa Monica Boulevard and Third, just off the Mall, and wrote:

> *31 May 1973*
> Lady, here is my hand
> This book, my eye, yr heart
> our home & space
> to be free & alive
> yr joy my hope
> the words you send

First, he had to get himself approved for public assistance. If his family life was over, so was his life of working for others; why go through the charade? Baragan's old shrink could be counted on to tell the welfare department that he was psychotic; the Supplementary Social Security checks would be small, but without a heroin habit to support, they would be enough.

He was fortunate to have anything recognizable to come home to. In the years since Perkoff's arrest, the improvement faction—those unamused people of property who, in the name of making Venice a normal community, had persecuted and eventually bulldozed the Gas House, driven the Venice West Café out of business, and sponsored the attempt to ban the bongos—had at last gone for broke, and had almost succeeded in pushing through the most ambitious local development scheme since Abbott Kinney's own.

Property owners and realtors had watched in amazement as a little imagination had transformed the pumped-out Del Rey oil sands into a 6,000-slip, small-craft harbor now known as Marina Del Rey. Why not do the same with the Venice canals? As early as 1961, 80 percent of the homeowners on the canals had signed a petition asking the City of Los Angeles to consider it. The initial plan had called for widening the canals, shoring them up with concrete, and dredging them out to a high-tide depth of eleven feet. Enthusiasts thought it could be done for a mere $3.85 million, and Mayor Sam Yorty loved the idea. (His predecessor, Norris Poulson, had cut his own political career short by invoking eminent domain in behalf of another private money-making scheme, but Chavez Ravine, now the site of Dodger Stadium, had been a fine old neighborhood, whereas Venice was only a slum.)

The project had stumbled from sticking point to sticking point throughout the sixties. The projected cost had shot up to around twenty million dollars, but money was not the only issue. The most sensitive point was the nature of occupancy in the area. Like 70 percent of the people in Venice, most canal dwellers were renters, not owners. The official sketches showed tidy canals with sheer concrete banks, sleek, flat "homes" (always a code word for expensive houses) with tiled roofs, and trim, rakish yachts plying broad waterways. It was certainly going to be neater than the strange old jumble of mooring posts, ducks, bushes, footpaths, wooden bridges, and eccentric rambling houses, but anyone with the barest spark of imagination could see that the Venice of the future would not be occupied by those who lived there now.

By the spring of 1971, the plan had grown from a waterways project into a renewal scheme that promised to renew the old Venice right out of existence. The target area included all of the Ocean Front area, from the Santa Monica line to the entrance to the Marina; all of the pedestrian streets; all of the predominantly black neighborhood north and east of Electric Avenue; all of "downtown" Venice, with its galleries, curio shops, restaurants, and liquor stores; and all of the canals, of course, along with Windward Avenue. The cost of all this had by now risen to $24.5 million, which was still only a friendly estimate.

Many property owners now realized that urban renewal included them, too. As Larry Lipton had once predicted, it was fast becoming a case of the "little realestateniks being gobbled up by the big realestateniks." One realtor dismissed a homeowner's objections as being prejudiced by the fact that "he doesn't think he will be able to live here." To a remarkable degree, old community antagonisms vanished at the prospect of having no community left to fight over. Protest actions attracted home-owners, renters, hippies, pensioners, architects, grocery store clerks, artists, transients, anarchists, nuclear families, junkies, left-wing revolutionaries, and radical lesbians.

The protesters found an improbable ally in the biggest "real-

estatenik" of all. The Hughes Tool Company owned thirty-four
parcels of land in the target zone and sued the City of Los Angeles for "illegally" promising to buy off renters with public
funds. At roughly the same time, the Western Center for Law
and Poverty filed a class action suit, which contended that the
project would "produce a community in which only the wealthy
would be able to live." These and other lawsuits soon merged
into a delaying action that dragged the crisis on into 1973.

Early that year several canal-dwellers built their own boardwalk along the canal banks and staked off a section of city land
for a "People's Park." When the city declared the walkway unsafe, a local activist, Abe Osheroff, chained himself to the railing. As expected, the police cut his chains, took him to jail, and
tore the outlaw boardwalk down. To Mayor Yorty, it was all
proof that "subversive forces" were trying to derail one of his
favorite projects; to the program's other backers, it was one
more indication that Venice was more trouble than it was
worth. When Judge Jerry Pacht ordered the city to submit an
environmental impact report on the proposed renovation, the
mayor sadly gave up.

So the Venice of the Holy Barbarians remained, and the more
its physical landmarks crumbled, the more its stubborn mental
landscape showed through. The exhibitionistic sixties had been
peculiarly kind to Venice, covering rot and raw brick with color
and imagination until the whole town had become the most in-
geniously painted-on surface in Southern California. Enormous
faces grinned from stucco walls and garage doors; mobiles and
God's-eyes dangled in windows; doors, fences, mailboxes, and
railroad ties alike were covered with birds, rainbows, poems,
smart remarks, and political symbols. Some of it was the work
of working artists, such as Terry Schoonhoven and the muralists
of The L. A. Fine Arts Squad, but most of it was simply an
expression of the way life was lived in Venice. One vast Windward Avenue mural offered a strikingly realistic view of what
was behind the viewer's head; in another, angels carried parked
cars away from a drive-in theater; still another portrayed the
Ocean Front knee-deep in snow. Even Gold's Gym, a simple
one-story structure where Arnold Schwarzenneger, Frank Zane,
Franco Columbu, and the rest of the world's best bodybuilders
trained every year for titles that might have been invented by

Abbott Kinney himself, was a bright, completely unapologetic study in red, white, and blue. It was all very garish and it was still a slum, but there was no doubt that Venice was alive.

It was also a place that understood a poet's vocation. Stuart Perkoff's face, along with a line from one of his poems, adorned Number Six of the locally published "Poetry Series Postcards." When some local studio owners arranged a public reading for him, he was flattered, though also intimidated, to learn that they planned to record it on videotape. The reading went well. "Many ears were opened," Perkoff wrote, adding that most of the kids in the audience had a lot to learn: "They think [Rod] McKuen is a poet."

Perkoff moved into a tiny apartment on Paloma Avenue, with a postage-stamp view of the sea. He also met Philomene Long, who was to be his friend, soulmate, and principal flesh-and-blood "lady" for the remainder of his life. Thirty-three, dark, mercurial, and very, very Irish, Long was an artist, a poet, a film-maker, a registered nurse, and a former nun. The daughter of a naval officer, she had grown up in San Diego, gone to Catholic schools, and graduated from Our Lady of Peace Academy. She had gotten her vocation as a nun at age seven, "from reading," and had two principal influences in common with Jack Kerouac: St. Theresa and Huckleberry Finn.

After entering the convent as "a rather wild teenager," she had stayed to become both a working nurse and a rather wild nun. In the evenings, from her cloister in the Bel Air hills, she would "read" Los Angeles from left to right, following the basin's natural lines to the sea, or, more precisely, to Venice. One of her closest friends in the convent, who claimed to have gotten *her* vocation while sitting in a coffeehouse in San Francisco, told Long what was *in* Venice and first described her as a "beatnik."

"Why am I a beatnik?"

"Because you spend so many hours looking at the sky."

In her friend's experience, that was what beatniks did; they sat, thought, and stared. Occasionally they spoke to each other, but only to orchestrate the staring. Long had heard about beatniks, of course, but it was the first time anyone had applied that term to her. People usually told her she was worldly; the Mother Superior certainly thought so. In time, concluding that the old woman was right, she simply went over the hill. To save the order from embarrassment, a dispensation was hastily obtained, and Philomene Long, still in her twenties and still, somehow, considering herself a nun, joined the world.

After a failed marriage, she moved to Venice to write poetry, shoot film, and live exactly as she chose. She had first met Stuart Perkoff before his arrest, sitting on a bench with hundreds of pigeons gathered around him. In 1973, a regular feature of the Ocean Front in her tennis shoes, black thrift-shop dresses, long, straight hair, alarm-clock pendant, and heavy silver cross, she met him again.

"Are you Stanley Perkoff?" she called to him from her window.

"No, I'm Stuart."

"Where's Jack Hirschmann? I want to go to his reading."

Perkoff knew Hirschmann, and invited himself along. Within a few days he had begun to joke that he was "'Stanley' to my close friends." Not all of his friends were amused. They tended to regard him as their totem—in other words, their property—and even if the two of them were "running together," women were supposed to inspire, to support, to admire, not make movies or write poems or have ideas of their own.

Long refused to let anyone dismiss her as Perkoff's latest. It made her furious when Tony Scibella, who was trying to be friendly, took her aside and explained that when Perkoff called her his "lady," that meant, "I'm supposed to keep my hands off you." When James Ryan Morris, now living in Black Oak, Colorado, told Stuart, "Write—and if you can't write, have your bitch type it for you," Long insisted that he "write this mug back and tell him he that he doesn't *speak* this way."

Much of the same bowling-alley mentality continued to operate in Stuart. He never pretended to restrict his own adventures, but he demanded the usual absolute fidelity from her. They were as much friends as lovers, which was rare for any of the old Venice West crowd. Philomene admired him, as Suzan had, without worshiping him. It was a mutual-discovery scene, not a domestic one, and she was at once bright, creative, selfish, and mysterious enough to keep it going. He never even agonized about her in his journals, which were now devoted almost exclusively to his art.

His poetry had entered a new and very Jewish phase. He had always meant to explore his heritage directly, and the outbreak of the Yom Kippur War in October 1973 lent the project a certain urgency. When he heard the news, he was being treated for a bladder infection in a Marina Del Rey hospital. "They're killing Jews again," he wrote, and it occurred to him that he did not know how to say Kaddish. Soon he was making plans to study Hebrew and become a "modern Hebrew poet." He expected his devotion to "a female goddess, his ancient enemy," to present some problems, but he thought he might "discover something abt that too."

He also began a long poem about Moses, opening with the leader's reluctance to lead and ending with the people's refusal to sink, like every other nation, into obscurity. It was to be a poem about mission, obedience, and the meaning of uniqueness. He was also working with another poet, Paul Vangelisti, on a single-volume collection of poems from all of his creative periods. Still not quite forty-four, he had begun to achieve the balance of peace, purpose, and non-destructive recognition that had eluded him all his life. He was also suffering from an unaccountable pain in his back. The doctors who had treated him for bladder trouble had said there was nothing else wrong with him, but he wanted to find out, he said, "why I feel so bad when I feel so good."

They kept him in the hospital overnight. The next day, when Long came bounding up the stairs to his apartment with her usual armload of books, he told her he had cancer. They were still pretending it might be something else, but the fact was that they were waiting for his family to fly in—his parents from Santa Barbara, his brother Jerry, the doctor, from St. Louis, and Si, Suzan, and his children from Marin County. Stuart had only discovered the truth by accident, when a nurse had told him matter-of-factly that some unfamiliar pills were his "cancer medicine."

The doctors wanted to be sure, of course. After a week of further testing, they sent him home with a pound jar of sleeping pills. "For me," he explained to Long, "and for whoever else wants to." It was rather like leaving a disgraced Edwardian gentleman alone in a room with a loaded pistol. The cancer had spread from his lungs to his spine, with no signs of stopping there; Perkoff wrestled with the idea of suicide, but decided it was "not allowed." Instead he asked Philomene to stay away for a day while he shot some heroin to "sort out this thing in my mind." Afterwards he asked her to help him through "this dying thing," and she proved to be the ideal co-conspirator. She managed to persuade his doctor to give him all the morphine he needed—what were they afraid of, getting him hooked?—and she drove him to his last reading, at Papa Bach's bookstore on Santa Monica Boulevard.

He arrived at the reading looking old and professorial in his tweed jacket, crew-necked sweater, and string of beads. Bob Alexander snapped a picture of him leaning on his cane, shy, emaciated, smiling. With his long pony tail and enormous black beard, he looked like an archetype of the grandfatherly hippie, a *mana*-charged bearer of . . . *tradition.* Among the poems he intended to read was his elegy for Gary Cooper, who had died of cancer the same week Mad Mike had hanged himself. After a good start, he found he was too weak to finish. Long took him home early; he threw up on the staircase, took to his bed, and stayed there.

"Don't despair," he scribbled on his wall, quoting Kafka, "not even over the fact that you don't despair. Just when you think all is lost, new forces will come to your assistance, and *just that* means that you are alive." Tony Scibella flew in from Denver to find Perkoff surrounded by girls, music, incense, and a seemingly endless stream of visitors. An enormous friend, Gary Paul, was in charge of carrying Stuart back and forth from the hospital and administering his drugs. "Give some to Tony," Perkoff told him, grinning with his shrunken, toothless mouth.

"Stuart," Scibella said, "you've always done everything first for us. Poetry, visions—*everything.* You've always done it first." But Jerry Perkoff was impatient with all the chaos, and began to insist on putting his brother into the hospital.

"The morning's grey is illuminated by pain," Stuart wrote.

> POEMS
> LADY SEND
> ME POEMS
> PLEASE!!!

They decided to take him to Brotman Memorial in Culver City, where Long knew the administrator well enough to obtain permission to stay with Perkoff more or less constantly. Most nights she even slept in his room. She watched, listened, played the chorus in the ancient sense of the word and helped him focus his thoughts.

"Do you ever curse, Stuart?"

"Sometimes, when I'm alone."

"What is the pain teaching you?"

"To obey."

Jerry Perkoff was seeing to it that he got all the painkillers he needed, but drugs were of no help when, just before his family arrived from the Bay Area, he abruptly lost the power of speech. With his false teeth out and his eyes wide, he tried to communicate with finger gestures and dark, oracular nonsense sounds, but after three days it was clear that he preferred that they not see him die. Rachel and Ben took the bus back to San Francisco; Sasha simply disappeared. Then, just as suddenly as it had vanished, Perkoff's voice returned.

"When I cannot speak," he rasped, "I am no longer human." He began to talk without stopping. By six the next morning Philomene had begun to doze, but he jarred her awake. "Hold on to your hat," he said. "Hold on to your chair. I've just seen the source of all knowledge. Now I'm ready to give Holy Communion." He asked her to leave for awhile, but to come back later with a tape recorder; he had a "poem in him."

She rushed back the following afternoon to find everyone waiting glumly in the hospital lobby. He was dying, and everybody seemed to agree that it was her role to "be with him." Upstairs, she found Perkoff "angry, fighting, impassioned," tearing at the air for breath and flailing weakly with his arms and eyes. She even heard him profaning the Lady.

"Don't let the Muse own you," he croaked when he saw Philomene.

"But, Stuart, she wrote poems through you."

He conceded that the Lady had given him everything—poems, visions, ecstasies, love, pain, and death. She had even permitted him to see her physical form—once in the sky, after he had eaten peyote, and once in the fire, the time he and Rios had written poems to burn in her honor. The cost, like his devotion, had been absolute, and it was now clear that whatever else she might be, the Muse was a goddess of purpose, not of mercy. The day the tumors had broken through his collarbones, Perkoff had written in a jagged hand, "O Lady, give me some slack!" He had loved the Muse, in part, for her unapproachability, for the fact that *she*, who could not be found by looking for her, had come to *him*. If she could make an angry man a poet, she could also leave an angry poet alone to die. What did he expect, a chariot of fire?

"I . . . *see* her," Stuart sighed to Philomene.

"I see her, too, Stuart."

"I love you. See me? *Easier.* Here I am."

As Long looked into his wide, unfocused eyes, Perkoff's face began to transform itself around them, as if he were passing back through all the people he had been. He raised his fist, but let it fall again. A full minute after his chest had stopped heaving, he lifted his arm, threw it down "with an orgastic sound," and closed his own eyes.

Philomene Long was not a part of the kitchen-table summit which convened hastily the next day to decide what to do with Perkoff's manuscripts. Suzan, Baza, Tony Scibella, Paul Vangelisti, and Stuart's mother were agreed on one thing: no more of his work should be allowed to "just go" the way so much of it already had. The novel he had started in Mexico had vanished when someone had "borrowed" it to read on a long road trip. The *Venice Poems* and *Round About Midnite*, Stuart's play for voices, were also missing, and would not be seen again until 1986. Perkoff and Vangelisti had already selected the poems for their anthology, but there were forty-odd journals and hundreds of scraps of paper to be dealt with. Money was not the issue; it was only a question of who could be relied on to do what.

Suzan wanted Tony Scibella to serve as Stuart's literary executor, since no one knew his work more intimately or understood it better. Perkoff's parents had their doubts about Scibella, however, and Vangelisti feared that some new arrangement might scuttle the plans he had made with the poet himself. There was also the matter of belief. Tony shared Stuart's faith in the Muse and the "magic"; Vangelisti despised all the shamanistic mumbo-jumbo and hoped to begin freeing Perkoff's art from its association with "the already worm-eaten corpse of Venice West." Too much of the man's talent, he would later write, had already been "sacrificed to fantasy."

So there would be two posthumous volumes. Vangelisti's collection, *Love Is the Silence*, would be the definitive Stuart Perkoff reader, a "masterpiece" in the ancient and literal sense of offering proof of the full range of the guildsman's abilities. Tony Scibella, after taking a year to put Perkoff's journals in order, would publish *How It Is, Doing What I Do*. For him there was no fantasy to be regretted; Perkoff had taught him to regard poetry as a condition above life, a walking, shouting, unsparing state of grace, and to try to separate the man's art from his life was unthinkable. Most of Scibella's own poems from those days had disappeared, but he had a shrewd appreciation for what remained. "It's not the man u love," he wrote, "but what he sd & showed u.... history & responsibility: u will tell the others what u know. this then is partly how i say my debt. the rest is how i live it."

There had been, to be sure, only a single Stuart Perkoff. In setting out to pursue his craft, he had never had any intention of standing for anything other than himself—certainly not anyone else's idea of a literary generation. In spite of himself, he had managed to embody all three sides of the beat equation: the private reality, the public fantasy, and the intimation of something even larger on the other side of the veil. As hard as it was to separate these elements in the Beat Generation, it was harder still to tell them apart in Stuart Perkoff. Nor would anyone who wanted to try have gotten any help from the poet. He had always considered each aspect of himself to be as authentic as all the rest, never daring to tamper with any part for fear of marring the whole. If the price of keeping faith with one's whole self was a strong streak of self-delusion, so be it. If there were never any more than that to the legacy of Venice West, it would still, as far as Stuart Perkoff was concerned, have been a triumph.

The night after the kitchen conference, Rachel Perkoff received a frantic telephone call from Santa Cruz. She already knew her father was dead, but the news had left her numb. All she could feel was embarrassment at feeling nothing. She was sixteen years old and she wanted her mother, but at the moment, her mother had far more need of her.

Philomene Long had driven Suzan Perkoff as far as Santa Cruz, where some friends of the Perkoffs lived. Once there, Suzan had "flipped out" again—absolutely, instantaneously, and with no warning at all. It was more than her friends could handle, and they wanted Rachel to come and get her immediately, which she somehow managed to do.

Suzan rode home alone in the back seat, chattering, laughing, and chanting little spells to herself. For the first time in her life, she seemed a stranger to her daughter. She kept snarling and telling her to keep away. Rachel took her home but refused to stay in the house with her. She spent the next few nights at a friend's, and was planning on doing her regular volunteer work at the temple when another friend called to say that Suzan was on a rampage in the kitchen, smashing things to the floor and tramping around barefoot through the broken glass. Rachel rushed home to find her mother tracking blood up and down the street, shouting quotations from the prophet Isaiah.

She called her uncle Si, who told her to "get the hell out of there" while he dashed out to start the car. After he and Sarah arrived, the three of them persuaded Suzan to go to the hospital. When Rachel returned the next day to fill out the usual stack of forms, she could hear her mother's screaming through all the layers of glass, steel, and drugs until her "lifelong enemies, the doctors," pounded her mind flat with lithium and achieved a kind of peace.

As Stuart Perkoff lay dying, in April 1974, Peter Orlovsky traveled to New York City to accept the National Book Award for Poetry in behalf of his companion of nearly twenty years, Allen Ginsberg. Ginsberg's acceptance address, which Orlovsky delivered for him in ceremonies at Lincoln Center, seemed political in nature—full of Watergate-era righteousness and blasts against the American "police state." His fellow writers had voted him the award, after all, for a book of poems called *The Fall of America*. The poet's advice to those who found post-Vietnam America intolerable was not to organize and smash the state, but to return to being solitary guerrillas of consciousness. In the hour of the Beat Generation's closest brush with respectability, Ginsberg came full circle back to the theme that had always been its essence: the absolute independence of the individual mind.

> There is no longer any hope for the Salvation of America proclaimed by Jack Kerouac and others of our Beat Generation, aware and howling, weeping and singing Kaddish for the nation decades ago, "rejected yet confessing out the soul." All we have to work from now is the vast empty quiet space of our own Consciousness. AH! AH! AH!

Lawrence Lipton survived Stuart Perkoff by slightly more than a year. Diabetic, hypertensive, and atherosclerotic, he had never recovered fully from the beating he had suffered in Chicago. He walked with difficulty, had undergone several painful courses of surgery, and owed his doctors far more than he could pay. His answer was to keep on inventing new projects for himself. His responsibilities at the *Free Press* had grown to include the editorship of what amounted to a newspaper within a newspaper, the Living Arts Supplement—far and away the *Freep's* best feature, but far more than a fragile seventy-six-year-old could continue to handle. Lipton got a lot of minimum-wage clerical support from John Thomas, who was also trying to help him make a readable autobiography out of a long, impassioned, and unmanageable narrative he had been working on for years. It was not enough, and his tenure at the *Freep* was just about over. Since 1971 his regular column had been moved to the paper's back pages—not because it was unpopular but because the editors could never be sure when, or if, the copy would arrive. In 1972, he gave up on the column entirely.

Incredibly, he then proposed to start his own nationally distributed newsletter, and he actually went so far as to write the old dean of independent muckrackers, I. F. Stone, for advice. He could never have brought it off. He still wrote poems and submitted them to publishers, but the more projects he planned for himself, the less work he was actually able to do.

He was poor as well. Instead of writing another trendy "youth book," he had spent the last decade soldiering on with the *Free Press*. Now, at seventy-six, he was forced to apply for a grant from the Carnegie Fund for Authors. He and his wife needed $10,000 in order to keep their home. They had looked at apartments, but without a garage to house his books, papers, and tapes, he would not have been able to keep working. Nettie Lipton earned $600 a month from her job at UCLA; Larry received only his Social Security checks. They owed $27,175 on their house, drove an eight-year-old Chevrolet worth $500, and were nearly $4,000 behind in their payments to only one of Larry's many doctors.

Where the application called for a list of his published works, he cited only the ones that had appeared under his own name since 1942—in other words, the ones written by the "real" Larry Lipton. The Fund was not snobbish; all its directors wanted was proof that he had actually made his living through writing. Lipton was not quite broke enough to list the movie scripts and potboilers that had once made him wealthy. He might have beaten the subject of dedicated poverty half to death, but he had meant every word he said.

On the other hand, his fellow Southern California writers still thought of him as a huckster. Although places were being found in the cultural firmament for some of the poets he had encouraged, none would be offered to him. While he and his wife lived within walking distance of Beyond Baroque, the literary foundation housed in the old Venice City Hall, they never attended its weekly poetry readings, even when John Thomas and Frankie Rios read there.

When Larry Lipton died in July 1975, the *Freep* ran a eulogy which included a poem by Fay Irving, whose husband Clifford had recently gone to prison for tricking a major New York publisher into buying a fraudulent biography of Howard Hughes. The Irvings had moved into 20 Park Avenue after the Liptons had moved out, hoping, as Fay had told Larry, that "something of the Beat way in living and writing might rub off on Cliff." The commercial impulse had won out in the young novelist, as it had, in quite another way, in Lawrence Lipton himself.

No one had done more than Lipton to turn an obscure and sincere doctrine of poverty and art into a recognized alternative to conventional life. On the other hand, he had promoted that way of life like any other consumer product, and his enduring gifts to the movement, and to those which had subsequently sprung from it, were oversimplification, a nearly incestuous relationship with the commercial media, and, most of all, the hard sell. He had made it seem possible to escape the grip of Moloch simply by deciding to turn in another direction, but it remained to be seen whether he had not merely offered the youth of the middle class a temporary way of pretending they were somebody else. If it had all happened before he arrived on the scene, it is easy to imagine him condemning his own movement on the very grounds of its marketability.

After he died, Nettie Lipton had no trouble selling the house on Burrell Street; it was near the Marina, after all. She moved first to Sherman Oaks, then to Santa Barbara, where Kenneth Rexroth had settled. A decade later, after Rexroth's death, she returned to the San Fernando Valley, where she engaged Jacob Zeitlin, the distinguished book dealer, to sell Lipton's uncatalogued papers and her own collection of limited-run books for enough money to establish an endowment for young poets. Shortly after she died, in 1986, the collection and the papers were purchased by the University of Southern California. Distribution of the proceeds was left to the executor of her estate. Nettie would have preferred that they go to a young poet living in Venice, but life was becoming so expensive near the water that it may have been hard to find anyone poor enough to qualify.

There was still one way to live cheaply near the water, and that was not to have a home at all. Even before the really massive influx of homeless people into Venice, dozens of people bedded down outdoors every night, and among them was Milton Bratton. Milton had first come to Venice in the very early fifties, and the rent inflation that had driven others away had merely driven him outdoors. He lived on the vacant lot at the corner of Ocean Front Walk and Sunset Avenue, hobbling out every day to sit in the shade of the Sunset Pavilion and discuss books, music, art, and all the other things he knew well. Crippled by a fall from a third-storey window, Bratton usually planted himself in one place for the whole day, leaning on his elegant eagle-headed cane and adjusting the angle of his broad-brimmed straw hat as the sun progressed across the sky. A lean, dignified black man, he stuttered so badly that it took some practice to understand him, although those who made the effort usually considered it well spent.

Bratton had never been an artist himself, but he knew a great deal about all the arts. He had spent his life reading and memorizing things, and his record collection, when he still had a place to keep it, had been the best on the beach—78s, 33s, old jazz, new jazz, thirties titles, blues. All of the Venice West originals had met in his living room, and his ex-wife, Bunny, had been the first to take an interest in Charlie Foster. Bratton had tried living in other places, but he had always come back to Venice.

July was not an especially cruel month for sleeping outdoors, but when a friend offered to let Bratton sleep in his van, Milton accepted gratefully. What his friend neglected to say was that he had just burned someone in a drug deal, and the cheated party wanted revenge. Not necessarily deadly revenge, but revenge enough to make a point; the man had no idea Milton Bratton was in the van when he set fire to it.

The following Sunday, 19 July 1987, Bratton's friends held an impromptu memorial at the corner of Sunset and the Ocean Front, on the sand lot where he had slept at night. It was two blocks south of the gallery that now occupied the site of the Venice West Café, and nine blocks north of the rusted Abbott Kinney-era pillar that still marked the site of the Gas House. By right of salvage, the pillar now served as a display rack for sunglasses, nose masks, plastic ninja weapons, and weird, flowing, brightly colored sand pictures.

John Thomas and Philomene Long, who were now married to each other, missed the ceremony—probably because it *was* a ceremony, and Thomas had never had much patience with the freewheeling spiritual intensity of Venice West. But the emphasis was not on "ceremony" at all. Tony Scibella was there with both of his wives; Bob Alexander, just out of chemotherapy and watched over zealously by his wife Anita, presided. Representing her mother, her brothers, her father, and herself was Rachel Perkoff, an actress and a UCLA graduate, now the manager of a firm which packaged rock music programs for satellite transmission around the world.

It was not intended to be a wake for the old days, nor did it become one. It was a ritual of respect for the elements that had briefly turned Venice, California, into Venice West: the sun, the water, the empty ground, the battered, preposterous architecture, the people who had known and celebrated each other completely. Around them, the Sunday crowd celebrated itself— street performers, street crazies, spiritual healers, drug dealers, gang members, bodybuilders, near-naked women, small children, Afghan hounds, chain-saw jugglers, and tourists with expensive cameras, all dodging skaters on neoprene wheels, all accepting each other as completely ordinary, all conspiring to keep the fantasy going.

As Stuart Perkoff had written in his final poem about Moses, the story had refused to end on cue. He was thinking, of course, about the Children of Israel, but he might as well have included everyone who defied the dominant version of reality and made their defiance stick. "They might," he wrote, "perhaps they shd, have quietly disappeared into the history of the land, as so many had, but they didn't. As it turned out, others besides themselves considered the same things important (for very different reasons), & so, here we still are."

"Well, *that's* not finished," Stuart Perkoff had scribbled in his journal underneath the poem. "Not sure it's even finishable. We'll see."

NOTES ON SOURCES

INTRODUCTION

Tony Scibella, whom I interviewed in his home in Van Nuys, California, on 9 June 1987, described the powerful "drive for nonrecognition" among Venice poets and artists, as well as his own dread, as a young man, of a life based on "the lunch box forever."

The term "poetry-spouting" is quoted, in this instance, from an unsigned *Newsweek* article, "California: Heat on the Beatniks" (16 August 1959, 32); references to "beatniks" in the popular press almost always included some allusion to poetry, as if that association alone were enough to establish them as hopelessly eccentric.

Paul O'Neil's "Life Among the Beatniks" (*Reader's Digest*, April 1960, 64–68; the illustration appeared on 64, "What have we done to deserve this?" on 68) was a "condensed" version of O'Neill's longer piece for *Life*, "The Only Rebellion Around" (subtitled "But the Shabby Beats Bungle the Job in Arguing, Sulking and Bad Poetry," 30 November 1959, 115–131). Francis J. Rigney and L. Douglas Smith describe the police crackdown on North Beach in their psychological study of the San Francisco Beat community, *The Real Bohemia* (New York: Basic Books, 1961, 160–161).

Allen J. Matusow characterizes the beat subculture in *The Unravelling of America: A History of Liberalism in the 1960s* (San Francisco: Harper & Row, 1984, 287–307; the long quote is from 287). William O'Neill's even briefer treatment of the beats is found on page 234 of his *Coming Apart: An Informal History of America in the Sixties* (Chicago: Quadrangle Books, 1971).

Douglas T. Miller and Marion Nowak devote far more attention to the beats in *The Fifties: The Way We Really Were* (Garden City, N.Y.: Doubleday, 1977). Direct references in the text are as follows:

"McCarthyist" tactics, 385; "bland journalese," 391; Mills, Hughes, Goodman, 398; attitude of U.S. intellectuals toward their own status in American culture, 220–247, esp. 242. Bernard Iddings Bell ("slavery to crowd culture," etc.) is quoted on 229. Theodore Roszak dismisses the beats rather quickly, on essentially political grounds, in *The Making of a Counterculture: Reflections on the Technocratic Society and Its Youthful Opposition* (Garden City, N.Y.: Doubleday, 1969).

Jack Kerouac included his "A" from Mark Van Doren among the vital personal details listed at the start of his memoir, *Lonesome Traveler* (New York: Grove Press, 1960; Black Cat edition, 1971, vi). Allen Ginsberg's counterattack on Ciardi, Dickey, and Hollander is quoted in Dennis McNally's *Desolate Angel: Jack Kerouac, The Beat Generation, and America* (New York: Random House, 1979, 241); Paul Vangelisti's low opinion of "Venice West," as opposed to his admiration for the best of its poetry, can be found in his introduction to Stuart Z. Perkoff's *Love Is the Silence: Poems 1948–1972* (Los Angeles and Fairfax: The Red Hill Press, 1975, unpaged).

The continuing search for communist teachers in Southern California schools was reported in a newscast which also included coverage of the Gas House case (KRCA-TV, Los Angeles affiliate of NBC, 23 September 1959, Tape #116, Lawrence Lipton Collection, USC). Southern California growth statistics are taken from Howard J. Nelson's *The Los Angeles Metropolis* (Dubuque: Kendall/Hunt Publishing Company, 1983, 186, 187, 240).

I have relied on the following biographies of Jack Kerouac: Ann Charters, *Kerouac: A Biography* (New York: Straight Arrow Press; rev. ed., Warner Books, 1974); Barry Gifford and Lawrence Lee, *Jack's Book: An Oral Biography of Jack Kerouac* (New York: St. Martin's Press, 1978; Penguin Books, 1979); Dennis McNally's *Desolate Angel*, already cited above; and Gerald Nicosia's *Memory Babe: A Critical Biography of Jack Kerouac* (New York: Grove Press, 1983).

As noted in the text, my sources for pre–World War I Greenwich Village are Robert E. Humphrey, *Children of Fantasy: The First Rebels of Greenwich Village* (New York: John Wiley, 1978; "materialism and respectability," 7; "excessively eccentric or uncouth," 8) and Arthur Frank Wertheim, *The New York Little Renaissance: Iconoclasm, Modernism, and Nationalism in American Culture, 1908–1917* (New York: New York University Press, 1976, "helped change the entire course . . . ," 246). John Wilcock, the *Village Voice* columnist, informed the world of the existence of Rosalind Constable in "The Village Square: The Whither Eyes of *Time* Magazine" (11 January 1962, 3).

Specific citations from Rigney and Smith's *The Real Bohemia* are as follows: "but only in their own way," 180–181; "psychic and physical distress," 180; "self-acceptance," 181; "encumbrance . . . enduringly human," 73; "minority phenomenon," 60; identification of alcohol as the most destructive drug among the beats, 180; "shabby to sloppy," 236; socioeconomic origins, 20–21; "intensity—real or fancied," 181–182; "hiding their own such impulses," ibid.; "not synonymous with health," 182.

CHAPTER ONE

"Mulled Murder, With Spice" was the cover article for the 28 January 1946 issue of *Time* (88–90). Lipton later confided to a friend (Lipton to Jack Lewis, 15 June 1953, Lawrence Lipton Collection, UCLA) that his wife had already relapsed into alcoholism by the time of the interview, largely as a result of the pressure put on both of them to keep producing books on schedule.

All of Lipton's letters to Rexroth from 1952 through 1958 are held in the Lawrence Lipton Collection, UCLA. Lipton recalled his bohemian past in detail in Lipton to Rexroth, 15 June 1953; a copy of the "Escalator Manifesto" is included in Lipton to Rexroth, 31 January 1953. Further details of his background are given in *The Beatniks*, a CBS Radio program aired late in the summer of 1959 (Tapes #452 and #453, Lawrence Lipton Collection, USC), in other letters to Rexroth, and in the author's interview with John Thomas and Philomene Long, 24 June 1987 (John Thomas supplied the anecdote about Frank Harris, which was told to him by Lipton himself). Lipton's lament about "looking like everything I was not" is included in Lipton to Rexroth, 26 January 1953.

Both ends of Lipton's correspondence with James T. Farrell and James Henle are held in the Lipton Collection, UCLA; his letters to and from Ken McCormack are to be found in the same collection, while the newspaper ad that led to their meeting is preserved in the Lawrence Lipton Collection, USC, along with notes of their meeting on 25 November 1940. Lipton's correspondence with Lee Wright is housed in the Lipton Collection, UCLA, and includes Wright's prematurely encouraging letters of December 1940.

Aswell and Lipton corresponded with each other, sometimes on a daily basis, from January through June 1942 (Lipton Collection, UCLA). Aswell explained what Lipton must do to purge his book of libel in Aswell to Lipton, 6 January 1942, and informed him of the decision of the company's lawyers in Aswell to Lipton, 20 February 1942.

All of the correspondence concerning the *Brother* controversy is now held in the Lipton Collection, UCLA. Sydney B. Lavine's letter to Harper's was quoted by Aswell to Lipton on 29 May 1942; Lipton replied to Lavine eight days later. Nathan Rothman wrote his letter of support to Lipton on 24 June 1942, while Sinclair Lewis wrote his gentle reprimand on 11 July. The Lipton Collection also preserves letters from Feuchtwanger, Mann, Brickner, and others named in the text. Lipton's letters to the publisher of *In Secret Battle*, Appleton-Century (Lipton to Schaefer, May through November 1944, Lawrence Lipton Collection, UCLA) deal almost entirely with his inability to meet his deadlines, and his willingness to cut artistic corners for the sake of seeing the book in print.

My abbreviated account of the founding and early history of Venice is drawn primarily from Tom Moran and Tom Sewell's *Fantasy by the Sea: A Visual History of the American Venice* (Venice: Beyond Baroque Foundation, 1979), but the main points are echoed by so many popular sources (textbooks, tourist brochures, etc.) as to be considered common knowledge in Los Angeles. The more personal-sounding descriptions are drawn from my own family history (both of my parents lived in Venice in the early 1920s), from impressions formed while researching this book in 1986 and 1987, and from my experiences as a twelve-year-old on the Venice boardwalk after dark in 1959.

Lipton's renewed correspondence with Craig Rice began in January 1951 (Lawrence Lipton Collection, UCLA) and ended in June 1952. During this time Lipton's confidante was Jack Lewis, who also lent Rice money and persuaded her to sign the television deal.

CHAPTER TWO

Lawrence Lipton corresponded with Lucy Kroll from November 1952 through December 1953, and with Selden Rodman in January and February 1953 (both sets of letters are contained in the Lawrence Lipton Collection, UCLA). Rodman's blunt "you-asked-for-it" letter was written on 29 January.

My source for the details of Dylan Thomas's life (including his belief that becoming a screenwriter would free him to write poetry) is Paul Ferris, *Dylan Thomas* (New York: Penguin Books, 1978), supplemented by my own inquiries while a guest of the people of Laugharne, Carmarthenshire, South Wales, in May 1971. Lipton's elegy for Thomas, "Death of a Poet," is included in his posthumous *Bruno in Venice West and Other Poems* (Van Nuys, Calif.: Venice West Publishers, 1976, 14), while the passages I have quoted from Rexroth's *Thou Shalt Not Kill: A Lament for Dylan Thomas* are from a very early mimeographed edition (Sunnyvale, Calif.: H. Schwartz, 1955).

Page references for the passages quoted from Lipton's *Rainbow at Midnight* (New York: Golden Quill Press) are as follows: ". . . world's remembrancer," 74; "Good omen . . . ," 50; "new hierogamy," 73. Parts of this long poem were published as "Excerpts from *Rainbow at Midnight*" in *California Quarterly* (Spring 1953, 16–42).

The Lipton-Rexroth correspondence, which underpins the bulk of this chapter, is preserved in the Lawrence Lipton Collection, UCLA, and includes letters from late 1952 through 1958. The most important letters, from an expository point of view, were exchanged from December 1952 to July 1953 (especially Lipton to Rexroth, 23, 25, and 31 January 1953; Rexroth to Lipton, 1, 6, and 15 February 1953; and Rexroth to Lipton, 3 July 1953, in which the author describes his working life, his politics, and his attitudes toward literature). Dennis McNally's reference to Rexroth's "shit list" is drawn from his biography of Jack Kerouac, *Desolate Angel* (New York: Random House, 1979, 205). Lipton expounded his concept of "dedicated poverty" in letters to Rexroth dated 4 February and 17 April 1953; Rexroth tried to explain what *he* meant by the term in Rexroth to Lipton, 22 April 1953.

The figure of forty dollars a month for a storefront apartment was provided by Tony Scibella in our interview of 9 June 1987; Scibella grew up in and around Venice. Scibella also describes the theory and practice of "just blowing" (with anecdotes about himself, Saul White, and Stuart Perkoff) in his interview with John Macker ("Conversation with Tony Scibella," *Moravagine 3*, Denver: Long Road Press, 1986, 19–29). Stuart Perkoff's unpublished poem, "Bird: an elegy for Charlie Parker," written in 1955 or 1956, is included in the Lawrence Lipton Collection, UCLA. James Boyer May recalled his conversation with Lipton about Curtis Zahn ("I don't know what to make of him") on *The Beatniks*, a CBS Radio broadcast aired in the summer of 1959 (Tapes #452 and #453, Lawrence Lipton Collection, USC).

Lipton's published articles on "dedicated poverty" and related themes include "Secession: 1953 (The State of the Arts on the West Coast)," *Intro* 2, no. 2, 1953, 32; "Disaffiliation and the Art of Poverty," *Chicago Review*, Spring 1956; "America's Literary Underground," *Coastlines* #6, Winter 1956; and "Youth Will Serve Itself," *The Nation*, 10 November 1956, 389–392. Rexroth urged Lipton to ease off a bit on his rhetoric in a letter dated 1 December 1953.

Rexroth's poem on Thomas is contained in *Thou Shalt Not Kill: A Memorial for Dylan Thomas* (Sunnyvale, Calif.: H. Schwartz, 1955).

My sources for the Six Gallery reading are Ann Charters, *Kerouac: A Biography*; Barry Gifford and Lawrence Lee, *Jack's Book: An Oral Biography of Jack Kerouac*; Dennis McNally, *Desolate Angel*; Gerald Nicosia, *Memory Babe: A Critical Biography of Jack Kerouac*; and Jack Kerouac, *The Dharma Bums* (New York: The Viking Press, 1958; Signet Books, 1959). The passages from "Howl" are drawn from Ginsberg's *Howl and Other Poems* (San Francisco: City Lights Books, 1956). Lipton wrote his unsent letters about the San Francisco poetry phenomenon on 7 May and 5 June 1956; both are preserved, along with the usual carbon copies, in the Lawrence Lipton Collection, UCLA.

I have reconstructed Ginsberg's "naked reading" from several sources: Lipton's highly partisan version in *The Holy Barbarians* (New York: Julian Messner, 1959, 194–199); Gene Frumkin's equally partisan, but less impassioned account in his article, "The Great Promoter: A Hangnail Sketch of Lawrence Lipton" (*Coastlines #15*, Autumn 1959, 4–6); and Anaïs Nin's diary (*The Diary of Anaïs Nin: 1955–1966*, New York and London: Harcourt Brace Jovanovich, 1966, 1976, 63–65), which also contains Ginsberg's letter inviting Nin to round up assorted celebrities for his reading. As for Ginsberg's fondness for taking off his clothes, Kerouac's novel *Desolation Angels* (New York: Coward-McCann, Inc., 1965; Bantam edition, 1966, 1971) includes a complaint from a character generally understood to be Corso about "having to look at naked men" every time the Ginsberg character happens on the scene (239).

Of the many versions of Perkoff's poem "the barbarian from the north," I have used the unpublished text found in his unnumbered diary (see notes to Chapter 3), apparently written in November 1956.

CHAPTER THREE

It was John Thomas who first pointed out to me that Stuart Perkoff "thought of himself as Moses" (author's interview with John Thomas and Philomene Long, 24 June 1987, Los Angeles), but references to Moses recur throughout Perkoff's poems and journals. The rabbinical story cited here was recalled by Perkoff in a footnote to his poem, "On Sinai" (unpublished, probably 1958, Lawrence Lipton Collection, UCLA). The version of "Feasts of Love, Feasts of Death" used here is the one published in the posthumous volume, *Love Is the Silence: Poems 1948–1972* (Los Angeles and Fairfax: The Red Hill Press, 1975, unpaged), edited by Paul Vangelisti.

Most of the account of Stuart's life through the early fifties is based on the author's interviews with Suzan Perkoff (28 June 1987) and Tony Scibella (9 June 1987; it was Scibella, in this conversation, who admitted that "you could easily hate the dude"), with additional details drawn from John Macker's "Interview with Tony Scibella" (*Moravagine #3*, Denver: Long Road Press, 1986, 19–29), and from Perkoff's own work (especially *The Venice Poems*, unpublished, 1958, Lawrence Lipton Collection, UCLA).

To trace the development of Stuart's attitudes toward both his family and his art, I have relied heavily on what appears to be the only one of his journals which is not a part of the Stuart Z. Perkoff Collection, and which is therefore not identified by a number. Filed among other "works by young authors" in the Lawrence Lipton Collection at UCLA, this diary covers the years 1956 and 1957, and includes the following passages quoted in the text: "responsibilities . . . that spring from love"; "send thoughts thru germinations . . . on stretched skin & chewed out hollowed wood"; "Now I see that the art & craft of poetry . . . "; "carriers of the blood . . ."; and the "Anniversary Poem for Suzan" which includes the lines, "I'm tired of poverty," etc., as well as working drafts of a number of poems, including "The Barbarian from the North." Stuart's observations about the limited effects of marijuana are to be found in the Journal of Stuart Perkoff #6 (August 1956), while his mother's objection to his use of pot is recorded in his Journal #22 (December 1956).

My depiction of Lawrence Lipton's literary salon is derived from Lipton's own descriptions in *The Holy Barbarians* (especially 18–25), from Stuart Perkoff's unnumbered journal, from my interviews with Suzan Perkoff and Tony Scibella, and from my conversation with Nettie Lipton in March 1986. Anaïs Nin's impressions are recorded in her diary (*The Diary of Anaïs Nin*, Vol. 6, 119–120). The Foster quotation ("a matchbox . . .") is from his untitled story of November 1957, Lawrence Lipton Collection, UCLA.

The long account of Suzan Perkoff's madness is based primarily on the interview we conducted over the telephone in June 1987, with support from Lipton's account of the events in *The Holy Barbarians* (pp. 80–81) and Stuart's version in *The Venice Poems* (1958, with drafts dated October 1956). Stuart's poem is a record of his own emotions during Suzan's ordeal, while Lipton's, though compassionate, is also rather self-serving. Except for those specifically attributed to other sources in the text itself, all direct quotations from Suzan Perkoff are derived from our long-distance interview. I was later allowed to read the diary she had kept at Camarillo, but since it contained no information not available from other sources, I have not quoted from it in this chapter.

Larry Lipton and Kenneth Rexroth continued to write each other on a regular basis through around 1958, and I have drawn on their correspondence from October through December 1957 for the background of the West Coast Poetry and Jazz Festival. The *Los Angeles Times* covered that event ("Jazz Hall Reopens Tonight," 3 December 1957, Part I, 224; George Wall, "Poor Staging Dampers Poetry, Jazz Festival," 6 December 1957, Part IV, 11), and Suzan Perkoff told me about the argument she and Stuart had about his participation. The Rexroth-Lipton "debate," which was aired as a segment of CBS

Radio's "Sunday Desk" on 15 September 1957, is preserved on Tape #166, Lawrence Lipton Collection, USC. Rexroth's affair with Susan Weire was related to me by Suzan Perkoff, and is confirmed by a letter from Rexroth to Lipton (26 December 1957), in which he expresses his almost horrified willingness to move to Southern California to be near her.

Principal sources for the account of the founding of the Venice West Café were the author's interviews with Suzan Perkoff and Tony Scibella (both conducted in June 1987), supported by photographs published in Lipton's *The Holy Barbarians*.

CHAPTER FOUR

This chapter's opening line is from F. Scott Fitzgerald's story, "The Rich Boy" (*The Stories of F. Scott Fitzgerald*, ed. Malcolm Cowley, New York: Charles Scribner's Sons, 1951, 177).

Lawrence Lipton's character "Chuck Bennison," who appears throughout *The Holy Barbarians* and is characterized at length on pp. 44–48, is obviously Charles Foster, and judging from Foster's own writings about himself, Lipton hardly found it necessary to "fictionalize" him. Two lengthy autobiographical stories by Foster—one written in semi-diaristic style in November 1957, and the other in more or less conventional narrative fashion, probably in 1959—were preserved by Lipton and presented to UCLA as part of the Lawrence Lipton Collection. I have relied heavily on these stories for the details of Foster's life and beliefs, cross-referencing them, where possible, with Lipton's portrayal, with the recollections of Tony Scibella, John Thomas, and Suzan Perkoff, and with editor Charles Potts's "Extroduction" to Foster's *Peyote Toad* (Salt Lake City: Litmus, "distributed by the Cosmic Aeroplane," 1975).

Apart from such outright fantasies as "The Troubled Makers" (*Evergreen Review* 1, no. 4, 1957, 9–28), Foster's writing is almost always confessional, both in nature and in form. This is especially true of such unpublished poems as "Bill of Divestment," dated 20 March 1957; "Riffs on Palm Trees, In So Far . . . No. 1," probably written in 1957; and "A WALK/ THRU PSYCHOSIS/ A TALK/ WITH GOD," which, according to Lipton, absorbed vast amounts of Foster's limited energy throughout 1958, but was never completed. While I am aware of the dangers of accepting any writer's self-revelations at anything approaching face value, no one has ever accused Foster of being the least bit kind to himself.

The fabrication of the "fifth volume" of Frank Harris's memoirs is described by Maurice Girodias himself in the paperback edition of that profitable work (*The Fifth Volume of Frank Harris' "My Life and Loves:" An Irreverent Treatment*, Paris: The Olympia Press, 1958,

1959; paperback edition, Olympia Press Companion Series #108, with Foreword by Maurice Girodias, 1966). *Young Adam*, Alexander Trocchi's first novel, is included in an anthology, *The Outsiders* (New York: Grove Press, 1960). I have drawn additional insights from his book of poems, *Man at Leisure* (London: Calder & Boyars, Ltd., 1972), and one of his better known pornographic titles, *White Thighs* (North Hollywood, Calif.: Greenleaf Classics, 1964). But *Cain's Book* (New York: Grove Press, 1959; Grove Press Outrider (paperback) edition, 1979; introduction to the latter copyright 1979 by Richard W. Seaver) remains, in Sir Walter Raleigh's words, Trocchi's "paternoster and his creed," and I have quoted several long passages from it because I doubt that anyone could have improved on them. Page references for direct quotes from *Cain's Book* are as follows: "... and, above all, *inviolable*" (10–11); "... chemistry of alienation" (33–34); " ... it is the pale rider" (76); "... one simply is" (11); "... *that these laws be changed*" (40–41). William Burroughs's observation that "NOTHING ever happens in the junk world" is taken from his essay, "Deposition: Testimony Concerning a Sickness" (introduction to his novel *Naked Lunch*, New York: Grove Press, 1962; Black Cat edition, 1966, xlv).

Of the Venice West participants I succeeded in interviewing, only Tony Scibella and Suzan Perkoff had any direct recollections of Trocchi; the former said he had been given his first fix by Trocchi in New York City, while the latter maintained that even though Trocchi had not given her husband his first shot of heroin, he had "turned him on intellectually." I was not able to discover the real identity of "Lyn." Charles Foster refers to her (by her first name only) in his untitled diaristic story of November 1957, and Trocchi dedicated *Cain's Book* to her without revealing her last name. Lawrence Lipton (*The Holy Barbarians*, 98–99) referred to her as "Diana Wakefield, Handmaiden of the Muse" (his name for Trocchi is "Tom Draegen"). The plan to leave Venice and have Lyn turn tricks in Las Vegas is mentioned in *The Holy Barbarians* (135) and confirmed by Tony Scibella, Nettie Lipton (in conversation, 19 March 1986), and Christopher Isherwood, whose friendship with Trocchi is documented in the transcript of the former's conversation with one of Lipton's young literary protégés, Kent Chapman (1959, Lawrence Lipton Collection, UCLA). At some time during his stay in Venice, Trocchi gave the older novelist a chair designed to ease the strain on his back while writing.

Although Charles Foster includes "Alex" among the people he wishes to "love like a brother" in his diaristic story of November 1957, he seems to have been less than awed by him as a literary figure.

My description of the Venice West Café, as indicated in the text, is drawn from the photo essay in the U.S. edition of *The Holy Barbarians* (unnumbered, between 304 and 305) and the German translation

(*Die Heiligen Barbaren*, trans. Helmut Degner [Dusseldorf, Federal Republic of Germany: Karl Rauch Verlag, 1960], two photographs opposite 176). The jazz artists are named on page 314 of the American edition; Jerome Lindsay is listed as playing trumpet, but does not appear in any of the pictures. Tony Scibella also described the café in our interview of 9 June 1987.

Stuart Perkoff's business failure, his break-up with his wife, his creative friendship with Tony Scibella and Frank Rios, and his growing addiction to opiates are described in the author's interviews with Tony Scibella (9 June 1987) and Suzan Perkoff (28 June 1987), John Macker's interview with Scibella, and a number of entries, most of them undated, in the Journals of Stuart Z. Perkoff #4, #5, and #23 (1959). My sources for the properties of Tussar and its active ingredient, hydrocodone bitartrate, are the 1959 (#13, 625, and 929–933) and 1983 (#37, 597–598) editions of the *Physicans Desk Reference* (Oradell, N.J.: Medical Economics Co.). As noted in the text, the information contained in the *PDR*, which serves as the standard reference work for the pharmaceutical industry, is provided by the manufacturers themselves.

CHAPTER FIVE

Caroline Freud's article on Lawrence Lipton, "Portrait of the Beatnik," appeared in the June 1959 issue of *Encounter*, 42–46. Lipton expressed his belief that she had been "out to do a hatchet job" to Professors Robert Kaplan and James Durban, of the University of Southern California's department of English, who interviewed him at his home on 23 January 1962 (American Literature Collection, Department of Special Collections, Doheny Memorial Library, USC).

Lipton was quoted as saying that the beats were "the conscience of the world" in *The Saturday Review of Literature*, 4 July 1959, 6. Among the reviews of *The Holy Barbarians* Lipton himself clipped for his files were Robert R. Kirsch, "Beat Generation's Voice Cries Out" (*Los Angeles Times*, 24 May 1959, clipping preserved in the Lawrence Lipton Collection, UCLA); Robert H. Glauber, "Who, What, and Why Are the Beatniks?" (*The New York Herald Tribune*, Sunday Book Review Section, 2 May 1959, clipping preserved in the Lawrence Lipton Collection, UCLA); William Leonard, "The Beatniks' Boredom with a Messed-up World" (*Chicago Sunday Tribune*, 7 June 1959, clipping preserved in the Lawrence Lipton Collection, UCLA); "Mentholated Eggnog" (*Time*, 1 June 1959, 88); Earl Lewis, "A Prophet of 'Beats' Explains His Flock" (*People's World*, 11 July 1959, 7).

Attacks on the Beat Generation, and on Lipton personally, included Norman Podhoretz's essay, "The Know-Nothing Bohemians," (*Parti-*

san Review, Spring 1958, 305–318); Kenneth Rexroth's comments in *Bird in the Bush: Obvious Essays* (New York: New Directions, 1959, ix); Curtis Zahn's letter to the editor of *Liberation* (9 June 1959, 10); Mel Weisburd's "Editorial: The Merchant of Venice" (*Coastlines #7*, Autumn 1959, 39–40); and Gene Frumkin's "The Great Promoter: A Hangnail Sketch of Lawrence Lipton" (*Coastlines #15*, Autumn 1959, 3–10). James Boyer May recalled Lipton's earlier dismay at Zahn's dress and demeanor in "The Beatniks" (CBS Radio broadcast, 1959, Tapes #452 and #453, Lawrence Lipton Collection, USC). Despite Lipton's strained relations with *Coastlines*, that journal continued to include "Venice West" in its coverage of the Los Angeles literary scene (e.g., "Blunderbuss: . . . From Venice West," *Coastlines*, Autumn 1958; Lipton is cited as the source of the information in this unsigned article).

Anti-Lipton feeling in Venice West was described for me by Suzan Perkoff (28 June 1987), Tony Scibella (9 June 1987) and John Thomas (17 June 1987). Stuart Perkoff suggested the title *Holy Horseshit* in the Journal of Stuart Z. Perkoff #5, Summer 1959, and described his break-up with his wife Suzan in a taped conversation with Lawrence Lipton (American Literature Tape #T66, Department of Special Collections, Doheny Memorial Library, USC; though catalogued as having been recorded in 1963, internal evidence and cross-references with Perkoff's journals makes it clear that the conversation took place in 1959) and in his Journal #12, Spring and Summer 1959, especially entry of 21 May. A copy of his rhyming "curse" was shown to me in San Francisco on 1 November 1987 by Suzan Perkoff, who added that she had shouted after him, "Besides, you didn't get 'em all!" Consistent references to Susan Berman in this time frame appear in the Journals of Stuart Z. Perkoff #4, #5, and #1. "The Magic Summer" is Tony Scibella's phrase.

Scibella describes the tourist invasion of 1959 in interviews with me and with John Macker ("Interview with Tony Scibella," *Moravagine #3*, Denver: Long Road Press, 1986, 19–29). Scibella, Perkoff, and William J. Margolis also discussed the phenomenon in a KPFK-Radio broadcast (reprinted in an unsigned obituary article, "Larry Lipton [1889–1975]," *Los Angeles Free Press*, 1/7 August 1975, 11). John Thomas admits to having been glad to receive "two dollars to read a poem to my girl" (interview, 17 June 1987); his own journey from Baltimore to Venice, along with experiences once he got there and the origins of the Gas House, are described in our two interviews (17 and 24 June 1987) and in his short piece, "All the Ben Talbert I Know" (Thomas, *Epopoeia and the Decay of Satire*, Los Angeles and Fairfax: The Red Hill Press, 1976, unpaged).

In addition to John Thomas's and Tony Scibella's recollections, my sources for Eric Nord's career in San Francisco and Venice are James Schock's *Life Is a Lousy Drag* (San Francisco: Unicorn Publishing Co., 1958, 11); the anonymous *Beatnik Dictionary and Who's Who in Venice West* (Venice: Beat Scene Press), said to have been published (or, more precisely, mimeographed) by Bob and Anita Alexander; Rigney and Smith, *The Real Bohemia* (160); Nettie Lipton, in conversation, 19 March 1986; and an unsigned magazine feature, "The Bored, the Bearded and the Beat" (*Look*, 19 August 1958, 64–68). He is also pictured in Sewell and Moran, *Fantasy by the Sea* (87), and in Philomene Long's film, *The Beats: An Existential Comedy* (Venice of America Films, 1980).

My two sources for Lipton and Nord's acting stint in are KNX Radio motion picture editor Josephine Layton (speaking on *The Beatniks*, CBS Radio broadcast, Summer 1959), and Tony Scibella (interview, 9 June 1987), who insisted they had used his conga drum.

Lipton recorded this episode of *The Romance of Helen Trent*, a long-running CBS radio soap opera, on 4 September 1959 (Tape #116, Lawrence Lipton Collection, USC).

Sources for the Gas House hearing are as follows: Affadavit "before the Board of Police Commissioners, City of Los Angeles . . . in re: Application of Al Mathews for Cafe Entertainment Permit at 1501 Ocean Front Walk, d/b/a Gas House," 8 October 1959 (Lawrence Lipton Collection, USC); "California: Heat on the Beatniks," *Newsweek*, 17 August 1959, 17; "Gas House Hearing," news broadcast, KRCA-TV (Los Angeles Affiliate of NBC), 23 September 1959 (Tape #116, Lawrence Lipton Collection, USC); "The Beatniks," CBS Radio broadcast, Summer 1959; two stories written by Jerry Hulse for the *Los Angeles Times*, "Beatniks Beat Bongoes in Basement, Hearing Told" (29 August 1959, Part I, 2), and "Wine, Nude Models Liven Up Beatnik Capital, Witness Says" (28 August 1959, Westside Section, 2, 10); an unsigned *Times* article, "Denial of Gas House Permit Seen" (27 December 1959, Westside Section, 1); Lipton's own recollections in his column for the *Los Angeles Free Press*, "The Wasp" (5 March 1965, 2); Tom Moran and Tom Sewell, *Fantasy by the Sea* (97); and my interviews with John Thomas (17 June 1987) and Tony Scibella (9 June 1987). Duhab, the popeyed robot, is pictured in Philomene Long's *The Beats: An Existential Comedy*.

CHAPTER SIX

Stuart Perkoff's trip to San Francisco is described in the Journal of Stuart Z. Perkoff #4, September 1959 (Perkoff described his withdrawal symptoms and decision to retreat to Venice on 15 September, one of the few precisely dated entries in all of the poet's journals). The presence of tour buses and other manifestations of the beatnik fad in North Beach—and the severity of the police department's reaction—are described by Francis J. Rigney and L. Douglas Smith, *The Real Bohemia* (New York: Basic Books, 1961, 4, 63, 161) and confirmed by my interviews with Tony Scibella (9 June 1987) and John Thomas (17 June 1987).

"Squareville U.S.A. vs. Beatville U.S.A.," an unsigned feature article, appeared in the issue of *Life* dated 21 September 1959 (31–37). The advertising rates in effect at that time were quoted to me on 5 January 1987 by a *Life* advertising sales representative; although the salesman preferred not to be cited by name, there was nothing secret about these prices, which were published, as always, both in the publication's media kit and by the Standard Rate and Data Service. On a one-time basis, a full page of black-and-white advertising in *Life* cost $15,000, and a page of full color, $19,980; if the advertiser's artwork extended to the edges of the page, an additional "bleed" charge of 15 percent was assessed. The client may have paid an additional fee for far-forward positioning, and may also have received a discount for running several times within the year. Tom Wolfe has described Henry Luce's commitment to Project Mercury, as well as the price paid for the astronauts' "story," in *The Right Stuff* (New York: Farrar, Straus & Giroux, 1979; Bantam edition, 1980, 116–118).

Letters concerning "Beatville . . . " appeared in the 12 October 1959 issue of *Life* (14–18); I have quoted from those of Alexander Gross (". . . poverty of American life," 14, 16), Mrs. R. A. Henkins ("these screwy beatniks," 16), and Mrs. Boyd Rustine (". . . ceramic art to ballet," 16).

The establishment of the Grand Hotel, including Lawrence Lipton's "screening" of would-be residents and the Frank Rios incident, is recounted by Stuart Z. Perkoff in the Journal of Stuart Z. Perkoff #4, Summer and Fall 1959; by John Thomas, in our interviews of 17 and 24 June 1987); and by Tony Scibella, in our interview of 9 June 1987. Perkoff described his first few days in the hotel in a conversation with Lawrence Lipton (American Literature Tape #T66, USC; catalogued as having been recorded in 1962, but internal evidence leaves no doubt that the discussion occurred in 1959). Ginsberg's command to "dig prosody" was included in a letter letter to the editor of *Liberation* (June 1959, 10).

The factionalism that made a disappointment of the Grand Hotel experiment was described for me by John Thomas and Tony Scibella (interviews, see above); Perkoff's observations are from the Journal of Stuart Perkoff #5, October 1959, and from his taped discussion with Lawrence Lipton (American Literature Tape #T66, 1959).

The Groucho Marx show segment is included in Philomene Long's documentary film, *The Beats: An Existential Comedy*, Venice of America Films, 1980). Nettie Lipton (in conversation, Burbank, 16 March 1986) and John Thomas (in conversation, Santa Monica Place, 17 December 1987) told me that Marx had subsequently contributed "a little money" to the project. Tony Scibella (9 June 1987) described Perkoff's appearance on Paul Coates's show; the letter to Coates, c/o KTTV-TV, Los Angeles, undated, 1959, is preserved in the Stuart Z. Perkoff Collection.

Perkoff's complaints about his fellow Grand Hotel residents are from the Journals of Stuart Z. Perkoff #23 (1959) and #1 (early 1960). Tony Scibella (9 June 1987), Suzan Perkoff (28 June 1987) and John Thomas (24 June 1987) all recalled the Kerouac visit in their respective interviews; John Montgomery, the model for "Henry Morley" in *The Dharma Bums*, confirms Kerouac's presence at Lipton's house (*Jack Kerouac*, Fresno, Calif.: The Giliga Press, 1970, 7) The long quotation about "rigid coolness" is from Kerouac's novel *Desolation Angels* (New York: Coward-McCann, Inc., 1965; Bantam Books, 1966, 1971, 328–329). Lipton desparaged Kerouac's work in *The Holy Barbarians* (New York: Julian Messner Inc., 1959, 251); John Thomas (interview, 24 June 1987) is of the opinion that the novelist snubbed him.

Perkoff describes the recording session at the Liptons' in the Journal of Stuart Perkoff #5 (October 1959), which was also captured on Tape #46 (1959), Lawrence Lipton Collection, USC. (Lipton himself can clearly be heard trying to make everyone pay attention to business.) Perkoff's fight with Tony Scibella was mentioned to me by John Thomas (author's interview with Thomas and Long, 24 June 1987) and is described in the Journal of Stuart Perkoff #5, October 1959.

The remainder of the chapter is based on the Journals of Stuart Perkoff #1, #4, and #25, 1959 and 1960. Perkoff's journey to the open-air junk market occurred in April 1960. No one I have talked to seems to have the slightest idea of who the "strange chick" who wrote in his diary may have been.

CHAPTER SEVEN

Stuart Perkoff's experiences in Venice and Mexico (as well as his description of Tamboo) are contained in the Journals of Stuart Z. Perkoff #1 (February and March 1960), #5 (October 1959), #18 (Summer 1960 through May 1961), #25 (April through September 1960), #30 (1961), and #44 (March and April 1960), supported by my interviews with Suzan Perkoff and Tony Scibella. All of Perkoff's numbered journals, along with his unpublished poem, "The Summer: An Elegy" (1961), are held in the Stuart Z. Perkoff Collection. Suzan

Perkoff described Stuart's immediate post-Mexico condition to me in a conversation in San Francisco on 1 November 1987.

The account of "Mad Mike" Magdalani's suicide is based on my interview with John Thomas, 17 June 1987; on John Thomas's poem, "Some of Them End as Suicides" (included in his *john thomas*, Fairfax, Calif.: The Red Hill Press, 1972, unpaged); on Perkoff's "The Summer: An Elegy"; on a radio interview with Magdalani in *The Beatniks*, a CBS Radio broadcast aired in the summer of 1959 (Tapes #452 and #453, Lawrence Lipton Collection, USC); on the Journal of Stuart Perkoff #18, May 1961; and on a taped discussion featuring Lawrence Lipton, Stuart Perkoff, Tony Scibella, and others (1 June 1962, American Literature Tape #T71, USC).

Charles Foster's long conversation with the Liptons is condensed, but not otherwise "reconstructed," from my transcript of Tape #126, Lawrence Lipton Collection, USC. The account of his stay at Camarillo is also taken from that source. Foster's "The Troubled Makers" was included by Richard Seaver, Terry Southern, and Alexander Trocchi, eds., in *Writers in Revolt: An Anthology* (New York: Frederick Fell Inc., 1963), although Lawrence Lipton continually refers to "Grove Press" on Tape #126. Foster's evolving attitudes and interests are described by the author himself in his "Patriotic Essay" (Foster, *Peyote Toad*, ed. Charles Potts, Salt Lake City: Litmus, "distributed by the Cosmic Aeroplane, 1975," 22), and by his posthumous editors Charles Potts (*ibid.*, 61) and Karl Kempton (afterword to Foster, *Outrider for the Lady*, Sacramento, Calif.: Rainbow Resin, 1974, unpaged). In the cover photograph for *Peyote Toad*, which could not have been taken, for obvious reasons, after 1967, Foster looks like an unhealthy man of sixty.

Two versions of Lawrence Lipton's screenplay about Paul Gauguin (*Love Walked Naked Once*; original title, *Because I Was Flesh*) are held in the Lawrence Lipton Collection, UCLA. Lipton explained that he was "prepared to go beyond the Beat Generation, if necessary," to Professors Kaplan and Durban, of the University of Southern California, in their interview of 23 January 1962 (American Literature Collection, Department of Special Collections, Doheny Memorial Library, USC). Carl Forsberg's poem, "Wanted: One Salvation Army" (unpublished, Lawrence Lipton Collection, UCLA) offers a tongue-in-cheek portrait of Lipton as the literary "doge" of Venice, still waiting for the right young poet to come along and fulfill his dreams of a literary renaissance.

Suzan Perkoff recalled Foster as having "lived on her couch" in our interview of 28 June 1987. The Liptons' modest financial status is corroborated by their own records (Lawrence Lipton Collection, USC) and by John Thomas in our interview of 24 June 1987. The sound of

Lipton ruffling the bill near the microphone is unmistakable in Tape #126, and he refers rather pointedly to its denomination in the course of the discussion.

CHAPTER EIGHT

The destruction of the Gas House is described in an unsigned story, "Venice Beatnik Haven Falls to Wreckers," in the *Los Angeles Times* (7 September 1962, Part I, 2), which had also run stories on the impending demolition on 18 and 22 April, 12 August, and 3 September of that year.

John Thomas (interviews, 17 June and 24 June 1987) told me of Lipton's journey to San Francisco to gather material for *The Growing Edge*; a copy of the program of the Pacific Coast Writer's Conference, held 24 June through 11 July 1963 at what was then Los Angeles State College, is preserved in the Lawrence Lipton Collection, USC.

Lipton forwarded the first installment of "The Wasp" to the *Los Angeles Free Press* on 22 July 1964 (Lipton to Kunkin, Lawrence Lipton Collection, USC). Paul Jay Robbins's review, "Op, Pop and Slop," appeared on 12 March 1965 (*Los Angeles Free Press*, 7); Kunkin's apology appeared in the *Free Press* one week later, as a sidebar alongside "The Wasp" (19 March 1965, 2). Letters to Kunkin about the unpleasantness included Thomas to Robbins, c/o editor, *Los Angeles Free Press*, undated, carbon copy in the Lawrence Lipton Collection, USC; Muchmore to editor, *Los Angeles Free Press*, 26 March 1965, 4; Ellison to editor, *Los Angeles Free Press*, 26 March 1965, 5.

John Haag's background and political career are described in a handbill, "Defend the Venice West!" distributed in January 1966 and preserved in the Lawrence Lipton Collection, USC; in Clay Carson's article for the *Los Angeles Times*, "Leader of the Beatniks" (25 June 1965, 3); and in a flyer issued by the Peace and Freedom Party in support of Haag's candidacy in November 1986 for state controller in 1986 (author's personal collection). John Thomas (interview, 24 June 1987) and Tony Scibella (interview, 9 June 1987) also provided background information about Haag and the last years of the Venice West. The issue of poetry in the Venice West was reported in the Venice *Evening Advertiser* ("Venice Poetry Reading OK'd," 4 March 1965, 1) and the *Los Angeles Free Press* ("Poetry Den Raided," 4 March 1965, 1; "Venice Poetry Den Wins Court Case," 25 June 1965, 1; Lawrence Lipton's column, "Radio Free America" [successor to "The Wasp"], 25 March 1966, 2; and Claude Hayward, "Venice West Café Faces Political Eviction Soon," 25 March 1966, 2).

Ridgely Cummings covered the anti-bongo ordinance story for the *Free Press*, with articles appearing on 3 December 1964 ("Ban on Bongos, Guitars at Beaches and Parks Proposed by City Council," 1) and 25 June 1965 ("City Hall Bongo Conference," 2); Erwin Baker seems to have had just as much fun covering the story for the *Los Angeles Times* ("Beatniks, Indians—Even Whales—Get into Council's Bongo Session," 1 December 1964, Part II, 1). The *Times* also published a fairly sympathetic article on 31 January 1965 ("Beach Music: Coffee House Owner Hits Ban on Bongoes,") which Lawrence Lipton, who was conspicuous by his noninvolvement in the proceedings, nevertheless clipped for posterity (Lawrence Lipton Collection, USC).

The Venice "urban renewal" effort is described in articles in the *Los Angeles Times* (Doug Mauldin, "Venice Sees Renewal Loan Gains: Officials Seek Federal Backing to Rebuild Area," 3 December 1964, Part 9, 9) and the *Los Angeles Free Press* ("Imminent Destruction of the St. Mark's Hotel," 20 August 1964, 1, and Lipton's column, "The Wasp," 24 September 1964, 2).

The *Free Press* gave a great deal of publicity to both the cancellation of Lipton's UCLA extension class and the foundation of the "Free University of California." Lipton also recorded a number of classroom sessions; the tapes are preserved in the Lawrence Lipton Collection, USC. Stuart Perkoff recorded his ambivalence about the FUC, and about Lipton himself, in the Journal of Stuart Perkoff #26, 1966. Jana Baragan's devotion to Astarte is recorded in a diary which is almost certainly hers (undated, Stuart Z. Perkoff Collection, UCLA)

The account of the Human Be-In, 14 January 1967, is based on my own observations as a participant. Luce's visit to the Haight-Ashbury district is related in an unsigned obituary article in *Time*, 10 March 1967, 33.

Alexander Trocchi's legal battles are alluded to on the jacket of his book of poems, *Man at Leisure* (London: Calder & Boyars, Ltd., 1972), which also contains an introduction by William Burroughs in which the senior literary junkie endorses Trocchi's claim to being a "cosmonaut of inner space" (9). Marion Magid describes her visit with Trocchi in "The Death of Hip" (*Esquire*, June 1965, 89–103), and Barry Farrell gives him pride of place in "The Other Culture" (*Life*, 17 February 1967, 86–102). Direct quotations from Farrell's article are as follows: "We're coming along at a perfect time," 97; "Time! Time! . . . world's second most famous junkie," *ibid.*; "a vast mosaic of underground friendships," 87–88. Trocchi mentions having tried "lysergic acid" in *Cain's Book*, 10.

My account of Perkoff's life just prior to his arrest is drawn from the Journal of Stuart Z. Perkoff #46 (1974) and from my interviews with John Thomas (17 June 1987) and Tony Scibella (9 June 1987). Thomas described the poet's intentions, Scibella the details of the "bust." John Thomas also recalled Lipton's intervention to save

Perkoff's literary estate in our interviews of 17 and 24 June 1987). Jana Baragan's acceptance by the Perkoffs is described in my interviews with Suzan and Rachel Perkoff (28 June and 21 July, respectively, 1987); the poet expressed his gratitude in Stuart Z. Perkoff ("12368") to Suzan Perkoff, 28 August 1967 (Stuart Z. Perkoff collection, UCLA).

Charles Foster's death is recounted by Karl Kempton, editor of Foster's *Outrider for the Lady* (Sacramento: Rainbow Resin, 1974, unpaged). The extent and relatively quality of Foster's literary estate is suggested by Charles Potts, who edited *Peyote Toad* (Salt Lake City: Litmus, "distributed by the Cosmic Aeroplane, 1975," 56, 61). The final quotation from Foster ("my neurosis i found out") is quoted by Potts in the latter work (58), and is taken from Foster's aptly named "notes toward a comprehension of chaos."

The Lawrence Lipton Collection, USC, contains a number of letters from admirers and supporters of his projected radio station (including the anonymous, undated note quoted in the text); it also includes a mailer addressed to "Friends of Radio Free America," dated 19 December 1967, attributed to the Radio Free America Interim Committee (membership: Lawrence Lipton, Art Kunkin, and Paul Dallas) and assuring its recipients that "Radio Free America has not died."

William Burroughs, Terry Southern, Jean Genet, and John Sack are shown together on the front cover of *Esquire*, November 1968. Lawrence Lipton's coverage of the Chicago convention for the *Los Angeles Free Press* appeared in two installments: "Lipton from Chicago" (30 August 1968, 6), and "Six Days in August: A Diary: The Old Order, a Chronicle of Disorder, Violence and Decay," (6 September 1968, 3–9). Both the long quotation and the account of his injury are from "Six Days in August," 3.

Stuart Perkoff recalled his parole interview (which took place in 1968) in the Journal of Stuart Perkoff #46, Winter 1974. Tony Scibella (interview, 9 June 1987) characterized him as having had "no tip" in prison. The poem which concludes the chapter is Perkoff's "Some Aspects of Prison, for Frank Rios, 5: The Human Flow" (Perkoff, *Love Is the Silence, Poems 1948–1972*, ed. Paul Vangelisti, Los Angeles and Fairfax: The Red Hill Press, 1975, unpaged).

CHAPTER NINE

Norman Podhoretz's syndicated opinion-page essay, "Spare Us a Revival of Kerouac and the Pied Pipers of Despair," appeared in the *Los Angeles Times* on 8 January 1987 (Part 2, 6). Podhoretz had, of course, attacked Kerouac nearly thirty years before in "The Know-Nothing Bohemians" (*Partisan Review*, Spring 1958, 305–318).

For my portrait of Kerouac in his last years I have drawn on James

McClintock's article, "This Is How the Ride Ends" (*Esquire*, March 1970, 139, 188–189), Gerald Nicosia, *Memory Babe* (New York: Grove Press, 1983, 696); Dennis McNally, *Desolate Angel* (New York: Random House, 1979, 343, 365); Carl Adkins, "Jack Kerouac: Off the Road for Good," in John Montgomery's *Jack Kerouac* (Fresno Calif.: The Giliga Press, 1970, 39), and Kerouac's own *Big Sur* (New York: Farrar, Straus & Cudahy, 1962, 4). Lawrence Ferlinghetti referred to "Old Sweet Jack" in his cover blurb for Jan Kerouac's *Baby Driver: A Novel about Myself* (New York: Holt, Rinehart and Winston, 1981; Owl edition, 1983).

The "Woodstock" edition of *Life* appeared as an insert in the regular weekly issue dated 29 August 1969 (14B-23), which also contained Norman Mailer's "Of a Fire on the Moon," Richard Schickel's review of *Alice's Restaurant*, and Albert Goldman's profile of the founder of Grove Press, "The Old Smut Peddler" (50). The insert was also sold as a separate publication for several weeks thereafter.

The Perkoff family's experiences from 1967 to 1973 are based on my interviews with Suzan Perkoff (28 June 1987) and Rachel Perkoff (21 July 1987), on photographs given or shown to me by Suzan Perkoff, and on my interview with Tony Scibella (9 June 1987). I have also drawn on the Journal of Stuart Perkoff #34, May and June 1973, and on John Macker's interview with Scibella.

My principal text for the history of the Venice renovation project is Tom Moran and Tom Sewell's *Fantasy by the Sea: A Visual History of the American Venice* (Venice, Calif.: Beyond Baroque Foundation, 1979, 102–105), supplemented by Horst Schmidt-Bruemmer, *Venice, California: An Urban Fantasy* (trans. Feelie Lee, New York: Grossman Publishers, 1973, 25–99), and, to a lesser extent, Charles Gaines and George Butler's *Pumping Iron* (New York: Simon and Schuster, 1974, 18–25). Most of the outdoor works of art mentioned in the text are still extant.

Stuart Perkoff sent Suzan at least four of the postcards mentioned in the text, and described his videotaped poetry reading in the Journal of Stuart Perkoff #34 (June 1973, Stuart Z. Perkoff Collection, UCLA). Philomene Long described her relationship with Stuart Perkoff, as well as his final illness and death, in our interview of 24 June 1987 (with additional comments by John Thomas). My accounts of the poet's death, and of the disposition of his literary estate, are also based on my interviews with Suzan and Rachel Perkoff, Tony Scibella, and John Thomas; on the Journals of Stuart Perkoff #34 and #46 (1973 and 1974), Paul Vangelisti's introduction to Perkoff's *Love Is the Silence: Poems 1948–1972* (ed. Paul Vangelisti, Los Angeles and Fairfax: The Red Hill Press, 1975, unpaged); and on Tony Scibella's preface to Perkoff's *How It Is, Doing What I Do: Poems and Drawings, Bowery*

#21 (ed. Tony Scibella, Denver: Black Ace, 1976, unpaged). Suzan Perkoff's breakdown after Stuart's death is described in my interviews with Suzan and her daughter, Rachel.

Allen Ginsberg's acceptance speech, read by Peter Orlovsky at the National Book Awards ceremony in 1974, was subsequently published as *"The Fall of America" Wins a Prize* (New York: Gotham Book Mart and Gallery, 1974).

I have based my account of Lawrence Lipton's last years on my interview with John Thomas, on my conversation with Nettie Lipton, and on the following documents in the Lawrence Lipton Collection, USC: State of California Certificate of Death, Lawrence Lipton, 10 July 1975; application of Lawrence Lipton to the Carnegie Fund for Authors, 31 January 1974; and Morton H. Maxwell, MD, To Whom It May Concern, re: Lawrence Lipton, 14 June 1974; Lipton to editor, *American Poetry Review*, undated, but filed among papers dated 1974; and on the Liptons' financial records for 1975. Nettie Lipton's intentions regarding the collection of books and papers that ultimately became the Lipton Collection, USC, were expressed to me by Mrs. Lipton herself, 19 March 1986, and by Jacob Zeitlin, the rare book dealer, in the office of the University Librarian, USC, in the spring of 1986. Lipton's obituary article in the *Los Angeles Free Press* ("Larry Lipton [1898–1975])," included, as noted in the text, a contribution by Fay Irving (9).

The news of Milton Bratton's death was conveyed to me by John Thomas in July 1987; my source for the memorial service was Rachel Perkoff. The final quotation in the book is from Stuart Perkoff's unfinished poem about Moses, included in the Journal of Stuart Z. Perkoff #34, 21 April 1974.

BIBLIOGRAPHY

ARCHIVAL SOURCES

Department of Special Collections, Doheny Memorial Library, University of Southern California

American Literature Collection, Department of Special Collections. Includes those Lawrence Lipton tapes which were held by the library prior to 1986.

Lawrence Lipton Collection. Includes Lawrence Lipton's manuscripts, correspondence 1960–1975, memorabilia, newspaper clippings, and tape recordings, 1958–1975. For the most part, these materials were used before they were acquired by USC, and before any formal attempt had been made to catalogue them. Cited in Notes on Sources and remainder of Bibliography as "Lawrence Lipton Collection, USC."

Department of Special Collections, University Research Library, University of California, Los Angeles

Avant-Garde Literature Collection.

California Ephemera Collection.

California Tape Collection.

Lawrence Lipton Collection. Includes correspondence to and from Lawrence Lipton, 1940–1958; drafts of several of his books, including *The Holy Barbarians*; screenplays and galley proofs; and copies of works by "various young authors," including Stuart Perkoff, Charles Foster, Bruce Boyd, William J. Margolis, Eric Nord, Kent Chapman, John Montgomery, Carl Forsberg, and Maurice Wilmer Lacy. Cited in Notes on Sources and remainder of Bibliography as "Lawrence Lipton Collection, UCLA."

Stuart Z. Perkoff Collection. Includes manuscripts, photographs, correspondence, and the Journals of Stuart Z. Perkoff (46 volumes, numbered, but not in chronological sequence).

Author's personal archives

1750 Yosemite Ave. #204B, Simi Valley Ca 93063.
Includes original recordings and transcripts of the author's interviews, along with recent and archival photographs and duplicated materials from all the collections mentioned above.

RECORDED INTERVIEWS BY THE AUTHOR

Rachel Perkoff, 17 July 1987, Los Angeles, California.
Suzan Perkoff, 28 June 1987; interviewed by telephone, the author in Los Angeles, the subject in San Francisco, California.
Suzan Perkoff, 1 and 2 November 1987, San Francisco, California.
Tony Scibella, 9 June 1987, Van Nuys, California.
John Thomas, 17 June 1987, Los Angeles, California.
John Thomas and Philomene Long, 24 June 1987, Los Angeles, California.

WORKS BY VENICE AUTHORS

Beatnik Dictionary and Who's Who. Venice, Calif.: Beat Scene Press, 1959, 1960.
Crosson, Robert, John Thomas, Paul Vangelisti. *Abandoned Latitudes. (Invisible City #3)*. San Francisco and Los Angeles: The Red Hill Press, 1983.
Foster, Charles. "Bill of Divestment." Unpublished poem, 20 March 1957, original in the Lawrence Lipton Collection, UCLA.
———. *Outrider for the Lady*. Ed. Karl Kempton. Sacramento, Calif.: Rainbow Resin, 1974.
———. *Peyote Toad*, Ed. Charles Potts. Salt Lake City: Litmus, distributed by the Cosmic Aeroplane, 1975.
———. "Preliminary Report on Rerum naturem." Poem, circa 1957, original in the Lawrence Lipton Collection, UCLA.
———. "Riffs on Palm Trees, In So Far . . . No. 1." Poem, original in the Lawrence Lipton Collection, UCLA.
———, "The Troubled Makers." *Evergreen Review* 1, no. 4, 1957, 9–28.
———. "A WALK/ THRU PSYCHOSIS/ A TALK/ WITH GOD." Unfinished, unpublished poem, 1957 or 1958, original in the Lawrence Lipton Collection, UCLA.

———. untitled, unpublished story. 1959, original in the Lawrence Lipton Collection, UCLA.

———. untitled, unpublished diaristic story. November 1957, original in the Lawrence Lipton Collection, UCLA.

Lipton, Lawrence. "America's Literary Underground." *Coastlines #6*, Winter 1956.

———. *Brother, the Laugh Is Bitter.* New York: Harper & Brothers, 1942.

———. *Bruno in Venice West and Other Poems.* Van Nuys, Calif.: Venice West Publishers, 1976.

———. "Disaffiliation and the Art of Poverty." *Chicago Review*, Spring 1956, 53–79.

———. *The Erotic Revolution: An Affirmative View of the New Morality.* Los Angeles: Sherbourne Press, 1965.

———. "Excerpts from *Rainbow at Midnight*." *California Quarterly*, Spring 1953, 16–42.

———. *Die Heiligen Barbaren.* Trans. Helmut Degner. Dusseldorf: Karl Rauch Verlag, 1960.

———. *The Holy Barbarians.* New York: Julian Messner, 1959.

———. *In Secret Battle.* New York: Appleton-Century, 1944.

———. "The Poetry of John Thomas," *Los Angeles Free Press*, 23 June 1972, 4, 6.

———. "Radio Free America." Weekly column (irregular after 1971), *Los Angeles Free Press*, 1967–1974.

———. *Rainbow at Midnight*, Francestown, N.H.: The Golden Quill Press, 1955.

———. "Secession: 1953 (The State of the Arts on the West Coast)." *Intro* 2, no. 2, 1953, 31–43.

———. "Six Days in August: A Diary." *Los Angeles Free Press*, 6 September 1968, 3–9.

———. "The Wasp." Weekly column, *Los Angeles Free Press*, 1964–1967.

———. "Youth Will Serve Itself." *The Nation*, 10 November 1956, 389–392.

Long, Philomene, *The Beats: An Existential Comedy.* Venice of America Films, 1980.

———. "Elegy for Stuart Z. Perkoff." Poem, undated, copy in author's collection.

Perkoff, Stuart Z. *Alphabet.* Los Angeles and Fairfax: The Red Hill Press, 1973.

———. "An Attempt at a Letter of Communication." Poem, 1959, Stuart Z. Perkoff Collection, UCLA.

———. "bird: an elegy for Charlie Parker." Poem, 1955 or 1956, Lawrence Lipton Collection, UCLA.

———. *Feasts of Love, Feasts of Death*. Unpublished, 1957 or 1958, carbon copy in the Lawrence Lipton Collection, UCLA.

———. *How It Is, Doing What I Do: Poems and Drawings, Bowery #21*. Ed. Tony Scibella. Denver: Black Ace, 1976.

———. *Love Is the Silence: Poems 1948–1972*. Ed. Paul Vangelisti. Los Angeles and Fairfax: The Red Hill Press, 1975.

———. *Only Just Above the Ground*. In *The Smith*. New York: The Generalist Association, 1973.

———. "On Sinai." Poem, probably 1958, Lawrence Lipton Collection, UCLA.

———. "A Plea to the Goddess to Implement This Curse on Those Who Cuckold Me." Poem, 21 May 1959, Stuart Z. Perkoff Collection, UCLA.

———. *Round About Midnite*. Unpublished verse play, 1957, Lawrence Lipton Collection, UCLA.

———. *The Suicide Room*. Karlsruhe: Jargon Press, 1956.

———. *The Venice Poems*. Unpublished, 1956–1958, Lawrence Lipton Collection, UCLA.

Rios, Frank T., *A Piece of Flight*. In *Bowery #24*. Denver: Black Ace/ Temple of Man, 1976.

Scibella, Tony, *The Backshooter*. "Bowery Press Broadsheet #6." Denver: The Bowery, 1969.

Seaver, Richard, Terry Southern, Alexander Trocchi, eds. *Writers in Revolt: An Anthology*. New York: Frederick Fell Inc., 1963.

Thomas, John, *Epopoeia and the Decay of Satire*. Los Angeles and Fairfax, Calif.: The Red Hill Press, 1976.

———. *john thomas*. Fairfax, Calif.: The Red Hill Press, 1972.

Trocchi, Alexander, *Cain's Book*. New York: Grove Press, 1960; Grove Press Outrider (paperback) edition, 1979.

———. *The Fifth Volume of Frank Harris' "My Life and Loves": An Irreverent Treatment*. Paris: The Olympia Press, 1958, 1959; paperback edition, Olympia Press Companion Series #108, with Foreword by Maurice Girodias, 1966.

———. *Man at Leisure*. London: Calder & Boyars, Ltd., 1972.

———. *White Thighs*. North Hollywood, Calif.: Greenleaf Classics, 1964.

———. *Young Adam*. In *The Outsiders*. New York: Grove Press, 1960.

BOOKS BY OTHER AUTHORS

Allen, Donald, ed. *The New American Poetry, 1945–1960*. New York: Grove Press, 1960.

Allen, Donald, and George F. Butterick, eds. *The Postmoderns: The New American Poetry Revisited.* New York: Grove Press, 1982.

Burroughs, William S. *Junkie.* New York: Ace Books, 1953.

———. *Naked Lunch.* New York: Grove Press, 1962; Black Cat paperback edition, 1966.

Burroughs, William S., and Allen Ginsberg. *The Yage Letters.* San Francisco: City Lights Books, 1963.

Carr, Roy, Brian Case, Fred Dellar. *The Hip: Hipsters, Jazz and the Beat Generation.* London, Boston: Faber and Faber, 1986.

Charters, Ann. *Kerouac: A Biography.* New York: Straight Arrow Publishers, 1973; Warner Books paperback edition, significantly revised, 1974.

Colby, Vineta, ed. *American Culture in the Sixties.* The Reference Shelf, vol. 36, no. 1. New York: The H. W. Wilson Company, 1964.

Cook, Bruce. *The Beat Generation.* New York: Charles Scribner's Sons, 1971.

Cowley, Malcolm. *Exile's Return: A Literary Odyssey of the 1920s.* New York: The Viking Press, 1951; Compass Books edition, 1956.

Del Zoppo, Annette, and Jeffrey Stanton. *Venice, California: 1904–1930.* Venice, Calif.: ARS Publications, 1978.

Dickstein, Morris. *Gates of Eden: American Culture in the Sixties.* New York: Basic Books, 1977.

Feldman, Gene, and Max Gartenberg, eds. *The Beat Generation and the Angry Young Men.* New York: Citadel Press, 1958.

Ferris, Paul. *Dylan Thomas.* New York: Penguin Books, 1978.

Fitzgerald, F. Scott. "The Rich Boy." In *The Stories of F. Scott Fitzgerald*, ed. Malcolm Cowley. New York: Charles Scribner's Sons, 1951.

Gifford, Barry. *Kerouac's Town.* Berkeley: Creative Arts Book Company, 1977.

Gifford, Barry, and Lawrence Lee. *Jack's Book: An Oral Biography of Jack Kerouac.* New York: St. Martin's Press, 1978; Penguin Books, 1979.

Ginsberg, Allen. *The Fall of America: Poems of These States, 1965–1971.* San Francisco: City Lights Books, Pocket Poets Series #30, 1972.

———. *"The Fall of America" Wins a Prize.* New York: Gotham Book Mart and Gallery, 1974. "This is the text of Allen Ginsberg's acceptance speech for the National Book Award in Poetry, delivered by Peter Orlovsky on 18 April 1974, at Alice Tully Hall, Lincoln Center, New York City."

———. *Howl and Other Poems.* San Francisco: City Lights Books, Pocket Poets Series #4, 1956.

———. *Journals, Early Fifties, Early Sixties.* Ed. Gordon Ball. New York: Grove Press, 1977.

————. *Kaddish and Other Poems, 1958–1960.* San Francisco: City Lights Books, Pocket Poets Series #14, 1961.

————. *Planet News, 1961–1967.* San Francisco: City Lights Books, Pocket Poets Series #23, 1968.

————. *Plutonian Ode and Other Poems, 1977–1980.* San Francisco: City Lights Books, Pocket Poets Series #40, 1982.

————. *Reality Sandwiches, 1953–60.* San Francisco: City Lights Books, Pocket Poets Series #18, 1963.

Ginsberg, Allen, and Neal Cassady. *As Ever: The Collected Correspondence of Allen Ginsberg and Neal Cassady.* Ed. Barry Gifford. Berkeley: Creative Arts Book Company, 1977.

Gruen, John. *The New Bohemia: The Combine Generation.* New York: Shorecrest, 1966.

Higham, John, and Paul. K. Conkin, eds. *New Directions in American Intellectual History.* Baltimore: The Johns Hopkins University Press, 1979.

Humphrey, Robert E. *Children of Fantasy: The First Rebels of Greenwich Village.* New York: John Wiley & Sons, 1978.

Kammen, Michael. *The Past Before Us: Contemporary Historical Writing in the United States.* Ithaca, N.Y.: Cornell University Press, 1980.

Kerouac, Jack. *Big Sur.* New York: Farrar, Straus & Cudahy, 1962.

————. *Book of Dreams.* San Francisco: City Lights Books, 1961.

————. *Desolation Angels.* New York: Coward-McCann, Inc., 1965; Bantam Books, 1966, 1971.

————. *The Dharma Bums.* New York: The Viking Press, 1958; Signet Books, 1959.

————. *Doctor Sax: Faust Part Three.* New York: Grove Press, 1959.

————. *Lonesome Traveler.* New York: Grove Press, 1960; Black Cat edition, 1971.

————. *Maggie Cassidy.* New York: Avon Books, 1959.

————. *On the Road.* New York: The Viking Press, 1957; Penguin edition, 1976.

————. *Pic.* New York: Grove Press, 1971.

————. *The Subterraneans.* New York: Grove Press, 1958; Black Cat edition, 1971.

————. *Tristessa.* New York: Avon, 1960.

————. *Vanity of Duluoz: An Adventurous Education, 1935–46.* New York: Coward-McCann, 1968.

————. *Visions of Gerard.* New York: Farrar, Straus, 1963.

Kerouac, Jan. *Baby Driver: A Novel about Myself.* New York: Holt, Rinehart and Winston, 1981; Owl edition, 1983.

Knight, Arthur, and Kit Knight. *The Beat Diary,* vol. 5 of *The Un-*

speakable Visions of the Individual. California, Pa.: Arthur & Kit Knight, 1977.

————. *The Unspeakable Visions of the Individual,* vol. 10. California, Pa.: Arthur & Kit Knight, 1980.

Larsen, Carl, and James Singer. *The Beat Generation Cookbook.* New York: Poets Press, 1961.

McDarrah, Fred, ed. *Kerouac and Friends.* New York: W. Morrow, 1985.

McNally, Dennis. *Desolate Angel: Jack Kerouac, The Beat Generation, and America.* New York: Random House, 1979.

McWilliams, Carey. *California: Island on the Land.* Salt Lake City: Gibbs M. Smith, Inc., 1973.

Matusow, Allen J. *The Unravelling of America: A History of Liberalism in the 1960s.* San Francisco: Harper & Row, 1984.

May, James Boyer, Thomas McGrath, Peter Yates, eds. *Poetry Los Angeles.* London: Villiers Publications, 1958.

Miller, Douglas T., and Marion Nowak. *The Fifties: The Way We Really Were.* Garden City N.Y.: Doubleday & Company, 1977.

Mohr, Bill, ed. *"Poetry Loves Poetry": An Anthology of Los Angeles Poets.* Berkeley: Momentum Press, 1985.

Montgomery, John, ed. *Jack Kerouac: A Memoir in Which Is Revealed Secret Lives & West Coast Whispers, Being the Confessions of Henry Morley, Alex Fairbrother & John Montgomery, Triune Madman of the Dharma Bums, Desolation Angels & Other Trips.* Fresno, Calif.: The Giliga Press, 1970.

Montgomery, John, ed. *The Kerouac We Knew: Unposed Portraits; Action Shots Compiled by John Montgomery Honoring the Kerouac Conference at Naropa Institute.* Kentfield, Calif.: Fels & Firn Press, 1982.

Moran, Tom, and Tom Sewell. *Fantasy by the Sea: A Visual History of the American Venice.* Venice, Calif.: Beyond Baroque Foundation, 1979.

Nelson, Howard J. *The Los Angeles Metropolis.* Dubuque, Iowa: Kendall/Hunt Publishing Company, 1983.

Newfield, Jack. *A Prophetic Minority.* New York: The New American Library, 1966.

Nicosia, Gerald. *Memory Babe: A Critical Biography of Jack Kerouac.* New York: Grove Press, 1983.

Nin, Anaïs. *The Diary of Anais Nin, Vol. 6: 1955–1966.* New York and London: Harcourt Brace Jovanovich, 1966, 1976.

O'Neill, William L. *Coming Apart: An Informal History of America in the 1960's.* Chicago: Quadrangle Books, 1971.

Parkinson, Thomas, ed. *A Casebook on the Beat.* New York: Crowell, 1961.

Partridge, William L., *The Hippie Ghetto: The Natural History of a Subculture.* San Francisco: Holt, Rinehart and Winston, 1973.

Rexroth, Kenneth, *American Poetry in the Twentieth Century.* New York: The Seabury Press, 1973.

———. *Bird in the Bush: Obvious Essays.* New York: New Directions, 1959.

———. *Thou Shalt Not Kill: A Memorial for Dylan Thomas.* Sunnyvale, Calif.: H. Schwartz, 1955.

Rigney, Francis J., and L. Douglas Smith. *The Real Bohemia.* New York: Basic Books, 1961.

Roszak, Theodore. *The Making of a Counterculture: Reflections on the Technocratic Society and Its Youthful Opposition.* Garden City, N.Y.: Doubleday, 1969.

Schmidt-Bruemmer, Horst. *Venice, California: An Urban Fantasy.* Trans. Feelie Lee. New York: Grossman Publishers, 1973.

Schock, James. *Life Is A Lousy Drag.* San Francisco: Unicorn Publishing Co., 1958.

Starr, Kevin. *Inventing the Dream: California Through the Progressive Era.* New York: Oxford University Press, 1985.

Szasz, Thomas. *Ceremonial Chemistry: The Ritual Persecution of Drugs, Addicts, and Pushers.* Garden City, N.Y.: Anchor Press/ Doubleday, 1974; Anchor Books paperback edition, 1975.

Vangelisti, Paul, ed. *Specimen 73: A Catalog of Poets for the Season 1973–1974.* Pasadena, Calif.: Pasadena Museum of Modern Art, 1973.

Veysey, Laurence R. *The Communal Experience: Anarchist and Mystical Counter-Cultures in America.* San Francisco: Harper & Row, Publishers, 1973.

Wertheim, Arthur Frank. *The New York Little Renaissance: Iconoclasm, Modernism, and Nationalism in American Culture, 1908–1917.* New York: New York University Press, 1976.

Wolfe, Tom. *The Electric Kool-Aid Acid Test.* New York: Farrar, Straus & Giroux, 1968; Bantam paperback edition, 1969.

———. *The Right Stuff.* New York: Farrar, Straus & Giroux, 1959; Bantam edition 1980.

BOOK CHAPTERS AND MAGAZINE ARTICLES

Dominis, John, and Ell Eppridge, photographers. "Woodstock." *Life*, 29 August 1969, 14B-23.

Farrell, Barry. "The Other Culture." *Life*, 17 February 1967, 86–102.

Freud, Caroline. "Portrait of the Beatnik." *Encounter*, June 1959, 42–46.

Frumkin, Gene. "The Great Promoter: A Hangnail Sketch of Lawrence Lipton." *Coastlines #15*, Autumn 1959, 3–10.

Goldman, Albert. "The Old Smut Peddler." *Life*, 29 August 1969, 49–53.

Hollinger, David A. "American Intellectual History: Issues for the 1980s." From "The Promise of American History: Progress and Prospects," ed. Stanley I. Kutler and Stanley N. Katz, special issue of *Reviews in American History*, December 1982, 306–317.

Kazin, Alfred. "The Alone Generation: A Comment on the Fiction of the 'Fifties." *Harper's Magazine*, "Special Supplement: Writing in America," October 1959, 127–128.

McClintock, James. "This Is How the Ride Ends." *Esquire*, March 1970, 139, 188–189.

Macker, John. "Interview with Tony Scibella." *Moravagine #3*. Denver: Long Road Press, 1986, 19–29.

Magid, Marion. "The Death of Hip." *Esquire*, June 1965, 89–103.

O'Neil, Paul. "The Only Rebellion Around: But the Shabby Beats Bungle the Job in Arguing, Sulking and Bad Poetry." *Life*, 30 November 1959, 115–131.

———. "Life Among the Beatniks." *Reader's Digest*, April 1960, 64–68.

Podhoretz, Norman. "The Know-Nothing Bohemians." *Partisan Review*, Spring 1958, 305–318.

Veysey, Laurence R. "Intellectual History and the New Social History." In John Higham and Paul K. Conkin, eds., *New Directions in American Intellectual History*. Baltimore: The Johns Hopkins University Press, 1979, 3–26.

Weisburd, Mel. "Editorial: The Merchant of Venice." *Coastlines #7*, Autumn 1959, 39–40.

Zahn, Curtis. "Blunderbuss: What's Going on Around L.A." *Coastlines #8*, Autumn 1958, 3.

———. "The Bored, the Bearded and the Beat." *Look*, 19 August 1958, 64–68.

———. "California: Heat on the Beatniks." *Newsweek*, 17 August 1959, 32.

———. "Fried Shoes." *Time*, 2 February 1959, 48.

———. "Mentholated Eggnog." *Time*, 1 June 1959, 88.

———. "Mulled Murder, with Spice." *Time*, 28 January 1946, 88–90.

———. News item on Lawrence Lipton. *The Saturday Review of Literature*, 4 July 1959, 6.

———. "Squareville U.S.A. vs. Beatville U.S.A." *Life*, 21 September 1959, 31–37.

Newspaper Articles

Baker, Erwin. "Beatniks, Indians—Even Whales—Get Into Council's Bongo Session." *Los Angeles Times*, 1 December 1964, Part II, 1.

Carson, Clay. "Leader of the Bohemians." *Los Angeles Free Press*, 25 June 1965, 3.

Cummings, Ridgely. "Ban on Bongo's, Guitars at Beaches and Parks Proposed by City Council." *Los Angeles Free Press*, 3 December 1964, 1, 9.

———. "Denial of Gas House Permit Seen." *Los Angeles Times*, 27 December 1959, Westside Section, 1.

George, Wally. "Poor Staging Dampers Poetry, Jazz Festival." *Los Angeles Times*, 6 December 1957, Part IV, 11.

Glauber, Robert H. "Who, What, and Why Are the Beatniks?" *New York Herald Tribune*, Sunday Book Review Section, 2 May 1959. Clipping preserved in the Lawrence Lipton Collection, UCLA.

Hayward, Claude. "Venice West Café Faces Political Eviction Soon." *Los Angeles Free Press*, 11 February 1966, 2.

Hulse, Jerry. "Beatniks Beat Bongos in Baemen, Hearing Told," *Los Angeles Times*. 29 August 1959, Part I, 2.

———. "Wine, Nude Models Liven Up Beatnik Capital, Witness Says." *Los Angeles Times*, 28 August 1959, Part I, 2.

Jares, Joe. "Gas House Passes on with Bongo Beat," *Los Angeles Times*, 3 September 1962, Part I, 2.

Kirsch, Robert R. "Beat Generation's Voice Cries Out." *Los Angeles Times*, 24 May 1959. Clipping preserved in the Lawrence Lipton Collection, UCLA.

Kunkin, Art. "Lipton Course Canceled." *Los Angeles Free Press*, 16 July 1965, 1.

Leonard, William. "The Beatniks' Boredom with a Messed-Up World." *Chicago Sunday Tribune*, 7 June 1959. Clipping preserved in the Lawrence Lipton Collection, UCLA.

Lewis, Earl. "A Prophet of 'Beats' Explains His Flock." *People's World*, 11 July 1959, 7.

Mauldin, Doug. "Venice Sees Renewal Loan Gains: Officials Seek Federal Backing to Rebuild Area." *Los Angeles Times*, 3 December 1964, Part IX, 9.

Olten, Carol. "Poetry of Beats Echoes a Venice Gone By." *San Diego Union*, 18 November 1980, A-14.

Podhoretz, Norman. "Spare Us a Revival of Kerouac and the Pied Pipers of Despair," *Los Angeles Times*, 8 January 1987, Part II, 6.

Robbins, Paul Jay. "Op, Pop and Slop." *Los Angeles Free Press*, 12 March 1965, 7.

————. "Coffee House Owner Hits Ban on Bongoes," *Los Angeles Times*, 31 January 1965. Clipping preserved in the Lawrence Lipton Collection, USC.

————. "Famed Beatnik Landmark May Be Torn Down," *Los Angeles Times*, 22 April 1962, Westside Section, 8.

————. "Gas House in Venice Faces Demolition Order," *Los Angeles Times*, 12 August 1962, Westside Section, 2.

————. "Jazz Hall Reopens Tonight," *Los Angeles Times*. 2 December 1957, Part I, 17.

————. "Larry Lipton (1898–1975)." Obituary, *Los Angeles Free Press*, 25–31 July 1975, 11.

————. "Larry Lipton (1989–1975.)" *Los Angeles Free Press*, 1–7 August 1975, 9–10, 27–29.

————. "Lipton from Chicago." *Los Angeles Free Press*, 30 August 1968, 6.

————. "Venice Beatnik Haven Falls to Wreckers," *Los Angeles Times*, 7 September 1962, part I, 2.

————. "Venice Gas House Under City's Fire," *Los Angeles Times*, 18 April 1962, Part II, 1.

————. "Venice Poetry Reading OK'd," [Venice] *Evening Vanguard Advertiser*, 4 March 1965. Clipping preserved in the Lawrence Lipton Collection, USC.

INDEX